AQA Business Studies

A2

Helen Coupland-Smith
Diane Mansell
Peter Stimpson

 Nelson Thornes

Contents

Contents

AQA introduction

Nelson Thornes has worked in partnership with AQA to ensure this book and the accompanying online resources offer you the best support for your A Level course.

All resources have been approved by senior AQA examiners so you can feel assured that they closely match the specification for this subject and provide you with everything you need to prepare successfully for your exams.

These print and online resources together **unlock blended learning**; this means that the links between the activities in the book and the activities online blend together to maximise your understanding of a topic and help you achieve your potential.

These online resources are available on **kerboodle!** which can be accessed via the internet at **www.kerboodle.com/live**, anytime, anywhere. If your school or college subscribes to this service you will be provided with your own personal login details. Once logged in, access your course and locate the required activity.

For more information and help visit **www.kerboodle.com**

Icons in this book indicate where there is material online related to that topic. The following icons are used:

Learning activity

These resources include a variety of interactive and non-interactive activities to support your learning. These include online presentations of concepts from the student book, worksheets and other interactive activities.

Progress tracking

These resources include a variety of tests that you can use to check your knowledge on particular topics (Test yourself) and a range of resources that enable you to analyse and understand examination questions (On your marks…).

Research support

These resources include WebQuests, in which you are assigned a task and provided with a range of web links to use as source material for research.

Case Study

These resources provide detailed coverage of business scenarios, some of which extend material from this textbook and some of which are exclusively online.

How to use this book

This book covers the specification for your course and is arranged in sequence approved by AQA.

The book content is divided in to chapters matched to the sections of the AQA Business Studies specification for Units 3 and 4. Sections 3.1 to 3.5 cover Unit 3 (Strategies for success). Sections 4.1 to 4.3 cover Unit 4 (The business environment and managing change). The chapters within each section provide full coverage of the AQA specification.

The features in this book include:

In this chapter you will learn to:

At the beginning of each chapter you will find a list of learning objectives that contain targets linked to the requirements of the specification.

Case studies

The first Case study in each chapter (Setting the scene) provides real-life context for the theories which are to be discussed in the chapter. The concluding Case study in each chapter focuses on testing the theories covered in the chapter. It will have five questions attached, each testing knowledge, understanding, application, analysis, evaluation and research.

Key terms

Terms that you will need to be able to define and understand. The definitions will also appear in an online glossary.

Links

Highlighting any areas where topics relate to one another.

Activities

Suggestions for practical activities that you can carry out.

Business in action

A real-life business example which demonstrates theory being put in to practice.

AQA Examiner's tip

Hints from AQA examiners to help you with your study and prepare for your exam.

In this chapter you will have learned to:

A bulleted list of learning outcomes at the end of each chapter summarising core points of knowledge.

Summary questions

Questions that will test your knowledge of the preceding chapter.

AQA examination questions are reproduced by permission of the Assessment and Qualifications Alliance.

Nelson Thornes is responsible for the solution(s) provided online. They may not constitute the only possible solution(s).

■ Web links for this book

As Nelson Thornes is not responsible for third party content online, there may be some changes to this material that are beyond our control. In order for us to ensure that the links referred to in the book are as up-to-date and stable as possible, the websites are usually homepages with supporting instructions on how to reach the relevant pages if necessary.

Please let us know at **kerboodle@nelsonthornes.com.** if you find a link that doesn't work and we will do our best to redirect the link, or to find an alternative site.

Introduction to A2 Business Studies

This is the only textbook that has been endorsed by the AQA examination board for use by students following the AQA A2 Business Studies specification. Assuming that you already have a copy of the AS textbook, this is the only additional book you will need to provide a comprehensive and all-inclusive coverage of Unit 3 and Unit 4 of the AQA specification.

We hope that you achieved the success that you deserved in the AS examinations. If you used the AQA endorsed AS textbook to help prepare for your Unit 1 and 2 examinations then don't dispose of it just yet! You must keep it and refer to it for two reasons:

- You may decide to retake one or both of the AS Units in order to improve your overall chances of a top grade.
- The assessment used at A2 draws upon AS material, which you should include, where appropriate, in your responses to A2 questions.

So, to recap, the two texts, AS and A2 Businesses Studies endorsed by AQA, are the only two textbooks you will need whilst preparing for your A2 examinations!

Why is it so useful?

They key feature of this text is that, because it is exclusively endorsed by AQA, it is the only text that can be used by Principal Examiners when defining what questions can be asked in the Unit 3 and Unit 4 assessments. If concepts and techniques are explained in this textbook – then they could be assessed in the Unit examinations.

Each chapter covers one AQA specification topic and takes the reader logically through the subject content and examination skills that will be needed for success. The user-friendly nature of the text is added to by:

- Clear explanation of all definitions required by the AQA specification.
- Constant reference made to actual businesses to allow application of understanding to the real world.

- Hundreds of revision and examination-style questions to test understanding at each stage of the course.

Differences between AS and A2

The final chapter on A2 examination skills is very important. The main purpose of this chapter is to demonstrate and reinforce the essential skills that students need to demonstrate in examination answers in order to gain a grade A. The emphasis of this chapter – supported by many of the assessment questions in previous chapters – is on the absolute significance of supporting relevant business knowledge with clear skills of application, analysis and evaluation. This was also the case at AS, but A2 assessment puts even greater stress on the latter two skills.

The other important difference between AS and A2 Business Studies is that the focus moves from business start-ups and small businesses to much larger organisations with a national and international dimension. You will notice this is reflected not just in the subject content of each chapter but also in the style and scope of the assessment questions that the book contains. This switch of emphasis is reflected in the type of supporting materials contained on the interactive Nelson Thornes website that your school may have obtained a licence to access.

Final thoughts

The authors believe that this textbook will give all students who work through it thoroughly the best possible awareness of what Business Studies is about and what AQA senior examiners expect from grade A students by providing:

- a huge variety and number of presentational methods used in the book
- a range and diverse style of exercises and examination questions
- a thoroughly accessible text.

Introduction

Chapters in this section:

At AS Level, you will have studied the planning, financing and managing of a small to medium-sized business. As part of this course, you will have discovered that as businesses grow, roles within the organisation become more specialised and eventually functional areas emerge: marketing, finance, human resources and operations.

As life becomes more complicated, the need for good planning and clear goals is important. People who do not really know what they want to do as a career may find it much more difficult to decide on the best university course, compared with those who have known that they want to be an accountant, engineer, journalist or social worker from the age of 12! In the same way, once a firm has become established and no longer has survival as its main objective, it is important to set long-term aims and short-term objectives for the business. Setting targets creates the basis for decision-making – how will the answer to this problem help the business achieve its goals? This could be whether to relocate to a low-cost country, to launch a new product range or to buy a larger piece of machinery.

So, the development of a business into functional areas and the need for a clear range of organisational aims and objectives combine to produce a strategy for success:

- Each functional area sets targets which reflect the aims of the company.
- A range of strategies are deployed.
- Performance is measured against the targets.

This short section introduces planning and management within functional areas of a business.

Chapter 1: Using objectives and strategies explains how functional objectives are derived from corporate objectives. A range of corporate objectives that larger businesses might pursue are analysed. The relationship between functional objectives and strategies is examined and how they lead to the achievement of corporate objectives is discussed.

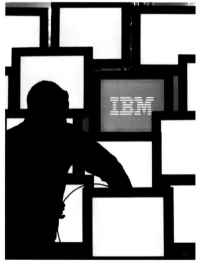

IBM offers businesses all over the world support in achieving their aims and objectives

Why might growing and larger organisations need help from a company such as IBM to achieve their corporate goals?

Using objectives and strategies

In this chapter you will learn to:

- understand how functional objectives are derived from corporate objectives

- analyse a range of corporate objectives that larger businesses might pursue

- explain the relationship between functional objectives and strategies

- evaluate the contribution of functional objectives to the achievement of corporate objectives.

Setting the scene

Reviving Marks & Spencer fortunes

Marks & Spencer appointed a new Chief Executive, Stuart Rose, in an attempt to improve disappointing business performance. He was given the task of reviving the company's fortunes with a new team and by producing a clear statement of the business's objectives. The aim of this corporate plan was to refocus the firm on its core values of quality, value for money, service, innovation and trust. The key objectives were: to **survive** in very competitive markets; achieve **growth** in sales value in key markets; to **increase market share** in all product areas; to **compete in new markets** and to **earn high enough profits** to satisfy their shareholders and prevent a hostile takeover bid. Success in achieving these objectives would be measured by reduced costs, increased sales revenue and market share by product group, successful new product development and higher percentage dividend payments to shareholders.

The functional areas within Marks & Spencer then set their own objectives in order to help the company achieve these goals, all focusing on the three key areas of product, service and environment. For example the finance department's objective was to deliver a range of financial solutions that were both simple and rewarding. Marketing worked on identifying how the range of products retailed by Marks & Spencer could be improved. The Human Resources function's objective was to ensure that the best employees were recruited and retained by the company. In IT, the goal was to create multi-channel retailing. The objective of operations was to improve the environment for customers and employees.

Marks & Spencer Chief Executive's Business Review 2007;
www.marksandspencer.com

Discussion points

1. Why would Marks & Spencer need to make its goals clear to all employees?

2. Why might Marks & Spencer have survival as a goal, even though it is a long-established, well-known retailer?

3. How might the marketing department at Marks & Spencer help the business to achieve its goal 'to compete in new product markets (goods and services)'?

4. Why is it important to set targets as part of the corporate plan?

5. For such a large organisation, which employs 68,000 in 30 countries in a very competitive market, will it be easy to ensure that the business achieves its objectives?

Fig. 1.1 *Marks & Spencer have had to change their traditional strategies to survive*

Corporate objectives

As a business grows, the founder(s) of the firm will become less involved in decision-making on a day-to-day basis. Their role is to establish long-term goals for the organisation and make the reasons for achieving these aims clear to key stakeholders in the business. Once the mission of the company and its aims has been set out, the **corporate objectives** can be established. These should be measurable targets so that the senior executives of the company can assess progress towards achieving the long-term goals of the business. They should also be clear, so that employees at all levels within the organisation are aware of what the company is trying to achieve. This should ensure that the daily decisions taken within each of the functional areas are based on the goals of the whole organisation, i.e. the corporate objectives.

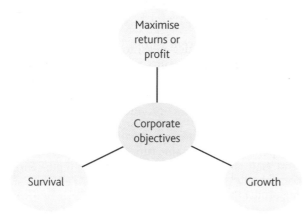

Fig. 1.2 *Some common corporate objectives*

Functional objectives

Every functional area, or department, within a business should use the corporate objectives to set its own targets. In this way the plans of all parts of the business can be focused on achieving the same longer-term goals. It is also important to stress that a particular plan, for example, for the marketing department, should not be seen as exclusive and separate from those of other departments. If the corporate objectives are to be achieved, all the **functional objectives** must be coordinated so that they do not contradict each other. Within any organisation, the success of any department will depend on the cooperation of all other areas of the business. This can be quite easy to achieve in small and medium-sized firms, but as companies grow larger and channels of communication become more complex, a coordinated approach to setting objectives and measuring performance can be difficult to maintain.

In this book, the financial, marketing, operational and human resource strategies available to larger businesses are examined. It should be noted that the functional areas used here are illustrative rather than definitive. Each company will have its own structure and therefore the departments which best meet its needs. However it is organised, it is very important to stress the interdependence of and possible conflicts between functional areas. Rather than viewing each department in isolation, businesses should appreciate that, whatever objectives each may set, they must all fit together. If there is no coordination of functional objectives, there is little chance of overall success.

For example, a manufacturing business may set itself the corporate objective of increasing profits by 15 per cent over the next five years. The Operations function may set the following as its objectives:

■ reduce waste to less than 1 per cent

■ reduce the workforce by 5 per cent.

The Marketing function may set these objectives:

■ increase sales by 25 per cent over the next three years

■ increase customer satisfaction to 95 per cent within two years.

The Human Resource function may decide on the following objectives:

■ reduce administration and managerial staff by 15 per cent

■ increase productivity per employee by 6 per cent.

The Finance function may set these objectives:

■ reduce adverse budget variances in every functional area

■ cut supply costs by 2.5 per cent within 18 months.

It is clear that, although all these functional objectives will contribute to the achievement of the corporate objective, they need to be discussed and coordinated so that time and effort is not wasted and conflict between functional areas does not arise.

In the above example, the Operations department wants to reduce the workforce by 5 per cent. At the same time, the HR department has the objective of increasing employee productivity by 6 per cent. These two objectives must be coordinated so that the most efficient size of workforce is retained.

Fig. 1.3 *The relationship between corporate and functional objectives*

Key terms

Functional strategy: the plan by which the department intends to achieve its functional objectives on a day-to-day basis.

Functional strategies

Once the functional objectives have been agreed, the detailed plans (**functional strategies**) of how they can be achieved must be developed. Again these plans must be specific and quantifiable so that managers can measure progress and, ultimately, success. These functional strategies should be the result of consultation with those involved in the implementation of the plans, otherwise there is a real possibility that the functional strategies may be unrealistic or too vague. Either of these situations could lead to delay and demotivation because they indicate that the channels of communication in the organisation are not effective.

In other words, the functional strategies need to include **SMART targets**. In fact, to be successful, the process of setting objectives, measuring performance and devising strategies should share this common theme.

Business in action

Marks & Spencer: functional strategies

These are some of the functional strategies Marks & Spencer have implemented since the formulation of Stuart Rose's plan:

- the acquisition of Per Una (previously a separate business used under a licensing agreement)
- negotiation of the sale of Marks & Spencer Money to HSBC while retaining 50 per cent of the profits
- heavy TV, newspaper and billboard advertising for Marks & Spencer products
- increasing the number of customer assistants and the amount of time they spend helping customers
- improvements to the rewards package, training and career paths
- launch of a new website
- a programme of store modernisation
- streamlining of product ranges to reduce costs and problems with high stock levels
- introduction of new products and services, for example home technology.

Key terms

SMART targets:

Specific – no confusion about what is required.

Measurable – a quantifiable goal is clear.

Agreed – the result of consultation with those involved in their delivery.

Realistic – an impossible goal is likely to demotivate employees at any level of the hierarchy in the organisation.

Time-based – so that progress towards achievement can be measured.

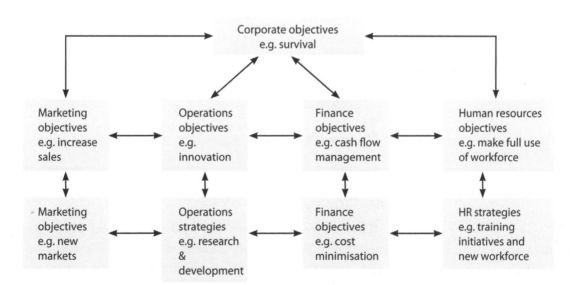

Fig. 1.4 *The relationship between functional objectives and strategies*

AQA Examiner's tip

Do not spend time in an exam explaining what SMART targets are. Assume the examiner knows, and apply the principle to your analysis of the business in question: the objectives it has set, how performance is measured and whether the strategies employed are feasible.

Case study

Greater output frames company strategy

In 2001, Rolls-Royce, the UK jet engine maker, cut 11.5 per cent of its workforce following the crisis in the world aviation and aerospace industries after the terrorist attacks on the US. In January 2008, Rolls-Royce announced that nearly 6 per cent of its global workforce would go, 2,300 support and clerical staff, but for very different reasons. Unlike seven years ago, the company is enjoying record order books, with an estimated £45bn backlog of work. Rolls-Royce has been trying to improve its productivity in the past two years, and on Friday the company insisted the job cuts were not so much a response to external factors, but part of a continuing programme to enhance its competitiveness. It stressed that it was continuing to recruit graduates and apprentices. Mike Terrett, the chief operating officer, said, 'We are determined to create a leaner and more flexible support structure, better suited to the global markets in which we operate.' In recent years, under the leadership of Sir John Rose, chief executive, Rolls-Royce has also tried to build a more global footprint. Although 23,300 of its 39,500 employees are still in the UK, it is expanding operations around the world. The company will invest £150m in two plants in Singapore and the US over the next five years to increase global manufacturing capacity, cope with surging new orders and reduce exposure to the weak dollar. In September, the company decided to site a new £30m test centre in Brandenburg, Germany, after being given a better financial package than that which was available in Britain. The company had considered locating the new centre in Derby, home to most of the company's UK manufacturing operations, which employs about 13,000 people. However, Friday's announcement is not related to this. In the past five years, Rolls-Royce has invested more than £800m in the UK. Bernie Hamilton of Amicus said, 'This is about a company trying to improve its operations.'

Adapted from The Financial Times *2008*

Questions

1. To what extent will the existence of functional objectives at Rolls-Royce contribute to achieving the corporate objective of 'enhancing its competitiveness'?

2. Analyse the range of functional strategies Rolls-Royce might pursue to achieve its functional objective of creating 'a leaner and more flexible support structure'.

3. To what extent will a coordinated approach to setting objectives and devising strategies be important to Rolls-Royce achieving its corporate objectives?

4. Analyse the difficulties a large organisation like Rolls-Royce might face in coordinating functional objectives.

5. Research task: Select two UK businesses operating in different markets and find the latest annual report online. Read through the Chief Executive's summary to identify the corporate objectives of the business. Investigate the functional objectives and strategies that have been put in place and find evidence of whether the company is on target to successfully achieve its goals.

✅ *In this chapter you will have learned to:*

- explain and illustrate how functional objectives are drawn from corporate objectives
- explain the relationship between functional objectives and functional strategies
- discuss the importance of a coordinated approach to setting objectives and devising strategies within a large organisation, and the difficulties such businesses may face
- analyse a range of functional objectives that a business might pursue to achieve its corporate objectives
- make a judgement about the extent to which the pursuit of functional objectives and strategies will enable a business to achieve its corporate objectives.

Summary questions

1. What is the relationship between functional objectives and functional strategies? (2 marks)

2. What should be the reference point for any department when deciding its objectives? (2 marks)

3. Explain why all objectives and strategies should be SMART targets. (4 marks)

4. New Look, the fashion retailer, may have the corporate objective of increasing market share. What functional objectives might be agreed to achieve this? (6 marks)

5. A UK pharmaceutical company has the corporate objective of growth in the global market. The Operations department has the objective of developing treatments for curable diseases in developing countries, while the Marketing department's objective is to increase the sale of products that slow down the ageing process. How does this situation illustrate why it is important to have a coordinated approach to setting functional objectives? (10 marks)

Introduction

Chapters in this section:

This section examines the range of financial objectives set by larger businesses. Many of these will be plcs and as a result the financial objectives set are likely to be informed or constrained by the need to maintain shareholder value. It will look at the ways in which financial performance can be measured, which will include interpreting published accounts and the use of ratio analysis. Finally, it will look at the financial strategies that large businesses may deploy to meet the objectives and the numerical tools available to aid decision-making.

Throughout this section you will be expected to carry out calculations and demonstrate an ability to interpret your findings. You will now be looking at the financial documents produced by larger businesses. This work does, however, follow on from your AS finance material.

Chapter 2: Understanding financial objectives
In Chapter 1, you were introduced to the concept of functional objectives and how these link to corporate objectives. In this chapter, you will take a more in-depth look at the range of objectives set within the finance function of large businesses. You will also look at how the setting of financial objectives is influenced by internal and external factors, such as the nature of the firm and the action of competitors.

Chapter 3: Using financial data to measure and assess performance
Having considered the range of financial objectives set by businesses, we now move on to look at how financial data can be used to measure performance against those objectives. This involves learning about the financial documents published by plcs, i.e. balance sheets and income statements.

Chapter 4: Interpreting published accounts
Having learnt about financial documents (published accounts) in Chapter 3, we take a more detailed look at how to interpret them. This is done through ratio analysis. Ratios allow for a more meaningful interpretation of accounts from a range of perspectives. Here we look at how ratios can help us to interpret key measures of business and financial performance, such as profitability and financial efficiency.

Chapter 5: Selecting financial strategies
This chapter looks at a number of financial strategies that are available to businesses in order to try to meet their financial objectives and improve their financial performance. Consideration is also given to the interrelationship between financial strategies and other functional areas.

Chapter 6: Making investment decisions
This is the final chapter on finance. It looks at how organisations look to measure the potential worth of an investment in order to inform decision-making. Three forms of investment appraisal are explained: pay back, average rate of return and net present value.

Understanding financial objectives

In this chapter you will learn to:

- understand the range of financial objectives typically set by larger businesses

- explain how internal and external factors can influence the setting of financial objectives.

Setting the scene

Domino's delivers bigger profits

Domino's opened its first UK store in 1985 and has since become recognised as the UK's leading pizza delivery chain. Domino's operates as a franchise allowing it to achieve rapid growth. By 2007 it operated from in excess of 500 stores and enjoyed a profit before tax of £18.7 million. In 2007 they opened 50 new stores and aim to continue to grow by opening 50 stores a year. As well as new stores, sales have also been increased by the introduction of new pizzas including the Meateor and rugby-themed Scrummy. Perhaps more significant has been the growth in online ordering, via both the internet and texting, which increased by 60.9% in 2007. The scooter delivery specialist predicted the trend for ordering food from home would continue.

In 2007 the company was faced with rising input costs and responded by raising prices by 4%. They have subsequently negotiated a fixed cost for flour until the end of the year and thinks that the cost of one of their other major ingredients, cheese, is starting to fall.

The Guardian, *February 2008*

Discussion points

1. Who do you think would set the financial objectives for individual Domino stores: the franchisee, franchisor or a combination?

2. How and why might the financial objectives vary between new and established stores?

3. What do you think the financial objectives of Domino's would have been in 2008?

4. Are there any factors outside of the control of Domino's that might influence its financial objectives?

Fig. 2.1 *Domino's is recognised as the UK's leading pizza delivery chain*

Financial objectives

Financial objectives refer to the monetary goals a business sets itself to achieve in a given time period, often a financial year. These provide both a target for the business to aim for as well as a mechanism against which to measure performance. For most plcs, their prime financial objective will be to maximise shareholder return. Although objectives are normally set on an annual basis, there is often a need to look at the greater strategic vision of the business. Large businesses will often set very focused objectives for one year or even a quarterly objective and then also longer-term five-year objectives. The five-year objective may be less specific and just focus on key headline figures such as revenue, costs and profits. Businesses will aim to maximise shareholder return by maximising their profits and undertake financial strategies to widen the gap between revenue and costs.

Link

Financial strategies are discussed in more detail in Chapter 5 — Selecting financial strategies, page 32.

Key terms

Cash-flow targets: a financial objective focused on maintaining a healthy cash balance.

Cost minimisation: the process by which businesses attempt to maximise profits by keeping costs low.

Activity

What is meant by the saying, 'cash flow is the oxygen of the business'?

Links

Business costs are explained in *AS Business Studies*, Chapter 11 — Calculating costs, revenues and profits, page 75.

Choosing suppliers is discussed in *AS Business Studies*, Chapter 26 — Working with suppliers, page 195.

Cash-flow targets

Financial objectives may focus on return on investment; however, this can only be achieved if the firm can meet a more fundamental objective of survival. It is therefore important for a firm to focus on cash flow as well as profitability. A firm that does not set or achieve a healthy **cash-flow target** may struggle to survive due to liquidity problems. Cash-flow targets may be as broad as to maintain a positive cash flow or more specific such as to maintain a cash balance of £x amount. When setting cash-flow targets, businesses must be aware, that although cash is the oxygen of the business, there is an opportunity cost associated with holding too much cash. Cash-flow targets may be focused on a more tactical aspect of cash-flow management and improving cash flow. Later in this unit, you will also look at ways of measuring financial efficiency which include debtor days (how long it takes on average to receive money owed from customers) and creditor days (how long on average it takes to pay money owing to suppliers).

Cost minimisation

Cost minimisation seems like a relatively straightforward objective. It is easy to see why a business may want to achieve this, because if they can minimise costs without having a negative effect on revenue, then the profit margins achieved will be improved. At AS Level, you would have identified that the costs of a business are wide ranging, from the fixed costs such as rent on premises to variable costs such as the wages of operatives. If a business sets a financial objective of cost minimisation, then it should look at all its costs for areas where savings can be made without affecting either their ability to operate or the customers' opinion of their goods and services. Cost minimisation could be achieved by a tactical decision such as changing suppliers or through a more strategic decision such as to relocate abroad.

■ Business in action

Cadbury's sweetened by mint sales

In the first half of 2008, Cadbury's profits rose by 28%, boosted by a rise in sales of chewing gum and throat lozenges.

The confectioner said it planned to cut costs to compensate for an expected 6% rise in the cost of ingredients.

Cadbury's said that despite challenging economic conditions, it was determined to deliver a strong performance for the rest of the year.

'We will take whatever measures are necessary in costs, prices, organisation structure and business portfolio to underpin and deliver [our] performance commitments,' said Cadbury's chairman Roger Carr.

news.bbc.co.uk

Fig. 2.2 *Cadbury's Dairy Milk now available in a whole host of flavours*

Return on capital employed (ROCE) targets

ROCE targets are a measure of the return achieved by a business, i.e. the operating profit as a percentage of the amount of capital tied up in the business; the capital employed. ROCE is a measure of a firm's profitability and performance. By setting a target for ROCE, a business will be stating the minimum percentage return it deems appropriate on its total investments. This target may be set in relation to an industry-standard ROCE achieved by other branches within a business or in recognition of the amount of risk being taken. As a minimum, it would be normal to see the ROCE target being set above the rate of interest that could be achieved if the capital employed were simply placed in a bank account.

Shareholders' return

Managing directors often refer to their prime financial objective as being to serve the interest of their shareholders or maximise shareholder value. This is an important objective as ultimately it is the shareholders who own the business. Although in large organisations, the influence of shareholders may not be obvious on a day-to-day basis, the need to maximise their returns will be a key factor influencing decision-making. If shareholders become dissatisfied, they have the option of selling their shares. If this is true of a number of shareholders or even of a few major shareholders, then the company shares will become freely available on the stock exchange, at a lower price. If sufficient shares become available, this can make the business vulnerable to takeovers. Shareholder value or **shareholders' return** has two distinct components:

▪ the market value of the share itself, i.e. how much could the shareholder get from selling their investment

▪ the dividend paid, i.e. how much do they receive from profits as a reward for their investment.

Shareholders also have the power not to reappoint members of the board of directors. It is therefore very much in the interest of the directors to look after the company shareholders.

▪ Internal and external influences

Financial objectives are set in a business by the board of directors and coordinated with the corporate objectives. However, the specific objectives set are also affected by a number of internal and external influences.

Internal influences

Characteristics of the firm

The size, status and, potentially, age of a firm can all have an influence on the financial objectives. At AS Level, for example, you will have predominantly studied small to medium-sized firms, many of whom would have had a financial objective of **satisficing**. At A2 level, however, you have moved on to look at larger organisations including plcs who will have an objective of maximising shareholder returns. The status of a business will also have an influence. For example, a business which is the dominant player in a market may strive to maintain this position through an objective of cost minimisation to improve competitiveness.

Owners

Financial objectives are likely to vary depending upon the relationship between owners and directors, the number of owners and their motives. If a

▪ **Links**

Further discussion on the strategies available to a business aiming to achieve cost minimisation can be found in Chapter 5 — Selecting financial strategies, page 32.

See also Chapter 14 — Operational strategies: location, page 102.

▪ **Key terms**

ROCE targets: the minimum percentage return a business strives to achieve from the capital employed in business activities.

Shareholders' returns: the financial rewards to a shareholder in return for their investment; this can include dividends paid and increased share value.

Satisficing: aiming to achieve a satisfactory level of profit.

▪ **Link**

Further details on the calculation of capital employed are given in Chapter 4 — Interpreting published accounts, page 22.

AQA Examiner's tip

If shareholders start to sell their shares, this does not have a direct impact on the amount of money available to the business, as the trading of shares takes place between the existing and future shareholders not directly with the company. Candidates often show a misunderstanding of this point in the examination.

Fig. 2.3 *The market value of shares change as they are bought and sold on the stock exchange*

business is fully floated on the Stock Exchange, it is likely that a substantial number of its shareholders will be pension or investment funds. Their objectives will therefore be the short-term maximisation of return on their investment. This will, in turn, allow the pension and investment funds to report a positive growth of funds to their own investors. If, however, the shareholders are fewer in number and are more directly involved with the business either as **executive directors** or **non-executive directors**, then they may be willing to set objectives linked to reinvestment of profits or expansion in order to maximise future potential returns.

Sector

The sector within which a business operates will also influence the financial objectives set. If, for example, the owners are private investors, i.e. the business operates in the private sector, then an objective of profit maximisation may be set. An organisation operating in the public sector, however, may have an overall objective of providing a service to the community but may set a financial objective to maintain a positive cash flow.

External influences

Competitors' actions

In order to maintain competitiveness, a business is often forced to set a specific financial objective. If, for example, an organisation is trying to gain market share via an aggressive pricing strategy, their competitors may be forced to set an objective of cost minimisation in order to also be able to afford to reduce prices.

Economic conditions

Directors will be aware of current and predicted future trends in the economy. If it is thought that the economy is unstable and that the degree of activity within it, i.e. the amount of buying and selling taking place, may decline in the future, then directors may be more cautious when setting financial objectives. A fall in economic activity may mean a fall in consumer confidence and consequently their willingness to spend. In these circumstances, a business may set their profit objective at a lower level than if they thought consumer spending was likely to increase in the future. Also when setting a ROCE target, a business will look at the current and predicted future rate of interest. If they suspect that the rate of interest will rise in the future, then this might lead to the setting of a higher ROCE target.

■ Key terms

Executive director: a member of the board of directors who also holds a position of responsibility in the business on a day-to-day basis, for example marketing director, finance director.

Non-executive director: a member of the board of directors who does not work for the business on a day-to-day basis but sits on the board in an advisory or consultative role.

AQA Examiner's tip

For the exam you will not need to have a detailed understanding of external influences and the economic environment. It is useful, however, to understand that when setting financial objectives a business will look at what is going on around it as well as what is going on within the firm.

■ Case study

Employee or shareholder satisfaction?

Optical Excellence plc manufactures and supplies fibre optical network equipment to the telecommunication industry. Despite the hi-tech, and hence capital intensive, nature of the industry, it also relies heavily on its employees. Without its dedicated team of engineers and technical experts, the business would fail to keep ahead in this technologically advanced and fast moving market.

As part of its annual employee satisfaction survey, it asked staff the following questions:

■ How happy are you with pay?
■ How happy are you with your working conditions?

■ Do you feel valued?

■ Would you recommend Optical Excellence as an employee to your friends?

The results came as somewhat of a shock with over 80 per cent of respondents stating they were slightly or very unhappy with the level of pay received. Despite this, they were happy with the working conditions and would recommend Optical Excellence to their friends.

At the next board meeting the directors met to discuss the findings of the survey. It was agreed that there should be a review of the pay scales. The Finance Director was, however, concerned about the impact that this would have on their financial objectives. They agreed that there was no need to change the objective of maximising sales revenue whilst minimising the cost of raw materials. It was, however, necessary to review the net profit objective downwards. The Managing Director was keen for this to be communicated to shareholders in a positive light as part of a long-term strategy to improve employee satisfaction and performance.

Questions

1. Briefly explain how internal influences affected the financial objectives of Optical Excellence plc.

2. How might external influences have affected the workers' attitudes towards their pay?

3. Analyse the impact of the board of directors' decision on both short and long-term returns to shareholders.

4. To what extent do you agree with the Managing Director that it was important to communicate the changes on objectives to the shareholders in a positive light? Justify your answer.

☑ *In this chapter you will have learned to:*

■ show understanding of the range of financial objectives set by larger businesses

■ understand how internal and external factors influence the setting of financial objectives.

Summary questions

1. With the use of an appropriate example, explain what the term 'financial objective' means to the directors of a hotel chain such as Marriott or Jarvis. (6 marks)

2. Briefly explain one advantage to a business of setting financial objectives. (6 marks)

3. Why might setting a cash-flow target be seen as crucial to the short-term survival of a business? (8 marks)

4. Outline two potential disadvantages to a manufacturer of high street fashions of an objective of cost minimisation. (10 marks)

5. Explain how failing to meet a satisfactory level of shareholder return may make a plc vulnerable to takeover. (8 marks)

6. Explain how the financial objectives of a hospital in the private sector may vary to those of one in the public sector. In what ways may this influence the day-to-day operations of the hospitals? (14 marks)

3 Using financial data to measure and assess performance

- analyse how income statements are used to assess performance and potential

- analyse how balance sheets are used to assess performance and potential

- understand the importance of working capital and depreciation

- understand the importance of profit utilisation and profit quality

- use financial data for comparisons, trend analysis and decision-making

- assess the strengths and weaknesses of financial data in judging performance.

Setting the scene

Life Leisure plc

New Financial Director Jack Barn is excited about the future prospects of Life Leisure plc. The company owns a number of gyms, cinemas and indoor adventure centres across the UK. It has recently sold off a hotel it owned in order to concentrate on its core interests of fitness and leisure. Jack is preparing for his first board meeting where the Board of Directors want to discuss proposals to upgrade the swimming pools within two of the gyms to Olympic standard. Jack is aware that all eyes will be on him when it comes to discussing the numbers behind the proposal. Jack has prepared a summary of the last two years' income statement to present to the Board.

Table 3.1 *Summary of income statement for Life Leisure plc 2008 and 2009*

	2009 (£m)	2008 (£m)
Revenue	54	52
Gross profit	32	35
Operating profit	3.5	4
Revenue from other sources *	12	
Profit for period	15.5	4

* Note to accounts: sale of hotels

Discussion points

1. As well as the income statement, what other financial information do you think Jack and the Board should be interested in?

2. What do you think the financial objectives of Life Leisure plc are likely to be?

3. Do you consider the performance of Life Leisure plc to have improved or deteriorated from 2008 to 2009?

4. Why should Jack and the Board of Directors be cautious of making an investment decision just based on the profit figure for 2009?

Activities

1. Why would shareholders, potential investors, banks and employees be interested in the annual report?

2. Who else might be interested and why?

Sources of financial data

Companies are required to produce an annual report which is a very important document. It is a formal report which outlines the company's performance in the previous year. For anyone wishing to research a company, this is probably the best starting point. The report will give details on how the company has performed financially as well as explaining the business's mission and management philosophy. The Director's report will summarise the business's performance over the last 12 months and list the financial highlights.

The annual report is produced for and distributed to shareholders but is also of interest to a number of other parties including potential investors, banks and employees.

Within a company's annual report, there are a number of financial documents. The two main documents are the income statement and the balance sheet.

Analysis of an income statement

An **income statement** is a summary of a business's trading activity and its expenditure over a period of time. Within the annual report this will normally be a year, but many businesses will also produce interim accounts to assess performance at a mid-year point. Ultimately, this statement shows the reader whether the business has made a profit or a loss.

Income statements often vary slightly in their format but Table 3.2 shows how the information may be laid out and what would be included.

Table 3.2 *Income statement for Ted Baker plc, for 52 weeks ending 27 January 2007*

	£000s	£000s
Revenue	125,648	
Cost of sales	51,986	
Gross profit		73,662
Operating costs	53,612	
Operating profit		20,050
Income tax expense	5,634	
Profit for the period		14,416
Attributed to: Equity shareholders of parent company		14,416

Adapted from Annual Report Ted Baker plc

When analysing the income statement there are a number of key points to consider: gross profit, operating profit, profit margins, profit quality and profit utilisation.

Gross profit

Profit after the cost of sales has been deducted but before deducting other expenses is called **gross profit**. Cost of sales are the costs incurred directly generating the revenue, for example raw materials and direct labour.

Operating profit

Profit after other expenses have been deducted, for example administration and distribution expenses, is called **operating profit**. It can also be referred to as 'net profit'. Removing tax from profit calculations can give a good impression of a company's profits from year to year, as tax may increase or decrease out of the control of business.

Key terms

Income statement: a financial document that summarises a business's trading activity and expenses to show whether it has made a profit or a loss.

Gross profit: profit after cost of sales has been deducted.

Operating profit: profit after all other expenses have been deducted, also referred to as net profit.

Fig. 3.1 *Ted Baker, a leading British fashion label*

■ Key terms

Gross profit margin: gross profit expressed as a percentage of sales revenue.

Operating profit margin: operating profit expressed as a percentage of sales revenue.

Profit quality: the sustainability of profit.

Profit utilisation: how profit is being used, i.e. whether it is being ploughed back into the business or distributed to shareholders.

Profit margins

At AS Level you would have learnt about net profit margins. When analysing income statements, it is worth looking at both **gross profit margins** and **operating profit margins**.

$$\text{Gross profit margin \% = Gross profit} \div \text{Sales revenue} \times 100$$

■ Activities

1 Using Table 3.2, calculate the operating profit margin and gross profit margin for Ted Baker plc in 2006.

2 What do these figures show you?

3 How significant do you think the Ted Baker brand name is in achieving the gross profit margin?

Profit quality

Profit quality is the degree to which the profit figure is sustainable in the future, i.e. what percentage of it is from routine day-to-day activity as opposed to a non-routine activity, such as selling off a division or an asset for a profit.

Profit utilisation

Profit utilisation is the way in which the profit is used, i.e. the split between how much is distributed to shareholders in the form of dividends and how much is reinvested back into the business, known as retained profit. When considering profit utilisation, it is worth considering the short v. long-term objectives of the shareholders.

The income statement is a summary of the company's financial performance and the annual report will contain a lot more detailed information that will help the company directors assess the performance of the company.

■ Business in action

Ted Baker plc

If we dig deeper into the Annual Report of Ted Baker plc, we find that the revenue figure of £125,648,000 can be subdivided in a number of ways as shown here:

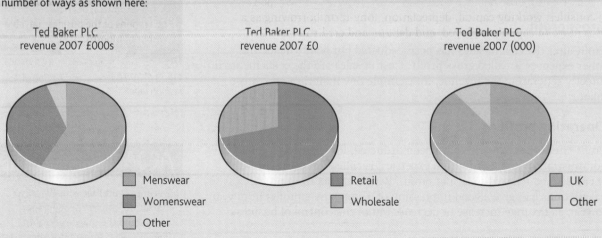

Fig. 3.2 *Subdivision of Ted Baker revenue*

Why would the information given in Fig. 3.2 be of interest to decision-makers within the business?

Analysis of a balance sheet

A **balance sheet** shows the net worth of a business at a set point in time by looking at what the business owns (its assets), for example premises and stock (**inventories**), and what it owes (its equity and liabilities), for example overdrafts and share capital. In order for a balance sheet to balance, total assets must equal **total equity** and liabilities.

Businesses own two types of assets. These are categorised as **non-current assets** and **current assets**. Fixed assets are those that have a useful life in excess of one year , for example cars and buildings, while current assets are expected to vary in value on a daily basis as a direct result of normal business operations, for example cash and inventories. **Intangible assets** are purchased assets of the business that are not physical, e.g. goodwill and brand names. Liabilities are also categorised into two types: **current liabilities** and **non-current liabilities**. Both are financial obligations of the business, but current liabilities are those that are expected to be paid within one year, for example creditors and bank overdraft, whereas long-term liabilities are those which will be paid over a longer period of time, for example bank loans. Assets and liabilities can be looked at in terms of **net current liabilities** and **net assets**.

All balance sheets vary slightly in their format, but Table 3.3 shows how the information may be laid out and what would be included.

Since 2005 there have been significant changes to the way that publi limited companies in the UK present their accounts. They now have to comply with International Financial Reporting Standards (IFRS). This means that:

1 Some old accounts or examnination papers you might see will use slightly different terms
2 The layout and terms used in this book and AQA A2 Business Studies examination papers will follow IFRS practice but will include familiar terms as well *where this aids student understanding.*

When analysing the balance sheet, there are a number of key points to consider: working capital, depreciation, long-term borrowing as a percentage of capital employed, and debtors and creditors.

 Examiner's tip

'Inventories' is the International Accounting Standards terminology for what you most commonly know as 'stock'. 'Inventories' will be used in this and the following chapter, as we will be discussing accounting data and so should use the accepted terminology. However, either 'inventories' or 'stocks' will be marked as correct in your examination.

Key terms

Balance sheet: a financial document that summarises the net worth of a business – it balances total assets with total equity and liabilities.

Inventories: the IFRS term for stocks.

Total equity: the total amount of money being utilised in the business from share capital and retained profit.

Non-current assets (fixed assets): items of value owned by the business that are likely to be kept for more than one year.

Current assets: resources owned by the business whose value varies as a result of daily business activities, e.g. cash, inventories.

Intangible assets: purchased items without physical form such as goodwill or brand names.

Current liabilities: financial obligations of the business payable within 12 months.

Non-current liabilities (long-term liabilities): debts that the business has more than one year to repay.

Net current liabilities: current liabilities plus current assets [do not forget th at current liabilities are a negative figure and shown in ( ) on the balance sheet].

Net assets: total assets minus total liabilities [also obtained by non-current assets plus net current liabilities minus non-current liabilites].

Key terms

Working capital: a measure of a firm's ability to meet day-to-day expenses.

Depreciation: an accounting practice which allows the value of a fixed asset to be spread over its useful life.

Link

See Chapter 4 — Interpreting published accounts, page 22, for further explanation of gearing.

Table 3.3 *Balance sheet for Lightening Hire plc as at 31 December 2009*

	£m	£m
Non-current assets:		
Intangible assets	71	
Premises	100	
Vehicles	105	
Fixtures and fittings	90	
Total non-current assets		366
Current assets:		
Inventories	11	
Trade receivables	101	
Cash	15	
Total current assets	127	
Current liabilities		
Trade payables	(92)	
Net current liabilities		35*
Non-current liabilities:		
Long-term Bank loan		(186)
Net assets		215
Equity:		
Share capital	61	
Retained profit	154	
Total equity		215

*If current liabilities exceed current assets then net current liabilities will be a negative figure.**

Working capital

Working capital is an indication of a firm's ability to meet its day-to-day expenses and hence survive in the short run. It is calculated as current assets minus current liabilities. If a business cannot generate enough cash in the short term to pay its short-term liabilities, then it may be forced to liquidate its fixed assets without which it cannot continue to operate.

Depreciation

Fixed assets are depreciated each year in order to ensure that the value shown in the balance sheet is a true and fair reflection of their worth. **Depreciation** is classed as an expense in the income statement to ensure that the cost of the asset is being spread over its useful life. This is in line with an accountancy concept known as the matching concept, i.e. matching the cost of an asset to its usage.

Non-current liabilities as a percentage of capital employed (or total equity plus non-current liabilities)

This is known as gearing. It is an indication of how reliant a firm is on borrowing and hence how at risk it is from an increase in interest rates. A firm which is heavily geared may find it more difficult to produce accurate budgets and cash flows, as a small rise in the interest rate could have a big impact on the amount they have to pay.

'Trade receivables' and 'trade payables'

If **trade receivables** from **debtors** are high, it may be because of fierce competition in the market and a need to offer favourable credit terms in order to achieve a competitive advantage or it may be a sign of internal weaknesses. It could be that credit control within the business needs to be improved.

If **trade payables** from **creditors** are low, a business may wish to consider whether it could improve its cash flow and working capital by negotiating more favourable payment terms with its suppliers. Alternatively it may be that the business is happy to keep creditors low and enjoy discounts offered for prompt payments helping their profitability.

> ### Key terms
>
> **Trade receivables:** amounts owed by debtors to the business.
>
> **Debtor:** someone who owes the business money, i.e. a customer who has not yet paid.
>
> **Trade payables:** amounts owed by the business to creditors.
>
> **Creditor:** someone the business owes money to, i.e. a supplier who has not yet been paid.

> ### Activities
>
> 1. What would happen if a business bought a new machine for £2.5m and put it in as an expense in the income statement in the year of purchase?
>
> 2. Why would this be an unwise thing to do?
>
> 3. What would happen if a business bought a new lorry for £200,000 and after four years still showed the value of the vehicle as £200,000 in the balance sheet?
>
> 4. Why would this not make sense from a business point of view?

Using financial data

Financial data is of interest to a large number of stakeholders both internal and external to the business. Within a business financial data will be used for a number of purposes, including inter-firm comparisons, intra-firm comparisons, trend analysis and decision-making.

Inter-firm comparisons

Inter-firm means between different firms and is likely to include comparisons with competitors or similar-sized firms. One firm might look at another successful firm in order to set targets for future performance. This is known as benchmarking. Intra-firm comparisons would also form an integral part of any takeover plans.

Intra-firm comparisons

Intra-firm means within the business and might include comparisons between branches, divisions, geographical locations or product ranges. A chain of fast-food restaurants, for example, might compare the profitability of like-sized restaurants within the chain to identify which ones are operating most efficiently. This would then allow them to improve overall performance by sharing good practice.

Trend analysis

Businesses will want to track their performance over time in order to assess whether they are operating efficiently or not and also to help extrapolate a trend into the future. If, for example, a business notices that over time its stock valuation each year is creeping up, but sales revenue is static, it may wish to investigate the cause of the rise in stock value.

Decision-making

All decisions made within a business are going to be influenced in some way by the current financial situation or influenced by the impact of the decision on future financial performance. Whether the decision be to invest in new capital equipment, automate a production line, increase staffing levels or launch a new product, financial data will form an integral part of the decision-making process.

■ Strengths and weaknesses of financial data

Published accounts arc a valuable source of information but should be read with care and in conjunction with the rest of the company's annual report and a consideration of external factors in order to gain a more detailed understanding of the company's performance. The annual report, for example, will also give details about the company's objectives, social responsibilities and cash flow.

Accounts published by plcs have to be audited by an independent auditor who will check their accuracy. The income statement looks back over the year's trading and should therefore be a true and fair picture of the company's activities. The balance sheet, however, will also be a true representation of the business's worth at the time at which it is drawn up, but it is only a snapshot and as such is only accurate at that moment in time.

One of the biggest problems with reading published accounts is that they may have been 'window dressed'. Window dressing is the process of manipulating accounts to make them look more favourable. This may include altering methods of inventory valuation, valuation of intangible assets and depreciation calculations. Window dressing is legal and should be easily identified by reading the notes to the accounts which explain how financial decisions were made, for example, how assets were valued.

Activity

1. How do you put a financial value on a brand name?
2. How do you decide how long an asset will last?
3. How do you determine the value of inventories held at the end of the year?

AQA Examiner's tip

Read the case study carefully for evidence of any window dressing that may have taken place. Window dressing is legal.

Case study

A difficult trading period!

David Bernstein, Chairman of Blacks Leisure Group plc, reported operating profit to be substantially lower in 2007 than previous years. He said that this reflected a difficult trading period for both the summer and Christmas seasons. The group, which includes Millets, Blacks Outdoor, Freespirit, Just Add Water and Outdoor, announced plans in the annual report to close approximately 45 loss making stores, predominantly Millets. It was estimated that closing these stores and exiting onerous leases would cost £13.9 million. This is shown as a provision for exceptional items in the accounts (Appendix A). David predicted that these initiatives together with continued tight controls on working capital and costs would lead to an improved performance in 2007/8.

Table 3.4 *Summary of financial highlights Blacks Leisure plc*

	2007	2006
Turnover	298.3m	297.2m
Gross profit	165.8m	169.1m
Operating profit before exceptional items	1.6m	22.4m
Operating (loss)/profit	(12.3m)	21.4m

Adapted from Blacks Leisure plc Annual Report 2007

Questions

1. Identify the potential costs associated with the closure of the stores.

2. With the use of a numerical example, explain the difference between gross profit and operating profit.

3. Explain why it is important for Blacks Leisure to continue to keep tight control of costs and working capital.

4. Analyse the changes shown in the firm's financial highlights from 2006 to 2007.

5. To what extent do you agree with David Bernstein that the strategy to close 45 stores will lead to improved performance in 2007/2008?

✔ *In this chapter you will have learned to:*

- analyse how both income statements and balance sheets are used to assess performance and potential

- understand and explain the importance of working capital and depreciation

- understand and explain the importance of profit utilisation and profit quality

- use financial data for comparisons, trend analysis and decision-making

- assess the strengths and weaknesses of financial data in judging performance.

Summary questions

1. What is the function of an income statement? (3 marks)

2. What is meant by the term 'profit quality'? (3 marks)

3. What is the function of a balance sheet? (3 marks)

4. With the use of an appropriate example, distinguish between a current liability and a non-current liability. (6 marks)

5. Explain why it is important for a firm to take account of depreciation in both the income account and the balance sheet. (6 marks)

6. Explain how businesses such as Marks & Spencer might use financial data for both inter-firm and intra-firm comparisons. (8 marks)

7. Analyse how a potential investor might use the accounts of a limited company to judge its performance. (10 marks)

4 Interpreting published accounts

In this chapter you will learn to:

- understand how to select, calculate and interpret financial ratios to assess business performance
- explain the value and limitations of ratio analysis in measuring a business's performance.

Setting the scene

Which supermarket?

Fig. 4.1 *Supermarkets operate in a very competitive market*

The 2006 annual accounts of Sainsbury and Tesco showed the following financial information:

Table 4.1 *Sainsbury and Tesco compared*

	Sainsbury	Tesco
Sales revenue	£16,061m	£39,454m
Operating profit	£229m	£1,788m
Dividend per share	7.8p	8.63p
Average share price for year	317p	350p

http://ftcom.ar.wilink.com

Discussion points

1. Based on the information above, which of these supermarkets would you invest in, and why?

2. Use the website given above to investigate the current financial position of each supermarket. Would your investment decision still be the same?

3. What other information would be useful in helping you make a more informed investment decision?

Conducting ratio analysis

The International Accounting Standards Committee (IASC) framework states:

> *The objective of financial statements is to provide information that is useful to a wide range of users in making economic decisions.*

The financial statements are the published accounts of plcs, i.e. their balance sheet and income statement. The potential users of the financial statements include investors, lenders, managers, employees, customers, the government and local community. Ratio analysis provides these users with a tool which allows for a more meaningful interpretation of published accounts. It does this by comparing one item of financial data to another.

The example in Table 4.2 will be used throughout this chapter to illustrate the accounting ratios as we discuss them.

Table 4.2 *Income statement and balance sheet for Alquimia plc as of 31 December 2009*

Income statement		Balance sheet		
	£m		£m	£m
Revenue	1390	Non-current assets:		
Cost of sales	(568)	Property, plant and equipment		3,001
Gross profit	822	Current assets:		
Other expenses	(277)	Inventories	42	
Operating profit	545	Trade receivables	135	
		Cash and cash equivalents	75	
		Total current assets:		252
		Current liabilities		
		Trade payables	(219)	
		Net current liabilities		33
		Non-current liabilities		
		Bank loans		(1,734)
		Net Assets		1,300
		Equity		
		Share Capital	450	
		Reserves and retained profits	850	
		Total equity		1,300

Notes to accounts:
The total dividend for the year was £300m.
Purchases on credit in the year were £845m.
All sales are made on credit.
Market share price on 31 December 2009 was £10.22.

Liquidity ratios

Liquidity is a measure of a firm's ability to meet day-to-day expenditure. It compares a firm's current assets to its current liabilities in order to assess whether a firm has sufficient short-term assets to cover short-term debts.

Two common measures of liquidity are the **current ratio** and the **acid test ratio**.

Fig. 4.2 *If a firm has liquidity problems it may have to close down and sell all its inventories to try and raise cash*

Current ratio

Current ratio = Current assets ÷ Current liabilities

This is also known as the working capital ratio. At Alquimia plc, the current ratio is:

$$\frac{252}{219} = 1:1.15$$

This means that, for every £1 of current liabilities, it has £1.15 in current assets.

Acid test ratio

Acid test ratio = (Current assets – Inventories) ÷ Current liabilities

At Alquimia plc, the acid test ratio is:

$$\frac{252 - 42}{219} = \frac{210}{219} = 1:0.95$$

This means that for every £1 of current liabilities, it has only £0.95 in current assets excluding inventories.

It is useful to note that 'curent assets – inventories' can also be referred to as 'liquid assets'.

Both the current ratio and the acid test ratio look at whether the business has enough short-term assets to be able to pay its short-term debts if immediate repayment was demanded. If it does not, then it may be forced to turn other assets, i.e. fixed assets, into cash and this would threaten the continued existence of the business.

The acid test ratio is more challenging to a business as it takes into account that it may be difficult for a firm to turn its inventories into cash quickly and that such action is likely to affect the price at which stock can realistically be sold.

There is not an ideal number above which a business is deemed to have a healthy liquidity position as this would very much depend upon the nature of the industry and other variables. It is, however, true to say that the higher the ratio, the more liquid a business. However, if a firm has high liquidity, this could mean that it is failing to find suitable, profitable uses for its cash.

■ Case study

Thomas Cook Group

The group states that it has an overall objective 'to ensure that it is at all times able to meet its financial commitments as and when they fall due'. An extract from the accounts is shown in Table 4.3:

Table 4.3 *Extract from accounts, Thomas Cook Group*

	2007	2006
Current assets	£2,321.4m	£1,433.4m
of which Inventories	£27.4m	£10.5m
Current liabilities	£3,737.9m	£207,709m

In 2006, its current ratio was 1:0.689 and its acid test 1:0.684.

■ Activities

Look at Table 4.3.

1 Calculate the Thomas Cook Group's liquidity ratios for 2007.

2 Comment on its ability to meet its overall objective.

3 Why do you think the two ratios are so similar?

4 How and why might liquidity ratios differ in other industries?

Profitability ratios

Profitability ratios allow for the analysis of a firm's profits in relation to either its trading performance, i.e. its sales revenue, or the capital utilised in generating that profit.

Two common measures of profitability are the operating profit margin and the **return on capital employed (ROCE)**.

Operating profit margin (OPM)

In the AS book, this was referred to as the Net Profit Margin as we were largely dealing with private limited companies which still use the term 'net profit'. Public limited companies use the term 'operating profit' instead, but the calculation of the ratio is still the same. Operating profit margin expresses the relationship between operating profit and sales revenue:

Operating profit margin % = Operating profit ÷ Sales revenue x 100

At Alquimia plc, the operating profit margin is:

$$\frac{545}{1,390} \times 100 = 39\%$$

■ Key terms

Profitability: the relationship between business's profits and sales revenues.

Return on capital employed (ROCE): a measure of how efficiently a business is using its capital to generate profits.

An operating profit margin of 39 per cent means that for every £1 of sales, 39p is left as profit after expenses have been paid. This allows a firm to compare its performance year-on-year, as well as against the performance of other firms in the same industry or even in the trading market as a whole. A declining OPM may indicate to a business that it is not managing its costs effectively or that sales are declining without a proportional fall in costs.

Return on capital employed (ROCE)

This is also known as the primary efficiency ratio as it shows the overall performance of a business expressed as a percentage of the total long-term capital invested into it. It measures how efficiently management is able to use the capital tied up in the business to generate profits.

$$\text{ROCE \%} = \text{Operating profit} \div \left(\begin{array}{l}\text{Total equity +} \\ \text{Non-current liabilities}\end{array}\right) \times 100$$

At Alquimia plc, the ROCE is:

$$\frac{545}{3{,}253} \times 100 = 16.7\%$$

This means that for every £1 capital invested, a profit of 0.167p was generated in that financial year. This figure will be compared with the firm's ROCE from previous years, that of other companies in the same industry and the return potentially achievable from other investments.

Financial efficiency ratios

Although financial efficiency ratios can be used for inter-firm comparisons, their dominant use is going to be internal: to assess how efficiently management are controlling the financial operations of the business. This may be management themselves assessing their own performance against pre-set targets or by other interested parties, such as shareholders or suppliers.

Four financial efficiency ratios are considered in this A Level specification: asset turnover, inventory turnover, creditor days and debtor days.

Asset turnover

Asset turnover measures how efficiently assets have been used to generate sales revenue. Businesses will generally aim to achieve a high asset turnover to show that assets are working hard for the business.

$$\text{Asset turnover} = \text{Sales} \div \text{Net assets}$$

At Alquimia plc, the asset turnover is:

$$\frac{1{,}390}{1{,}300} = 1.07$$

This means that for every £1 invested in assets, the business was able to generate sales of £0.43 in one year. The rate of asset turnover will vary substantially between industries depending upon the degree of capital intensity. A highly technical business with high value of assets in relation to sales will have a much lower asset turnover than a service industry where assets may be relatively low, for example an advertising agency. Asset turnover is, however, particularly useful when looking at the operational efficiency of firms in the same industry or for intra-firm comparisons, i.e. to compare the performance of one branch of a retail chain against another.

■ **Key terms**

Asset turnover: a measure of how effectively a business is using its assets to generate sales.

Capital employed: capital employed = total equity + non-current liabilites. It is the total capital invested in the business from long-term sales.

■ **Link**

For more about capital intensity, see Chapter 12 — Operational strategies: scale and resource mix, page 90.

Inventory or stock turnover

Inventory turnover is a measure of how many times a business turns over its inventories in a year. A high inventory turnover indicates that a firm is selling inventories frequently to generate revenue. The rate of inventory turnover is, however, very much dependent upon the nature of the firm. For example, a fish monger may have an inventory turnover of 300 times.

$$\text{Inventory turnover} = \text{Cost of sales} \div \text{Inventory}$$

This ratio may also be calculated by using the 'average inventories held' figure. This is calculated by finding the average of inventories held at the start and the end of the year.

At Alquimia plc, the inventory turnover is:

$$\frac{582}{42} = 13.5 \text{ times}$$

This means that the business is selling its inventory 13.5 times per year, i.e. on average it holds inventories for less than one month.

Payables (creditor) days

Payables days is a measure of the average amount of time it takes to pay for supplies purchased on credit and is expressed as a number of days.

$$\text{Payables days} = (\text{Payables} \times 365 \text{ days}) \div \text{Credit purchases}$$

At Alquimia plc, the payables days are:

$$\frac{219 \times 365}{845} = 94 \text{ days}$$

If the figure for 'credit purchases' is not available, 'cost of sales' is used instead. This means that on average Alquimia pays for supplies approximately three months after receiving them. Businesses often look to negotiate long credit payment terms in order to help with their own cash flow. Some firms, however, set themselves internal targets to pay all debts within a set amount of time. This can feature as part of a business's corporate governance if they want to show that they treat their suppliers well. Suppliers may also be interested in creditor days to see whether a potential customer pays within the payment terms stipulated. A business may, for example, agree to pay within 30 days, but a look at the creditor days from their accounts may tell a different story.

Receivables (debtor) days

Receivables days is a measure of the average number of days it takes to receive payments from customers.

$$\text{Receivables (debtor) days} = (\text{Receivables} \times 365 \text{ days}) \div \text{Revenue}$$

At Alquimia plc, the receivables days are:

$$\frac{135 \times 365}{1,390} = 35 \text{ days}$$

This means that on average Alquimia can expect to receive payment for their sales 35 days, approximately one month, after the sale has taken place. Businesses often look to negotiate short debtor payment terms in order to help with their own cash flow. Some businesses will offer discounts for prompt payments of invoices in order to try and avoid cash-flow problems. Small businesses dealing with large customers may, however, be forced to offer long payment terms in order to secure an order or contract.

 Activity

What do you think would be an acceptable rate of inventory turnover for the following businesses? Explain your answer.
- Interflora
- Top Shop
- Boeing
- Waterstones
- BMW dealership

Key terms

Inventory (or stock) turnover: a measure of how many times per year a business turns over its stock through sales.

Payables (creditor) days: a measure of the average number of days taken to pay suppliers.

Receivables (debtor) days: a measure of the average number of days taken by a business to collect its debts from customers.

AQA Examiner's tip

If possible try to look at creditor days and debtor days in relation to each other. Businesses will normally aim for their debtor days to be lower than their creditor days.

Fig. 4.3 *High gearing is particularly risky if interest rates are high*

Gearing ratio

There is only one **gearing ratio**. This is a measure of the percentage of a firm's capital that is financed by long-term loans–or compulsory interest bearing sources that the company has to pay interest on regardless of profit.

$$\text{Gearing ratio \%} = \frac{\text{Non-current}}{\text{liabilities}} \div \left(\begin{array}{c}\text{Total equity +}\\ \text{non-current liabilities}\end{array}\right) \times 100$$

At Alquimia plc, the gearing ratio is:

$$\frac{1,734}{3,253} \times 100 = 53\%$$

This means that for every £1 invested in the business, 53p is from a long-term liability where interest payments are compulsory. If the rate is high, then the business may be at risk if interest rates were to rise, as this means payments on loans would rise. However, if a firm has a low gearing, this may mean that it is being overly cautious and missing out on potential investment opportunities. What is an appropriate gearing ratio will be dependent upon a number of factors, including stability of interest rates, age of the business, policy of the owners and the nature of the firm and product.

Shareholder ratios

In Chapter 2, you studied the importance of shareholder returns as a financial objective. Here we look at **shareholder ratios** that help measure the value of the return to a shareholder: dividend per share and dividend yield.

Dividend per share (DPS)

Dividend per share is a calculation of how many pence per share a shareholder can expect to receive in dividends. Dividends can be paid on an interim basis as well as at year end, but it is the total dividend for the year that is of interest here. This is calculated by dividing the total number of shares by the total amount paid out in dividends in a financial year.

$$\text{Dividend per share} = \text{Total dividends} \div \text{Number of issued shares}$$

At Alquimia plc, the DPS is:

$$\frac{£300m}{450} = 66.7p$$

This means that for each share owned, a shareholder will receive 66.7p. A shareholder may be willing to accept a lower dividend per share in the short run if profits are being reinvested for the long-term good of the business rather than distributed to shareholders. It is, however, difficult to make a judgement upon this without knowing either how much the shareholder paid for the share or more significantly the current market price of the share. The latter is taken into account by the next ratio.

Dividend yield

Dividend yield is a measure of the dividend received as a rate of return compared to the current market share price.

$$\text{Dividend yield} = (\text{Dividend per share} \div \text{Market share price}) \times 100$$

At Alquimia plc, the dividend yield is:

$$\frac{0.667}{10.22} \times 100 = 6.5\%$$

This allows for a more meaningful comparison of the value of the investment in relation to alternative investments. A yield of 6.5 per cent means that if a dividend of £1 was received, the expected value of the share would be £6.50. A shareholder could compare this to other share dividend yields and also to the rate of interest that could be achieved if the shares were sold and the money invested in the bank. Unlike the other ratios where all the information is available in the company accounts, the current market share price will be quoted on the Stock Exchange. The dividend yield can therefore go up or down even when the dividend paid remains constant.

Business in action

International Accounting Standards

Ratios are produced as part of management accounts and are therefore produced for internal use. Published accounts of companies are, however, published for external use as well as internal. They therefore have to follow the conventions of International Accounting Standards (IAS). If you were to look at a set of published accounts for a business, you would find that some of the terminology used is different. Table 4.4 gives some examples.

Table 4.4 *Examples of UK and IAS equivalent terms*

UK term	IAS term
Profit and loss account	Income statement
Fixed assets	Non-current assets
Stock	Inventories
Debtors	Trade receivables
Cash at bank and in hand	Cash and cash equivalents
Trade creditors	Trade payables

Value and limitations of ratio analysis

Ratios are a valuable tool when analysing financial documents because they provide structure and put figures into a context. If both Company A and Company B have a sales revenue of £1m, it is not possible to comment upon which one has greatest profitability or financial efficiency without looking at the £1m in relation to net profit or total assets. Ratios therefore provide a framework from which we can make meaningful comparisons between a firm's performance from one year to the next, between branches within a firm or between firms in the same industry. Ratios therefore also provide management with a tool to compare performance and set targets.

There are, however, limitations to ratio analysis. The first limitation comes from the sources used, i.e. the financial documents. As discussed in Chapter 3, financial documents may have been manipulated (window dressed) to improve the picture they show. This will affect the ratios calculated. Also, when looking at ratios from the balance sheet, it is necessary to consider that the balance sheet is a 'snapshot' and as

AQA Examiner's tip

Do not try to state whether a ratio is good or bad without first of all reflecting on the nature of the firm and, secondly, thinking about what it is good or bad in relation to. Look at any trends in the ratios, for example; is performance improving or worsening?

such only true on the day it is drawn up. It may also be necessary to break down the components making up the accounts. If, for example, a balance sheet is shown for a business as a whole, then this may disguise underperforming departments or branches.

Finally, like all quantitative techniques, ratio analysis only takes into consideration the financial performance of a firm. Ratio analysis may show a firm to be liquid, profitable and financially efficient but would not alone inform a potential investor, supplier or customer about their ethical behaviour, future plans or green credentials.

Case study

Persimmon Homes

Persimmon Homes is one of the UK's leading house builders. It offers a wide choice of quality new homes in locations across the UK. In the annual accounts for 2007 chairman, John White, reflected upon the achievements of Persimmon in the financial year. He stated that, 'During the last 6 months we have continued to apply the necessary basic disciplines of our business to ensure we achieve the best possible results.' Within these disciplines he includes:

- investment in land at a sensible price
- maximising sales revenue through careful planning and marketing
- the application of firm controls on building costs.
- A summary of Persimmon's financial performance is shown in Table 4.5.

Table 4.5 *Summary of financial performance, Persimmon Homes*

	June 2007	December 2006	June 2006	December 2005	June 2005
Revenue (£m)	1,514.5	1,591.9	1,550.0	1,192.7	1,093.0
Operating profit (£m)	315.3	343.6	293.7		251.8
Unit sales*	8,002	8,475	8,226	6,682	5,954
ROCE (%)	22.9	23.1	24.4	28.8	30
OPM (%)	20.8		18.9	23.1	23
Gearing (%)	29	33	50	16	12

*Unit sales refers to the number of individual units sold. In this case, the number of properties sold.

corporate.persimmonhomes.com

Questions

1
a Calculate net profit for December 2005.
b Calculate OPM for December 2006.
c Calculate the average price of a Persimmon house in June 2007.

2 Explain one potential advantage to Persimmon of presenting interim as well as year-end figures in their accounts.

3 Should the chairman, John White, be pleased with or concerned about Persimmon's profitability in 2007? Justify your answer.

4 Outline one factor that could have contributed towards the higher gearing in June 2006.

5 Analyse how the disciplines adopted by Persimmon would help it achieve the reported financial results in 2007.

☑ *In this chapter you will have learned to:*

- select, calculate and interpret financial ratios
- analyse the value and limitations of ratio analysis in assessing business performance.

Summary questions

1 Briefly explain the difference between the current ratio and acid test ratio. (5 marks)

2 Why would the acid test ratio be of greater significance to a retailer of ladies' fashion than a provider of health and safety training? (4 marks)

3 What is meant by the term ROCE? (3 marks)

4 Explain why a business might want receivables (debtor) days to be shorter than creditor days. (6 marks)

5 With the use of examples, explain why the acceptable level of inventory turnover will vary widely from business to business. (6 marks)

6 Explain how the use of window dressing may affect the usefulness of ratio analysis to a potential investor. (6 marks)

7 Briefly explain why an existing shareholder would be interested in dividend yield as well as dividend per share. (8 marks)

5   Selecting financial strategies

In this chapter you will learn to:

- understand the meaning and significance of specific financial strategies

- understand how the specific financial strategies interrelate with other functional areas

- assess the suitability of specific financial strategies in a given context.

SOL-utions solution

Fig. 5.1 *Solar panels make use of renewable energy from the sun*

SOL-utions is the European market leader in the supply of solar panel solutions to industry. It boasts the ability to provide solar panels to factories and offices across Europe, enabling them to improve their carbon footprint whilst reducing energy costs to a fraction of their former levels. SOL-utions has, however, enjoyed less success in America. With little room for further growth within Europe, Managing Director, Stef Ascough, believes that it is essential it finds a way of breaking into the American market. Operation Director, Ged Stephenson, is less keen and believes there is scope for growth within the European housing market. His R&D team have been working to develop a cheaper version of its solar technology that could be used in houses and flats.

Determined to go ahead with his battle to capture a healthy share of the American market, Stef calls a board meeting. He has identified two established businesses within America which he thinks could be targets for a takeover. The first, Smart Solar, has a foothold in the market with 20 years worth of steady sales to its name. Its product is, however, now a bit dated with little investment in R&D. The second, Innov8, is struggling to achieve sales but does have an innovative solution to solar panels for the housing market.

Stef presents the Board of Directors with four potential strategies:

- an aggressive strategy to capture a share of the American market through price penetration
- buy out Smart Solar
- buy out Innov8
- buy out Smart Solar and Innov8.

Discussion points

1 How might SOL-utions raise finance to implement any of these strategies?

2 What might the finance director see as the advantages and disadvantages of the first strategy over the other three?

3 What is the relationship between a decision to adopt penetration pricing in America and the need to implement a strategy of cost minimisation?

4 How will the amount of capital expenditure vary between these proposed strategies?

5 Which strategy would you adopt? Justify your answer.

■ Financial strategies

Financial strategies are plans of action that will help a business to develop and maintain a competitive advantage and achieve financial objectives. An example of a financial objective may be to lower costs to a point where they are below those of key competitors. The corresponding financial strategy would have to plan for how this objective could be met.

Sources of finance

Businesses need finance for short, medium and long-term purposes. Long-term finance is normally required to fund capital expenditure in either fixed assets or long-term projects. At AS Level you will have studied the sources of finance available to fund small business start-ups. Here we are more interested in the main **sources of finance** available to a business to fund strategic development, or retrenchment. Typically the largest source of finance for many companies is retained profit. However, if there is insufficient retained profit then an alternative source of finance may be required. There are two main external sources of long-term finance available to a business: equity share capital and debt (loans). The main distinctions between these two sources of finance are shown in Table 5.1.

Key terms

Financial strategy: the long-term financial plan of action to achieve the financial objectives of the business.

Sources of finance: the range of options available to firms to fund business operations including banks, venture capitalists and share capital.

Table 5.1 *Contrasts between equity share capital and debt*

Equity share capital	Debt
Exists for an unlimited term	Exists for a fixed term, e.g. a 10-year loan
Carries a voting right	Does not carry a voting right
Dividends payable dependent upon company performance	Interest payable regardless of company performance
Dividends paid after tax and therefore do not affect tax liability	Interest paid before tax and therefore reduces tax liability
Ordinary shareholders are towards the bottom of the list when payments are being made following the closure of a company	Lenders are towards the top of the list when payments are being made following the closure of a company
Not secured	Will be secured against an asset

Equity share capital

Unlike sole traders and partnerships, companies are able to raise capital through the sale of shares. A company will decide upon the maximum amount of capital it is likely to need in the future from the sales of shares and will set this as the authorised share capital. It will then decide upon the percentage of this that will be needed in the short to medium term. Shares will then be issued to raise this predetermined amount of capital. This is known as the issued share capital. This means that if a company issues 250,000 ordinary shares at £1, once these are all sold and paid for, it will have a fully paid up share capital of £250,000. This, however, assumes that the shares are originally sold at their face value of £1. If they were sold for more than this, for example £1.50, the company would have £250,000 of share capital plus a share premium account worth £125,000.

Additional share capital can be issued by releasing more of the authorised share capital. This can be done through a rights issue whereby existing shareholders are offered the right to buy a number of new shares. The number offered to each shareholder is dependent upon the number of shares they already hold. These shares are normally offered at a price below their market value. If new shares are to be offered to parties outside of the existing shareholders, then a company will normally seek the permission of existing shareholders as doing so will reduce their share of the company.

Debt

Finance obtained from banks and other financial institutions is called loan or debt capital. For the lender, there is less risk than equity capital as the loan will be secured against an asset. This means that if the company fails to meet the terms of the loan agreement, the asset can be seized in order to recoup the money still owed by the company. However, the risk to the company is greater as interest payments are compulsory regardless of company performance. A company which relies heavily on debt capital is referred to as being highly geared.

Link

For an explanation of gearing, see Chapter 4 — Interpreting published accounts, page 22.

Business in action

HBOS rights issues

HBOS is the financial group that owns Halifax and Bank of Scotland. In April 2008, it announced that HBOS was planning to raise £4 billion through a rights issue. This meant that HBOS's existing shareholders were invited to purchase new shares. A rights issue was a way of HBOS strengthening its balance sheet by providing it with additional capital. This action may have seemed necessary as a result of increasingly tough liquidity conditions resulting from the credit crunch. (HBOS was acquired by Lloyds TSB in September 2008.)

Fig. 5.2 *High street banks face tough trading conditions in 2009*

Implementing profit centres

If financial objectives are to be a meaningful form of control, then it is important for a business to be able to measure its performance against these objectives. In order to be able to make strategic decisions, it therefore makes sense to be able to identify the performance of individual subsections within a business. For example, if directors can identify which products or which branches are underperforming or failing to meet objectives, then decisive action can be taken.

Profit centres involve devolving responsibility for revenues and costs, and hence profits, to identifiable subsections within a business. Not only does this help to achieve financial objectives but it also makes it easier to monitor financial performance, allows for greater delegation of responsibility and acts to motivate managers. Profit centres may be identified by product, department or geographical location. If each subsection within a business is working to achieve their targets and is aware of the responsibility they have for maximising revenue and minimising costs, then this will help the business achieve a competitive advantage.

Profit centres are only appropriate when a subsection of a business can take responsibility for it s own revenues as well as costs. A marketing department or Research and Development department for example could be given responsibility for its own costs but it would be difficult to accurately allocate revenue to its actions.

Cost minimisation

Cost minimisation was identified as a financial objective in Chapter 2. Here we are interested in the strategic approaches a business can adopt to achieve this objective. A strategy of cost minimisation will allow a business to compete on price.

A business that has a high market share or is a market leader will be in a position of power when it comes to negotiating terms and conditions with suppliers. It may, therefore, adopt a strategy which includes an aggressive approach to negotiating prices for goods and services. Lower input and processing costs can then be passed onto the consumer in terms of lower output costs.

Alternatively, a business may aim to reduce the cost of managing resources through the adoption of a strategy involving just-in-time. If stocks of raw materials are received as and when they are needed, and finished goods despatched upon completion to the customer, then a business can avoid the costs associated with holding stocks. However, if such a strategy puts excess strain on the suppliers, this may have the opposite and undesired effect of pushing costs up. It can also cause additional pressure on production staff that have production targets to meet and are relying upon an excellent relationship with, and service from, suppliers.

Key term

Profit centres: a section of a business for which costs and revenues and therefore profit can be identified.

Capital expenditure: the purchase of assets that will remain in the business in the medium to long term, accounted for in the balance sheet.

Activity

For each of the following businesses, identify a suitable basis for establishing profit centres, i.e. product, department or location:

- Nestlé
- McDonalds
- National Express
- BBC
- Sony
- Reeds Recruitment.

Business in action

Mini to get 'Italian Job' in cost-cutting deal with Fiat

In July 2008 talks between BMW and Fiat were underway to try an establish joint cost cutting schemes through the development of joint components and platforms. It could mean the next generation of Oxford-built Minis share key parts with a new, small Alfa Romeo.

Mr Eichiner, BMW's director of brand development said, 'We are currently examining with the Fiat Group possibilities for the joint use of components and systems in Mini and Alfa Romeo vehicles in order to achieve economies of scale and thus cost reductions.'

Adapted from www.thebirminghampost.net

Allocating capital expenditure

Capital expenditure refers to the purchase of assets that will remain within the business for a long period of time, for example a machine, delivery van or shop fittings. These are accounted for in the company's balance sheet,

Fig. 5.3 *Friedrich Eichiner, CFO of BMW*

allowing them to spread the cost of the asset over its useful life. Expenditure on day-to-day items, such as raw materials or staff wages, is referred to as revenue expenditure. This is accounted for in the income statement.

Expenditure on capital items is very important to a business and due to the often large amount of money involved decisions regarding capital expenditure are taken very seriously. Large organisations often have a 'sign off chain'. This means that as the amount of money spent increases, permission must be sought to make the purchase from higher up the hierarchy.

Link

Chapter 6 — Making investment decisions, page 38, looks at the numerical techniques available to a business when assessing the worth of capital expenditure.

Activity

Within a business, permission to buy a new printer costing £550 can be given by the Financial Director (North West), permission to buy a new company car costing £23,000 can be given by the Financial Director (UK) and permission to buy a new building costing £280,000 can only be given by VP Finance (Europe).

Why might a 'sign off chain' be used by a business as in the example above?

Capital expenditure on new equipment or to support new projects is important not only to maintain shareholder wealth but also to increase it. The financial benefits from capital expenditure can, however, be difficult to measure as they will be achieved over a long period of time. It is therefore important that capital expenditure is closely monitored to ensure that the expected benefits are actually achieved over time. Like all items of expenditure, there is also a need to consider the opportunity cost involved. If, for example, a business chooses to spend money on new equipment, it cannot spend the same money on staff training. The capital available to a business will be limited and how this is spent will have a direct effect on the future performance and growth of the organisation.

Case study

Red Square Industries plc

Red Square is a leading manufacturer of cement and building-related products in the UK. As the result of a strategy of growth through diversification and mergers, it now manufactures bricks, kitchen appliances, bathroom fittings and heating appliances, as well as having interests in property development, land reclamation and effluent treatment. In April 2009, it had a group turnover of £1,125m, with operating profits of £213.3 million. Its accounts show this split between major interests (Table 5.2).

Table 5.2 *Extract from accounts, Red Square plc*

	Turnover (£m)	Operating profit (£m)
Cement and building materials	886	148.1
Home products	139.8	22.6
Property	28.8	24.8
Bricks	16.2	6.1
Others	54.2	11.7

The following extract from its accounts shows examples of profit centres used within the organisation:

Domestic Heating

The main activities assigned to this profit centre are the design, manufacture and sale of gas boilers for domestic wet central heating systems, i.e. systems which circulate hot water around the premises.

Commercial/industrial

This profit centre covers the research, design (or design modification), sale, assembly, commissioning and servicing of a range of cast-iron commercial/industrial boilers, the components for which are purchased from independent suppliers in the United Kingdom and abroad.

Red Square's policy of operating each function as a profit centre is part of its overall strategy to keep costs down. Managing Director, Reg Doonan, is pleased with the group's performance in 2009 and plans to achieve further growth in 2010 by the acquisition of a small house-building company, HomeStart Ltd.

Questions

1 Analyse the advantages to Red Square plc of operating profit centres.

2 Explain why a strategy of cost minimisation is important for Red Square to achieve growth and remain competitive.

3 Suggest a suitable source of finance for Red Square to fund future expansion. Justify your answer.

✔ In this chapter you will have learned to:

- explain the meaning and significance of specific financial strategies
- understand how specific financial strategies interrelate with other functional areas
- assess the suitability of specific financial strategies to a given context.

Summary questions

1 What is meant by a financial strategy? (3 marks)

2 Explain why decisions about financial strategies should be taken carefully. (6 marks)

3 Why might a chain of high street coffee shops, such as Costa Coffee, choose a strategy of operating each shop as a profit centre? (8 marks)

4 What is the difference between capital expenditure and revenue expenditure? (5 marks)

5 Why are capital expenditure decisions so important to businesses? (6 marks)

6 If Primark was to set an objective of 20 per cent growth over the next five years, would you recommend a strategy of cost minimisation of capital expenditure? Justify your answer. (4 marks)

Making investment decisions

In this chapter you will learn to:

- understand the ways in which investment can help businesses to reach functional objectives

- select and use investment appraisal techniques

- interpret investment appraisal findings

- identify and apply appropriate investment criteria

- assess the risks and uncertainties of specific investment decisions

- evaluate quantitative and qualitative influences on specific investment decisions.

Setting the scene

New beginnings at Chester Zoo

Fig. 6.1 *The new entrance to Chester Zoo*

Chester Zoo has invested £1m in its New Beginnings project designed to transform the main entrance. The £1m investment has allowed it to landscape the main entrance, including an iconic oak tree as the centrepiece which is the same age as the Zoo. The facilities at the main entrance now include:

- a new wheelchair and buggy hire facility
- upgraded guest services area
- improved souvenir shop, The Ark.

Discussion points

1. What might the financial objectives of Chester Zoo be?

2. How could this investment help it to achieve its financial objectives?

3. How can Chester Zoo assess whether its investment was a worthwhile one?

4. What factors might contribute towards Chester Zoo being able to cover the costs of the investment?

The importance of investment

The term 'investment' is used in relation to capital expenditure, i.e. the purchase of assets that will stay in the business in the medium to long term. Investments, therefore, often involve spending substantial sums of money. Managers do not take investment decisions lightly as there is no such thing as a risk-free investment and all investments have both financial and opportunity costs.

Investment is important, as it is through investments that a business will strive to achieve its objectives. If, for example, an objective is one of growth, this may involve investment in new machinery or larger premises in order to move into a new market. Similarly, when weighing up the financial merits of an investment, managers will have to focus on the objective of maximising shareholder returns. A business with the objective of being market leader is likely to have an ongoing programme of investment in the most up-to-date machinery or extensive Research and Development (R&D).

Link

Shareholders' return is discussed in Chapter 2 — Understanding financial objectives, page 9.

Business in action

Wetherby Racecourse

Wetherby Racecourse has an ongoing programme to update the racecourse. As part of this, it has invested £1.4m in building a new conference and event venue. The venue took seven months to build and offers accommodation for 500 delegates theatre-style, 300 guests for a banquet, first-class catering, unlimited parking and a professional events management team. The design includes ground floor access and wide doorways to allow vehicular access for exhibitions such as motor shows.

AQA Examiner's tip

When assessing an investment decision, try to consider how it could contribute towards the functional objectives of the business. This will help you show the skill of application.

Investment appraisal

Investment appraisal techniques are scientific decision-making tools used to analyse whether a capital investment is worthwhile or, if there are a number of options, which one is the best investment. The quantitative results of these techniques should be considered alongside qualitative factors. The three investment appraisal techniques included in the AQA A2 specification are payback, average rate of return and net present value. These all involve estimating the total cash outflow and cash inflows over the expected life of an investment.

Table 6.1 shows the data that will be used to demonstrate and practise each of these techniques within this chapter. The data refers to a printing company trying to decide between two machines.

Key term

Investment appraisal: the process of analysing the financial merits of a possible future investment.

Table 6.1 *Appraising a printing investment*

	Machine A	Machine B
Initial cost	£750,000	£310,000
Inflows:		
Year 1	£150,000	£125,000
Year 2	£200,000	£127,000
Year 3	£260,000	£140,000
Year 4	£260,000	£140,000
Year 5	£300,000	£130,000
Maintenance costs	£7,500 per year	£15,000 per year

All three methods require this data to be placed in a table to show net cash flow (Table 6.2). The net cash flow is calculated by deducting the cash out from the cash in.

Table 6.2 *Net cash flow for Machine A*

Year	Cash out	Cash in	Net cash flow
0	£750,000	0	(£750,000)
1	£7,500	£150,000	£142,500
2	£7,500	£200,000	£192,500
3	£7,500	£260,000	£252,500
4	£7,500	£260,000	£252,500
5	£7,500	£300,000	£292,500

Activity

Using Table 6.1, draw a table to show the net cash flow for Machine B.

Payback

The **payback** method calculates the length of time it will take to pay back the initial cost of the investment. This is done by first calculating the year in which the cost will be paid back and then calculating the month in which it will be paid back.

Key term

Payback: calculation of how long it will take to recoup the cost of an initial investment.

Step 1:

Add up the net cash flows for Machine A until you have enough to cover the initial investment:

£142,000 + £192,500 + £252,500 = £587,800

£142,000 + £192,500 + £252,500 + £252,500 = £840,000

This means that by year 4 enough money has come in from the investment to cover the initial investment of £750,000. Payback is therefore three years and x months.

Step 2:

Calculate the amount still needed for Machine A in the year of payback and divide by the net cash inflow for that year and multiply by 12 to calculate the month of payback:

£750,000 Cash investment minus £587,800 cumulative net inflow at end of year 3 = £162,200

Remaining cash required: $\dfrac{£162,200}{£252,500} \times 12 = 7.7$ months, rounded up to 8 months

Net cash inflow in year 4:

Payback for Machine A is three years and eight months.

The shorter the payback period, the less risk there is involved in the project and the quicker the business can start to generate profit from its investment. Payback is the most commonly used form of investment appraisal because of its simplicity. It is also very important to businesses with potential cash-flow problems or if the investment is in technical equipment that may become obsolete or out-of-date quickly. Payback may be particularly important if the investment is to be funded by external sources of finance. In reality, however, payback is rarely used in isolation because of its simplicity.

The disadvantages of payback are that it fails to take into account any cash inflows after payback and in effect ignores the overall profitability of the project. It also assumes that in the year of payback the inflow of cash is steady across the year which for many firms will not be true. Imagine if the business in question was of a seasonal nature with cash inflows only in the final three months of the year.

Average rate of return (ARR)

Average rate of return assesses the worth of an investment by calculating the average annual profit as a percentage of the initial investment.

Step 1:

Calculate average annual profit by adding up all the net cash flows divided by the number of years:

Average annual profit = Total net cash flow ÷ Number of years

Total net cash flow for Machine A = (£750,000) + £142,500 + £192,500 + £252,500 + £252,500 + £292,500 = £382,500

Average annual profit = $\dfrac{£382,500}{5}$ = £76,500

Step 2:

Calculate the average rate of return for Machine A by dividing the average annual profit by the initial investment and express as a percentage:

Average rate of return = (Average annual profit ÷ Initial investment) × 100

Average rate of return = $\dfrac{76,500}{750,000} \times 100 = 10.2\%$

Average rate of return for Machine A is 10.2 per cent.

The higher the ARR, the more potentially profitable the investment. The advantage of ARR is that it allows for easy comparison with alternative forms of investment, such as the interest rate offered by a bank. It can also be easily compared to current or target ROCE. The disadvantage of ARR is that it does not take into account the timings of the cash inflows. An investment may appear very profitable, but if it takes four years before a positive net cash flow is achieved, this might pose too great a risk to the firm's short-term survival.

Activities

1. Calculate the payback for Machine B.

2. Based on the payback method, which machine do you think represents the better investment?

AQA Examiner's tip

When evaluating payback, do not just state its weaknesses but try to think about it in relation to the business being dealt with, i.e. look for hints such as expected lifespan of the project, seasonality and cash inflows, technical issues and the cash-flow situation.

Key terms

Average rate of return (AVR): average annual profit expressed as a percentage of initial investment.

Net present value (NPV): the total net return of an investment stated in today's monetary value.

Activities

1. Calculate the ARR for Machine B.

2. Based on the ARR method, which machine do you think represents the better investment?

Link

ROCE is explained in Chapter 4 — Interpreting published accounts, page 22.

Activities

1 Calculate the NPV for Machine B.

2 Based on the NPV method, which machine do you think represents the better investment?

Net present value (NPV)

Net present value takes into account the total return from an investment in today's terms. It recognises that £100 received today is worth more than £100 received in the future. If the £100 received today was invested in the bank, it would grow in value each year. This is done by the use of a **discount factor**.

Step 1:

Multiply each year's net inflow by the relevant discount factor, to calculate NPV.

Step 2:

Add up all the NPVs to calculate the net cash gain from the project expressed in today's terms.

Table 6.3 *Five-year NPV calculation for Machine A*

Year	Net cash flow	10% discount factor	NPV
0	(£750,000)	1	(£750,000)
1	£142,500	0.91	£129,675
2	£192,500	0.83	£159,775
3	£252,500	0.75	£189,375
4	£252,500	0.68	£171,700
5	£292,500	0.62	£181,350
Net present value			£81,875

If the project is predicted to produce a positive NPV, then it should be accepted. If choosing between two or more projects, then the one with the highest positive NPV should be accepted. If the present value of the future cash inflows is less than that of the outflows, then the NPV will be negative and the project should be rejected. This simple rule of 'positive NPV accept, negative NPV reject' provides managers with an easy guide to decision-making. The other advantage of NPV is that it takes account of the **time value of money**. The failure to do this by the previous two techniques can be seen as a weakness of them. The disadvantages are that it doesn't take into account the speed of repayment of the original investment, it can be difficult to choose the correct discount factor and non-financial managers may find the concept hard to understand.

Activities

1 Draw a table to summarise the results of all three techniques for Machine A and Machine B.

2 Based on these quantitative results, which machine do you think represents the better investment?

■ Investment criteria

Before carrying out investment decisions, managers will have a pre-determined set of **investment criteria** against which to judge the investment. These are minimum targets, known as criterion levels, that a possible investment must be able to reach before it is accepted. By setting these criterion levels in advance, it gives a clear rule on what is or is not an acceptable investment and prevents bias in decision-making.

The specific criteria set will depend upon the nature of the business and the investment. It will also be influenced by the culture of the business organisation, whether it is one of risk taking or risk aversion. Possible investment criteria could be:

- payback less than half the predicted life expectancy of the project
- ARR 3 per cent above rate of interest
- NPV at least 25 per cent of initial investment
- NPV positive with shortest payback period
- ARR equal to current ROCE.

Risks and uncertainties

Investment decisions carry with them risk and it is the potential gain achieved from that risk that carries reward. If, for example, the ARR is higher than the rate of interest to be gained by placing the money in the bank, this higher return is the reward for risk taking. Uncertainty exists because of the need to estimate the costs and revenues involved in an investment. It is the decision-makers' job to assess the risks associated with such uncertainties.

The degree of risk associated with a project will be dependent upon a number of factors. Key points to consider will include:

- the sum of money to be invested as well as the source of that money
- the length of time the business must commit to the project
- the impact of the investment on other aspects of the business, for example day-to-day funding
- the ease or difficulty with which an investment can be reversed
- the impact of the decision on other future strategic choices.

The degree of uncertainty associated with a project will be dependent upon a number of factors. Key points to consider will include:

- the stability of the market and associated likely accuracy of sales forecasts
- the credibility of the source of the estimated costs and revenues
- the stability of the economic environment in which the business operates
- the potential competitors' reactions to the investment
- the overall time period of future projections.

Qualitative influences on investment decisions

Investment appraisal techniques look at the quantitative aspects of an investment decision, but these are not sufficient alone to make a fully informed decision. Managers must also consider the qualitative factors. These include the impact on the image of the firm, the workers, ethical considerations, consumer perceptions and the impact on the wider society. A decision, for example, to invest in relocating manufacturing abroad may look very good on financial grounds but could lead to redundancies, negative publicity in the media, exploitation of cheap labour sources abroad and a fall in the image of the firm.

AQA Examiner's tip

Look for possible qualitative issues in the case study, i.e. would automation lead to a loss of quality in a product?

Lowfare Airways plc

Lowfare Airways plc is a UK-based budget airline which two years ago bought another budget airline, Vlodair, based in Poland. This expansion gave Lowfare airport operating bases in several Eastern European countries. The expansion, however, resulted in frequent communication failures and profit performance was disappointing. Despite this, the directors were determined to make Lowfare a major force in the airline industry. Research had showed them that the long haul market was the area where growth was expected.

The Board of Directors commissioned a report to investigate whether the company should expand into the long haul market. The report found that the new project would not be cheap but that profit margins were likely to be much higher. It recommended that a long haul project of four trial routes should be established. Initially, it would run for four years and require a capital investment of £25million.

The Board of Directors is now meeting to discuss the recommendations.

Table 6.4 *Data analysed by the Board when considering the proposal for the long-haul project*

Initial capital cost	£25m
Forecast annual net cash flow in:	
Year 1	£5m
Year 2	£10m
Year 3	£15m
Year 4	£15m
Projected payback	2 years 8 months
Forecasted increase in global long haul flights	8% per year for next 4 years
Forecasted increase in short haul EU flights	4% per year for next 4 years
Current interest rate on borrowed capital	10%
10% discount factors:	
Year 1	0.91
Year 2	0.83
Year 3	0.75
Year 4	0.68

Questions

1. What is meant by the term 'capital investment'?

2. Analyse how this investment decision could help Lowfare to achieve its functional objectives.

3   Recommend to the Board of Directors appropriate investment criteria that could help in deciding on whether to go ahead with this project. Justify your recommendations.

4   Calculate the average rate of return and net present value of the long-haul project, using the data in Table 6.4.

5   Should Lowfare go ahead with the long haul project? Use your results from question 4, data from Table 6.4 and any other information to support your answer.

☑ *In this chapter you will have learned to:*

■ explain the ways in which investment can help businesses to reach functional objectives

■ select and use investment appraisal techniques

■ interpret investment appraisal findings

■ identify and apply appropriate investment criteria

■ assess the risks and uncertainties of specific investment decisions

■ evaluate quantitative and qualitative influences on specific investment decisions.

Summary questions

1   What is meant by the term 'investment appraisal'? (3 marks)

2   Briefly explain, with the use of an example, how investment could help a business achieve its financial objectives. (6 marks)

3   Identify one advantage and one disadvantage of each method of investment appraisal. (12 marks)

4   What is meant by the term 'time value of money'? (3 marks)

5   Explain why it is appropriate to compare the ARR to

    a interest rates and

    b ROCE. (8 marks)

6   An internet-based stationery wholesaler is looking to move to a larger warehouse and has identified two potential locations. What qualitative factors should he consider alongside his investment appraisal? (10 marks)

Marketing strategies

Introduction

Chapters in this section:

Section 3.2 ended with an assessment of the risks involved in making investment decisions. This section concentrates on how the marketing function can reduce the risks involved in achieving objectives. Marketing is not an exact science. However, statistical methods and models have been developed to improve the decision-making process. Large organisations are less likely to take big risks with new products and new markets than smaller businesses, and will spend large amounts of time and money to ensure marketing success. This does not mean that there are fewer risks; they are just on a larger scale. When considering the external influences on marketing decisions, for instance, large corporations must take into account international competitors. In the same way, the pace of technological change will be different in markets across the world and successful businesses will take these differences into account. The other important factor to consider throughout this section is the reliability of data in decision-making. There may be a temptation to assume that all data and predictions are accurate and unchanging. All information should be treated with caution. It would be wise to revisit the AS marketing syllabus before starting this section.

Chapter 7: Understanding marketing objectives

It is very important in a large or growing business for the objectives of the marketing function to reflect the overall objectives of the business, and for these to be communicated effectively to the other functional areas. There are regularly examples of where this has apparently not been the case and there is an obvious lack of communication between marketing and operations (for example, supply of products unable to meet demand generated by a very effective marketing campaign). In the same way, the marketing function must take into account external factors, such as the activities of competitors and the state of the economy, in order to ensure that objectives are achieved successfully.

Chapter 8: Analysing markets and marketing

When entrepreneurs start up a new business, although they may undertake some market research, the chances are that they will rely on intuition or a 'gut feeling' that there is a gap in the market which can be exploited successfully. Large organisations, with greater resources, can reduce the risks involved by spending more time and money on collecting primary and secondary data about a market. This ensures that when decisions are made, they are based on reliable information as well as the experience of the senior managers. This use of statistical analysis is referred to as scientific decision-making.

Chapter 9: Selecting marketing strategies

Decision-making can be very difficult in large organisations, particularly where delegation is part of the culture and the management style is democratic. It is very helpful, therefore, to have a model which can be used as a basis for assessing alternative strategies open to a business: the risks and benefits involved. Ansoff's Matrix is used to assess marketing

Marketing is finding the best way to meet the customer's needs

strategies in a national and international context. Of course, there are the normal internal and external constraints that you should be familiar with by now.

Chapter 10: Developing and implementing marketing plans

When the marketing objectives have been decided and the strategies have been selected, the tactics to be used have to be implemented. This chapter analyses the internal and external influences on marketing plans and identifies strategic issues which will have an impact on how plans can be implemented.

A still from an Oreo advertisement

US manufacturer, Kraft, wants to break into the UK market with its 'twist, lick and dunk' Oreo biscuit, and is spending £4.5m on its first UK advertising campaign. So can this Goliath of a global brand crack what is the largest biscuit market in Europe? After all, Brits' biscuit tastes – digestives, Rich Tea, Hob Nobs, malted milk, fig rolls – are notoriously patriotic. How can the success of this marketing strategy be assured?

7 Understanding marketing objectives

In this chapter you will learn to:

- describe the range of marketing objectives typically set by larger businesses

- explain and analyse how internal and external factors can influence marketing objectives.

Setting the scene

Parkdean Holidays

Parkdean Holidays is a UK-focused self-catering family holiday park operator, with 24 parks spread across England, Wales and Scotland, in some of the most picturesque locations in the British Isles. In 2005, its corporate objective was to sell more holidays. This translated into clear marketing objectives: to support its business goals by creating and implementing an online marketing strategy that brought the right audience to it through the use of key terms such as 'holiday park' and 'family holiday uk' and allowed it to quickly and measurably convert these people into customers.

FlameDigital.com

Discussion points

1 What other corporate objectives might Parkdean Holidays have as well as 'sell more holidays'?

2 What other objectives might the marketing department at Parkdean Holidays set to help the business achieve its corporate goals?

3 How might technological change have influenced Parkdean Holidays' marketing objective of developing an online marketing strategy?

Marketing objectives

At AS you learnt about marketing and the competitive environment, with the emphasis on small businesses. At A2, you will use this knowledge to consider the **marketing objectives** and strategies developed by larger organisations. Revisit your AS work to remind yourself of market research, understanding markets and the elements of the marketing mix before moving on.

Successful organisations base their functional objectives and strategies on the organisation's overall targets (corporate objectives). In this section, the emphasis is on the marketing function, but you should remember that no area of the business can work in isolation and there will be a range of factors, from within the organisation and from outside, that will have an impact on the objectives that the business hopes to achieve through marketing.

The planning process within the marketing function should follow the following stages.

1 Corporate objectives (see Chapter 1)

2 Marketing objectives (this chapter)

3 Market and marketing analysis (see Chapter 8)

4 Marketing strategies (see Chapter 9)

5 Marketing plans (see Chapter 10).

Possible marketing objectives

Although the marketing objectives will develop from the corporate objectives, they are likely to include some of the following:

■ To maintain or increase market share: A business might want to ensure that it does not lose ground to competitors who are threatening to take customers away. On the other hand, the objective might be to increase the percentage of the total market it controls.

■ To target a new market segment of an existing market or a new market: When one market becomes saturated or sales begin to decline, a firm may consider whether the product could be aimed at a different target audience within the home market or at the same market in other countries.

■ To develop new goods and services as a result of market research findings or technological developments: This could also be because existing products are reaching the end of their product life cycle or the business is facing fierce competition in existing markets.

Whatever the marketing objectives are, they should always be quantifiable targets so that success can be judged. For example, has market share increased or been maintained? Have sales to the new target market been achieved within the specified timescale?

■ **Business in action**

Britannia Hotels

■ In 2005–6 Britannia Hotels had the following marketing objectives:

■ increase online bookings by 20 per cent year-on-year

■ increase brand awareness as measured by website visits.

Latitude Group

■ **Business in action**

Eurostar

In November 2007, Eurostar moved its London terminal from Waterloo International to St Pancras International, opening up travel on Eurostar to new UK markets, whilst retaining the existing traveller relationships. Gaining deeper knowledge and understanding of travellers was a key factor in a successful move. In 2005 Eurostar's marketing objective had been to increase data about its customers, in order to increase understanding of, and improve relationships with, them. A secondary objective, ahead of planned station changes in London in 2007, was to profile Eurostar travellers to understand the effects the changes would have on existing and future customers.

OCCAM Direct Marketing

Internal factors influencing the setting of marketing objectives

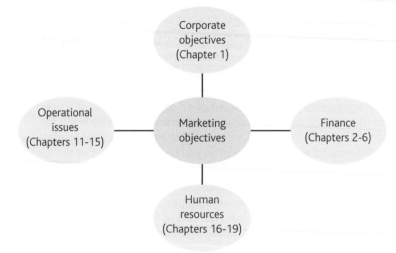

Fig. 7.1 *The internal influences on marketing objectives*

Finance

This refers to the amount of money available to the marketing function to spend on its activities for a given period of time. Factors which will have an impact on the final marketing expenditure budget include the organisation's financial position and the expected return on a marketing project.

■ The organisation's overall financial position is obviously very important. It might be assumed that the size of the budget will reflect the success of the business: the more profitable the company, the higher the spending on marketing. However, it could be argued that when the firm is in difficulty and sales are falling or market share is decreasing, the marketing budget should be increased. Of course, this logic is of little help if there is not the finance available.

■ The expected return is particularly important when deciding on the marketing expenditure budget. If marketing objectives have been successfully achieved in the past, this can increase the likelihood of finance being made available in the future. If the expected return on a marketing project is relatively low, there is less chance of funding being made available.

Human resources

The skills and abilities of the workforce will have an impact on the marketing objectives because they can potentially limit what the business is able to do. There is no point planning to make use of technological developments if the employees of the organisations do not have the necessary skills. On the other hand, the workforce might well be an under-utilised resource that has the potential to give the business a competitive advantage over its rivals in the market.

Operational issues

It is very important that the marketing function takes issues such as quality and capacity into consideration when setting objectives. For example, if the decision is taken to introduce a new product to the range, it is essential that the business has the manufacturing capacity or the space to cope with extra customer numbers. In the same way, an operational objective of quality improvement should be incorporated into marketing planning.

External factors influencing the setting of marketing objectives

Just as there are internal factors that the marketing function must consider, there are also very important external influences on decision-making.

Fig. 7.2 *External factors affecting the marketing objectives of a large organisation*

Competitors' actions

When making decisions about marketing objectives, the current and/or future actions of major competitors must be taken into consideration. This should involve an assessment of all the elements of their marketing mix, pricing, promotion, distribution and product policies, as well as overall spending on marketing. For example, if a main competitor in the market is developing e-commerce as a major channel of distribution, it will be difficult for a business to ignore this policy without running the risk of losing market share. You may notice that a major promotion by one firm in a competitive market is often followed by equally large-scale campaigns by rivals.

Technological change

Computer-aided manufacturing can significantly reduce production times and labour costs. This may open up new markets or increase a company's ability to compete in a low-cost market. On the other hand, technological developments can lead to shortened product life cycles which have implications for product development. Ultimately, it can lead to products becoming obsolete which can have a major impact on the marketing objectives of the business.

Business in action

Kodak

With the slogan 'You press the button, we do the rest', George Eastman put the first simple camera into the hands of a world of consumers in 1888. In so doing, he made a cumbersome and complicated process easy to use and accessible to nearly everyone. Since that time, the Eastman Kodak Company has led the way with an abundance of new products and processes to make photography simpler, more useful and more enjoyable. In fact, today's Kodak

Activity

How might internal factors influence the marketing objectives set by Parkdean Holidays (page 48)?

Activity

How did Sky Sports and Setanta compete for the pay-per-view football audience at the end of 2007?

AQA Examiner's tip

Don't assume that you have to include all possible factors when analysing internal and external influences on marketing objectives. The question to ask yourself is 'how relevant is this to the scenario I have been given?'

is known not only for photography, but also for images used in a variety of leisure, commercial, entertainment and scientific applications. Its reach increasingly involves the use of technology to combine images and information, creating the potential to profoundly change how people and businesses communicate.

Adapted from kodak.com

Market factors

These include the economic climate, social change, legislation and consumers' need.

- The economic climate should be considered, as economic recession or growth could have a direct impact on demand, for example a recession in a company's main market may encourage the development of a new market overseas.

- Social change can have an impact on marketing objectives, for example increased awareness of fair trade issues has increased the demand for products sourced from fair trade producers.

- Legislation has an increasing effect on marketing, for example regulations about recycled packaging based on EU directives has encouraged firms to change the materials they use to package their products.

- Consumers' needs may change and effective marketing objectives should anticipate these changes (based on good market research). For example, children staying in the family home for longer (one in four parents have adult children still living in the family home) changes the type of housing demanded.

Case study

Volvo's marketing objective

In 2005 Volvo's primary marketing objective was to encourage consumers to reappraise the brand. They wanted people to associate their cars with a sophisticated lifestyle.

Channel4.com provided Volvo with a monthly lifestyle channel, Real, and a dedicated 4Car channel. Real enabled C4 to deliver its content with hints of Volvo's brand values. In contrast the 4Car area gave Volvo a way to communicate with an identified target market, centred on a road test format with news and videos, and providing links to brochure and test drive requests throughout.

Results

Since the launch in May 2005, the sites collectively have generated more than 500,000 page impressions with more than 17,000 competition entries and an average opt-in rate of 42 per cent.

www.ukaop.org.uk

Fig. 7.3 *An example of Volvo's range*

Questions

1 To what extent is Volvo's marketing objective, in 2005, 'to encourage consumers to reappraise the brand' typical of the marketing objectives set by larger businesses?

2 Analyse how finance and operational issues may have influenced Volvo's marketing objective.

3 Analyse the possible influence of market factors on Volvo's marketing objectives.

4 To what extent would the actions of competitors be the major influence on Volvo's marketing objectives?

5 Prepare a report on the internal and external influences on the marketing objectives set by Nintendo.

✓ *In this chapter you will have learned to:*

- examine typical marketing objectives set by larger businesses

- describe and analyse how finance, HR, operational issues and corporate objectives influence marketing objectives

- explain and analyse how competitors' actions, market factors and technological change have an impact on marketing objectives.

Summary questions

1 What are marketing objectives? (2 marks)

2 What are the basic features common to all marketing objectives? (2 marks)

3 Explain three marketing objectives of a retail business, of which you have knowledge, wishing to increase its market share. (6 marks)

4 How might falling profits in a holiday company influence the setting of marketing objectives? (6 marks)

5 Analyse the impact of the signing of a new player on the marketing objectives of a Premier League football team. (10 marks)

6 A shoe manufacturing company wishes to develop a new range of canvas boots and shoes, after market research indicated that this was a major fashion trend amongst its target market. Analyse the influence of operations function on this marketing objective. (10 marks)

7 An independent radio station, Yoof fm, wishes to increase its share of the 14–25 market, and discovers that its main rival has just signed a recent winner of *Big Brother* to present its morning show. To what extent will this have an influence on the choice of marketing objectives it sets? (18 marks)

8 Analyse the impact of the fair trade movement on the marketing objectives of a clothes retailing business. (10 marks)

9 Assess the relative importance of internal and external factors influencing the choice of marketing objectives for a bank operating in a competitive market. (18 marks)

10 Why should the marketing function consider internal influences when making decisions about its objectives? (10 marks)

8 Analysing markets and marketing

In this chapter you will learn to:

- explain the reasons for market analysis
- assess the value of market analysis
- analyse market data and trends
- use correlation to analyse markets
- discuss the difficulties in analysing marketing data
- assess the use of information technology in market analysis.

Discussion points

1. Why might analysing marketing activities such as the Office Shoes website be of benefit to the business?

2. What other market information might be useful to Office Shoes?

3. Why might Office Shoes need to analyse the market on a regular basis?

Why analyse the market?

As you discovered at AS Level, marketing is about identifying, anticipating and satisfying customers' needs and wants. As you now know, this should also fit in with corporate objectives. To have a good understanding of customers, firms can use primary and secondary market research, practical experience and a detailed **market analysis**. This examination of the features of the market is very important in the planning process because it will enable the business to assess the situation and hopefully identify opportunities to be explored and threats to be overcome.

The following are aspects of the market which can be analysed:

- The size of the market can be measured in terms of value – How much is spent in the market as a whole (by all companies operating

Key terms

Market analysis: a detailed examination of the features of a market such as market size and sales used to predict future trends.

in the market) and by volume? How many items are sold? These statistics may be available from the Office for National Statistics at www.statistics.gov.uk. and are important because a firm must be sure that the market is big enough to be worth competing in.

- Growth in the market is also important as it gives an indication of future activity and potential profits. For example, in June 2007 www. greencarsite.co.uk announced that sales of hybrid cars in the UK had doubled in the previous 12 months, making cleaner cars the fastest growing sector in the industry. Year-to-date results for the hybrid market showed an increase in sales from 3,117 to 6,568 cars – or 111 per cent.
- Is the market divided into segments so that easily identifiable groups of consumers with similar wants and needs can be targeted?

Reasons for analysing the market include:

- *Gathering evidence for devising a new strategy*: It might be that an existing marketing strategy has to be changed. This could be because the corporate objectives have changed as a result of a takeover or merger, leading to new marketing objectives. As we saw in Chapter 7, it could also be because of changes in competitor behaviour, technological developments or market conditions. Whatever the reason, as much information as possible about a market should be made available to those planning a new strategy.
- *Identifying patterns in sales*: This is a process where past and current trends are used as the basis for making predictions about future sales. Businesses try to measure and forecast sales to try to identify the underlying trend, whether that is upward, downward or constant. This information can then be used as part of the strategic decision-making.

Methods of analysing the market

Moving averages

Moving averages plot the underlying trend of sales which may change on a weekly, monthly or quarterly basis. The aim is to take out the impact of extreme variations in figures, for example seasonal factors, by calculating an average from an agreed number of weeks or months. The timescale chosen will depend on the business and the product they are selling. Firms with a high turnover of stock or high daily sales, for example food retailing, are likely to use shorter periods of time such as weekly or monthly moving averages, compared to businesses where timescales are much longer e.g. construction.

A popular way of using moving averages is to calculate a 12-month average: figures for a 12-month period are added together and divided by 12. At the end of the next month the oldest figure is removed and the latest data is added. Once calculated, the figures can be plotted on a graph, with the moving average shown in the mid-point between the first and last months, for example in the sixth month of the 12.

Worked example

Table 8.1 shows figures for retail sales in the UK between June 2006 and May 2008 being analysed by a large national retail company considering further UK expansion. This information is also shown in Fig. 8.1 on page 57.

Activity

Refer to the 'Office Shoes' case study on page 54. Why might it be important for Office Shoes to analyse growth in its market?

Link

Identification of sales trends and strategic decision-making is discussed in Chapter 9 — Selecting market strategies, page 66.

Key term

Moving average: a technique for identifying an underlying trend by smoothing out fluctuations in data.

Table 8.1 *UK retail sales June 2006–May 2008*

Year/month	UK retail sales £b	Year/month	UK retail sales £b	Year/month	UK retail sales £b
2006/06	120.1	2007/02	114.7	2007/10	127.9
2006/07	121.1	2007/03	119.7	2007/11	141.5
2006/08	118.5	2007/04	123.8	2007/12	170.
2006/09	117.8	2007/05	123.4	2008/01	117.9
2006/10	124.1	2007/06	124.6	2008/02	122.2
2006/11	137	2007/07	124.7	2008/03	124.7
2006/12	167.8	2007/08	122.6	2008/04	125.5
2007/01	111.5	2007/09	122.7	2008/05	131.9

Table 8.2 *Quarterly moving averages*

Year/month	Quarterly moving average	Year/month	Quarterly moving average
2006/06		2007/07	123.97
2006/07	119.90	2007/08	123.33
2006/08	119.13	2007/09	124.40
2006/09	120.13	2007/10	130.70
2006/10	126.30	2007/11	146.47
2006/11	142.97	2007/12	143.13
2006/12	138.77	2008/01	136.70
2007/01	131.33	2008/02	121.60
2007/02	115.30	2008/03	124.13
2007/03	119.40	2008/04	127.37
2007/04	122.30	2008/05	128.73
2007/05	123.93	2008/06	
2007/06	124.23		

The table and graph seem to indicate that there is an upward trend in retail sales, but there are big variations between the monthly figures.

The use of moving average calculations can help to identify the underlying trend. Table 8.2 and Fig. 8.2 show the quarterly moving averages. Note that the moving average is shown in the middle month of the three used in the calculation, for example the June 2006–August 2006 average is shown in July:

$$(120.1 + 121.1 + 118.5) \div 3 = 119.9$$

The quarterly moving average line smoothes out the effect of seasonal variations in sales.

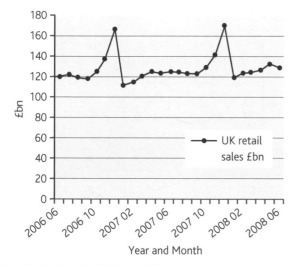

Fig. 8.1 *UK retail sales June 2006–May 2008*

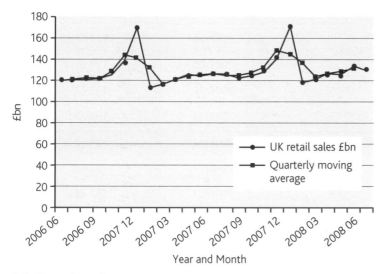

Fig. 8.2 *Quarterly moving averages*

In Table 8.3, the six-month moving average is shown in the third month of the six used in the calculation, for example the figure for June–November 2006 is shown in August:

$$(120.1 + 121.1 + 118.5 + 117.8 + 124.1 + 137) \div 6 = 123.10$$

Fig. 8.3 compares the **trends** using quarterly and six-month moving averages. The trend is clearer with a six-month moving average and shows that there has been little change in the underlying spending pattern of UK consumers over the two-year period.

The use of moving averages is important when a business wants to assess its current market situation to inform marketing planning.

Extrapolation

Extrapolation involves taking past and present data about a market and using an identified underlying trend to predict future sales. As Fig. 8.4 shows, despite monthly fluctuations in sales, the underlying trend is upwards. If we assume that this trend will continue, future sales figures can be predicted.

Key terms

Trend: a general direction in which something tends to move, e.g. sales are increasing.

Extrapolation: a prediction of a future trend based on an identified current trend.

Activity

Should the national retail company continue with a proposed expansion based on the data provided above?

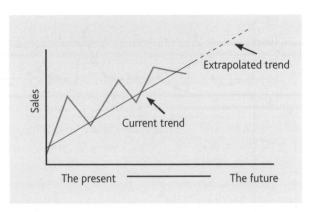

Fig. 8.3 *Extrapolation*

Table 8.3 *Six-month moving averages*

Year /month	Six-month moving average	Year/month	Six-month moving average
2006/06		2007/07	124.32
2006/07		2007/08	127.33
2006/08	123.10	2007/09	134.90
2006/09	131.05	2007/10	133.77
2006/10	129.45	2007/11	133.70
2006/11	128.82	2007/12	134.03
2006/12	129.13	2008/01	133.63
2007/01	129.08	2008/02	132.03
2007/02	126.82	2008/03	125.17
2007/03	119.62	2008/04	
2007/04	121.82	2008/05	
2007/05	123.13	2008/06	
2007/06	123.63		

AQA Examiner's tip

Remember that the benefits of data analysis rely on accurate and meaningful figures. For example, a trend can only be identified if there is sufficient data, covering a significant period of time.

Benefits of extrapolation

Forecasting increasing or falling sales can help not only the marketing function with distribution and promotional strategies, but also the other functional areas. Budget setting, workforce and production planning will all be better informed if the business has an idea of future sales.

Drawbacks to extrapolation

This method of predicting future trends relies on what has happened in the past continuing into the future. This may well be the case in stable, slow-moving markets, such as dental care. However, in high-technology dynamic markets where change happens very rapidly and products tend to have relatively short product life cycles, extrapolation is less useful and can be misleading. Similarly, health scares and severe weather conditions are very hard to predict yet can have a devastating impact on the sales of a wide range of goods and services.

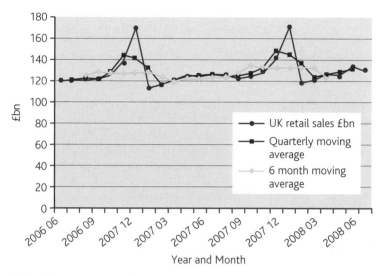

Fig. 8.4 *Comparing trends using moving averages*

Correlation

This involves trying to establish whether or not there is a link between two variables. For marketing, the aim is to find out whether there is a **correlation** between one factor and sales, for example good weather can have a positive impact on the sale of ice cream. Using this technique can help firms identify the most significant factors affecting demand for their product and therefore the level of sales. This can then become part of the marketing tactics employed to achieve the marketing objectives. However, as with other predictive techniques, apparent correlation between two factors should be treated with caution, because it is almost impossible to isolate one element of the consumer decision-making process and an observed link might just be a coincidence. Obviously the more rigorous the research and the more often the relationship is observed, the more reliable the findings.

There are three types of correlation:

- Positive correlation means that there is a direct relationship between the two variables, for example an increase in spending on advertising a family-run restaurant leads to an increase in bookings (Fig. 8.5).

- Negative correlation means that there is an inverse relationship between the two factors, for example if the interest rate goes up, new house purchases goes down (Fig. 8.6)

- No correlation means that there is no discernable link between factors and no pattern is evident when the data is plotted on a graph, for example the link between the price of fish and the sales of cinema seats (Fig. 8.7).

Correlation can be expressed numerically as a value between +1 and –1, with 0 being no correlation. Therefore the closer to either +1 or –1 the stronger the positive or negative correlation. It may be calculated using the Spearman Rank Correlation Coefficient or the Pearson Correlation Coefficient.

Key term

Correlation: an apparent (statistical) relation between two factors (variables) which can be either positive or negative.

Activity

Refer to the Setting the scene case study on page 54. What type of correlation would Office Shoes expect to find between visits to its website and online sales of shoes?

AQA Examiner's tip

You will not be expected to calculate moving averages or the correlation coefficient. However, you need to be familiar with what all these terms mean and how they affect the measurement and forecasting of sales.

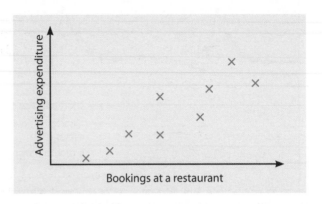

Fig. 8.5 *Positive correlation: a positive relationship between advertising expenditure and bookings at a restaurant*

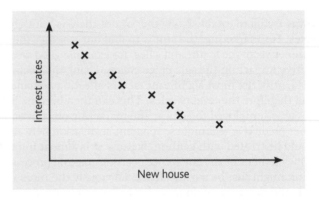

Fig. 8.6 *Negative correlation: a negative relationship between interest rates and the purchase of new houses*

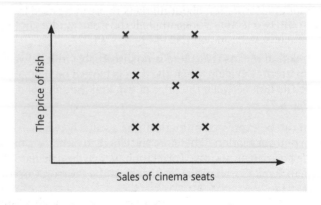

Fig. 8.7 *No correlation: this shows no apparent link between the price of fish and the sales of cinema seats*

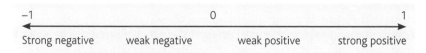

Fig. 8.8 *Correlation expressed numerically*

▦ Benefits of market analysis

Marketing success can be based on many things, including 'gut' feelings or intuition. However, answers to the following questions are the basis for good marketing planning and are easier to answer if a thorough examination of the market has been conducted first:

▦ What opportunities are there in the market?

▦ What is likely to happen to this market in the future?

▦ What are the most significant influences on demand in this market?

All the methods described above will aid the business in answering these questions with some degree of certainty.

▦ Business in action

Jarvis Rail

Jarvis Rail was interested in buying Estonia Railways, whose main business is the export of Russian oil products. Before making the purchase, they asked PDC (Petroleum Development Consultants Ltd) to prepare forecasts of:

▦ Russian refinery output (knowing supply helps to calculate price)

▦ Russian oil product consumption (demand)

▦ oil product exports by route.

In this way, Jarvis Rail reduced the risk involved in purchasing the Estonia Railways business.

Source: www.pdc.uk.com

Difficulties of analysing marketing data

There is a lot of information about markets that can be used by businesses, which will give a general analysis of the market and help with strategic planning, for example market share, sales trends and competitor actions. However, a business will also need to analyse the data collected about its own marketing activities (its **marketing data**), and this can be much more difficult.

Test markets

Part of the information-gathering process to support marketing planning is the practice of testing a market prior to launching a new or improved product. The aim is to simulate a full-scale launch on a representative sample of the target market. This can be achieved geographically, for example by television region or by type of customer through a limited number of outlets. The goal is to achieve results that represent the response of the whole market.

> ▦ Key term
>
> **Marketing data:** information gathered about the response to the marketing activities of a business.

Key term

Test market: to replicate all elements of a product launch including promotion, distribution and price, to a geographic region or demographic group to judge the viability of the product in the market before a full-scale launch.

Although this sounds straightforward, in reality it can be very difficult to select a suitable **test market**, particularly if the company is planning to expand abroad. If the geographical area chosen is not a typical representation of the whole market, then the data collected will be at best inadequate, and at worst misleading. Similarly, it is difficult to isolate the impact of a new or updated product on consumers. Reactions might be affected by external influences, such as a competitor launching a new product or starting an advertising campaign or something as simple as an item on the television – think of Jamie Oliver's healthy eating campaign. Whatever the cause, misleading results could be produced.

Secondly, there is a danger that a rival firm will gain details of the new product or service and produce a copy which will reduce any first mover advantage that the business was hoping to achieve. This is of particular concern in fast moving markets where there is a lot of competition. The business must decide whether or not it is worth the risk.

Fig. 8.9 *Innocent smoothies*

Business in action

The Innocent story

In the summer of 1998, when we had developed our first smoothie recipes but were still nervous about giving up our proper jobs, we bought £500 worth of fruit, turned it into smoothies and sold them from a stall at a little music festival in London.

We put up a big sign saying 'Do you think we should give up our jobs to make these smoothies?' and put out a bin saying 'YES' and a bin saying 'NO' and asked people to put the empty bottle in the right bin. At the end of the weekend the 'YES' bin was full so we went in the next day and resigned.

This extract is reproduced by kind permission of Innocent Drinks. It can be reached through its website at www.innocentdrinks.co.uk

Primary market research

Primary market research is a source of marketing data which can be used to gather information when devising a new strategy. This is a very expensive form of data collection and will involve the use of extrapolation to predict future sales, with the potential drawbacks this entails. The type of research conducted is also important and the business will be looking for a high level of confidence in the results if it is to use it as the basis for decision-making. Product recognition after an advertising campaign is an example of data which can be useful to a business in determining future marketing strategies. This can be conducted using consumer panels or through sampling the target market. However, it is very difficult to isolate the impact of the campaign from other factors that affect buying behaviour and as such should be treated with caution.

Reasons why marketing data might be incorrect or misleading include the following:

■ If it is backdata (historical information), it might not reflect a change in consumer buying habits and suggest a trend which is unrealistic. For example, airlines which used past sales figures to predict trends for the start of the new millennium could not have anticipated the impact of the attack on the Twin Towers which had a devastating effect on air travel. Although this is an extreme example, the point is that consumers do not always behave in predictable ways and historical information alone should be treated with caution.

- The data might be biased, for example if information about consumer demand is provided by a company supplying materials. It is in this firm's interest to portray future demand in a very favourable light in order to secure a lucrative contract.

- If the forecasts are for too far into the future, the chances of them being accurate are greatly reduced. As we have seen throughout this chapter, the possibility of an external factor having an impact on consumer behaviour increases as time passes, and therefore predictions become less and less reliable.

The use of information technology in analysing markets

The use of IT in the collection and analysis of data, and therefore markets, has increased rapidly over recent years. Businesses are now able to obtain valuable information about consumers through store cards. Market research can be conducted through EPOS and online questionnaires. Once data is collected, software packages are available to process and present information. More recently the growth of business 'blogs' as a way to obtain feedback from customers has become common.

Advantages of IT

- Information can be processed very quickly and used for sales forecasting techniques such as extrapolation, moving averages and correlation.

- Information can be used to build up an electronic database of consumer buying behaviour, as well as a detailed profile of each customer so that future products and promotions can be targeted more effectively.

Disadvantages of IT

- There is a possibility of information overload which can slow down the decision-making process because the opportunity to actually reach a conclusion never appears, just a continual stream of data. This could mean that the company misses a business opportunity which is then exploited by more decisive competitors.

- Data is available very quickly which may cause decision-makers to overreact or misinterpret apparent trends leading to unfortunate decisions being taken. For example, a business might believe that a product has reached decline stage of the product life cycle based on data showing a trend of falling sales, when in fact the loss of business is due to the actions of an aggressive competitor in the market.

Case study

A blooming business

Tregory Growers Ltd, based in Cornwall, had supplied bulbs and cut flowers for many years. Early summer flowers had long been their best sellers. They had generated a small, but declining profit by supplying mainly small retailers with traditional varieties of cut flowers. However, increasing competition from abroad and changing consumer tastes meant that the company needed to rethink its strategy. Yewande's appointment as Managing Director was a turning point for the company. In her first major presentation to the Board of Directors, she set out her strategy for the future of Tregory Growers Ltd:

'This market is changing and we have ignored it. Sales of cut flowers are increasing and customers are changing. Flowers grown overseas are becoming very popular. We must expand our product range and deal with bigger retailers.'

Yewande highlighted some statistics she had researched:

'The UK cut flower market is worth more than £1 billion per annum and sales have risen by 10 per cent yearly since 2001. Increasing amounts of cut flowers are imported by air. Women now account for nearly two-thirds of the UK market. These views are supported by research we have carried out recently. In the past we have not invested in market research. We simply tried to sell more of our existing products by increasing our marketing expenditure, especially on advertising in trade magazines, on the Internet and using mailshots. My research (see Appendix A) shows that increasing our market budget beyond the current figure of £650,000 will not work. We cannot continue to base marketing decisions on guesses. We must take a more scientific approach to our decision making in this area.'

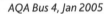

AQA Bus 4, Jan 2005

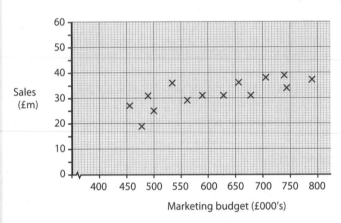

Fig. 8.10 *Appendix A*

Questions

1 Analyse the correlation between the marketing budget and sales as shown in Appendix A.

2 To what extent is analysing the market important for a business like Tregory Growers?

3 Analyse the disadvantages to Tregory Growers of relying on statistical analysis of the market.

4 Using all the information:
a Analyse the case for Tregory Growers Ltd basing its strategy on marketing data.
b Analyse the case for basing the strategy on other factors including guesswork and hunches.
c Make a justified recommendation about whether Tregory Growers Ltd should support 'a more scientific approach' to decision-making.

5 Look on the internet, for example www.thetimes100.co.uk, and write a short marketing case study with three or four possible exam-style questions, using the example above for guidance.

☑ *In this chapter you will have learned to:*

- examine the reasons for market analysis: gathering evidence for devising a new strategy and identifying significant patterns in sales
- discuss the value of market analysis
- use your familiarity with moving averages, extrapolation and test markets to discuss measuring and forecasting sales
- explain how correlation is used in analysing markets
- discuss the difficulties in analysing marketing data
- assess the use of information technology in market analysis.

Summary questions

1. What is market analysis? (2 marks)

2. Explain the benefits of using moving averages in market analysis. (6 marks)

3. What is extrapolation? (2 marks)

4. Explain the difference between a negative and a positive correlation. (4 marks)

5. What is a test market? (2 marks)

6. A traditional wellington boot manufacturing company has just appointed a new marketing director in an attempt to revive its fortunes.

   a Explain which elements of the market should be analysed. (6 marks)

   b Analyse the advantages to the business of analysing the market. (10 marks)

   c Describe three methods the new director could employ to analyse the wellington boot market. (6 marks)

7. Why might it not be beneficial for a computer game manufacturer to test market its latest product? (6 marks)

8. Discuss the difficulties facing EMI Records in analysing marketing data. (10 marks)

9. A large US fast-food retail business is planning a UK launch. Discuss the use of moving averages, extrapolation and test markets to measure and forecast sales. (18 marks)

10. How useful is information technology in market analysis for a specialist travel company such as Travelbag? (18 marks)

Selecting marketing strategies

In this chapter you will learn to:

- describe a range of marketing strategies

- explain the meaning and significance of Ansoff's matrix in assessing marketing strategies

- evaluate the suitability of Ansoff's competitive strategies in a given context

- analyse the risks and benefits involved in entering international markets.

Setting the scene

Marks & Spencer explore new opportunities

In his Chief Executive's Business Review, Stuart Rose identified these strategies that Marks & Spencer would be pursuing in 2007/08:

- new product opportunities in stores and online to encourage our existing customers to spend more with us. Opening more Simply Food stores than ever before, working towards our aim to have more than 400, in addition to selling our food in BP Connect service stations under the Simply Food banner in up to 200 locations within five years

- increase sales through the new website five-fold in the next five years

- trialling more widely new product and service offers, such as home technology, new formats for men's shoes, and new eating offers, such as our 'eat over delicatessens'

- develop our overseas business at a faster pace. We have teams exploring opportunities both in markets where we already perform well and in new locations.

Marks & Spencer Chief Executive's Business Review 2007;
www.marksandspencer.com

Discussion points

1 What evidence is there that Marks & Spencer is aiming to sell new products to its existing customers?

2 Is there any evidence to suggest that Marks & Spencer is hoping to sell more of its current product portfolio to new customers?

3 Why might it be more risky to develop the overseas business in new locations rather than in markets where Marks & Spencer already operates?

Link

For more information on market analysis, see Chapter 8 — Analysing markets and marketing, page 54.

Marketing strategies

So far we have looked at the marketing objectives of a business which come from the corporate goals and are influenced by internal and external factors. The necessity of analysing the market before attempting to devise a marketing strategy has already been discussed. In this chapter, we move on to look at the marketing strategy: the plan of how the marketing objectives are going to be achieved.

At AS Level, you looked at niche and mass marketing: the decision about which type of market to aim for is an important part of the strategic decision. However, there are other factors which should also be considered:

- Is the business going to develop a low-cost strategy and try to undercut its rivals, or should the company aim to achieve product differentiation and added value?

- Does the strategy have a national or international context?

Low cost versus differentiation

Low cost

In both niche and mass markets, there is the option to go for the cheaper end of the market. If this is the strategy adopted by the business, the aim is to offer products at a lower price than competitors in the market. To achieve this, the business must be able to reduce its own costs, for example through economies of scale, by finding the lowest cost suppliers or by moving its own operations to a low-cost location.

Differentiation

This strategy again applies in both the niche and mass markets. The purpose is to make one product appear different and somehow superior to others on the market, and thereby encourage consumers to choose that particular make or model when making their purchasing decisions. A differentiation strategy involves all elements of the marketing mix and includes patenting a new invention, developing a USP or building a strong brand image. The pricing will reflect the exclusivity and superiority of the product and the distribution will be strictly controlled if possible to maintain this image.

■ Business in action

easyGroup

easyGroup companies, including easyJet, easyCruise and easyPizza, all operate as part of a brand which is known to represent value for money and is aimed at the many rather than the few. Visit www.easy.com.

■ Business in action

Morgan Cars

Morgan Cars operates in a niche market making exclusive cars at its factory in Malvern, Worcestershire. Visit www.morgan-motor.co.uk to find out more.

Is the context national or international?

Whichever marketing strategy or strategies a business opts for, it is increasingly likely that there will be an international aspect to the plans. The growth of e-commerce has enabled small to medium-sized firms to attract customers from all around the world, so the opportunities for large organisations should be even more attractive. The expansion of the European Union will also encourage UK companies to think in an international rather than a domestic context.

■ Ansoff's competitive strategies

Igor Ansoff developed a model, known as **Ansoff's matrix**, which presents the product and market choices available to a business and divides them into four combinations, each shown by a different quadrant in the matrix. Choice is the basis for developing a clear marketing strategy, and the matrix allows managers to discuss the strategies for

■ Link

For more information on economies of scale, see Chapter 12 — Operational strategies: scale and resource mix, page 90.

■ Activity

How are Tesco and Asda able to offer products at such low prices?

Fig. 9.1 *Two companies that compete by offering customers the 'lowest prices'*

■ Activity

Refer to the Setting the scene case study on page 66. How might a new web presence help Marks & Spencer develop its international marketing strategy?

■ Key term

Ansoff's matrix: a way of classifying marketing strategies in terms of existing and new products in existing and new markets. The degree of risk involved in each strategy is an important element of the analysis.

achieving corporate objectives through the marketing function. With every choice, there comes an element of risk, and the matrix suggests that the level of risk increases as the strategy moves further away from the present product, present market option.

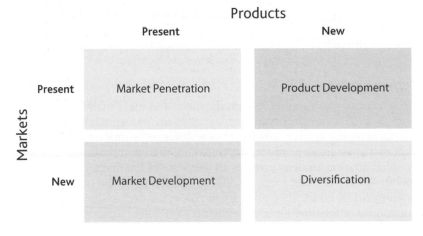

Fig. 9.2 *Ansoff's product–market growth matrix*

Ansoff (1959, 1989)

Based on Ansoff's matrix, a business can select one or more strategies: market penetration, product development, market development and diversification. As the focus at A2 is on larger organisations and more complex scenarios, particular consideration is given here to entering international markets.

Market penetration

The **market penetration** strategy aims to increase the sales of current products to existing customers and to entice consumers away from competing brands. In the past, this strategy would have referred to the national market in which a firm operates, but increasingly businesses operate in larger markets such as the European Union or pan-European market. The largest companies may consider the market for their leading brands to be global. This strategy involves using the elements of the marketing mix more effectively:

■ reducing prices to encourage customers to buy more or entice consumers from other brands in the market

■ increasing promotional spending to remind customers about the product range

■ launching a loyalty scheme

■ increasing the activity of the sales force

■ making small changes to the products on offer, for example a greater range of sizes or different levels of service

■ giving customers a greater range of buying options by increasing the places from which the product can be purchased.

This is the lowest risk strategy, because the business has experience of the market and should know the characteristics of the customers very well. However, if the market is large, assuming that customers share similar characteristics and will all respond in the same way, it may be dangerous. The existence of up-to-date market research will be invaluable.

Business in action

Cellbond Composites Ltd

Cellbond Composites Ltd, Huntingdon, looked to Anglia Polytechnic University for expertise to improve the production process for its aluminium honeycomb crash test energy absorbers for the motor industry. This collaboration produced benefits in terms of improved profitability and product reliability. Cellbond's Managing Director said, 'I am delighted with the results: It made a major contribution to the company gaining market share from its competitors and increasing market penetration in Europe and the Far East.'

Source: Association of Universities in the East of England

Product development

This is a higher risk strategy which involves selling new products to existing customers. Note that **product development** refers to a significantly new product line, not minor changes to an existing product. This strategy often looks favourable, because it might allow the company to utilise excess production capacity, respond to a new product launch from a competitor, maintain the company's reputation as a product innovator, exploit new technology or protect overall market share. When discussing this option, senior managers will take into consideration the size of the market and whether or not the business views it in national or international terms. This can be clearly seen when you buy goods that have instruction leaflets in more than one language, for example. This strategy might include:

- developing related products or services which market research has identified as being part of the buying decisions of customers
- introducing new models of existing products with significant modifications, new functions or services.

Key terms

Product development: offering new and improved products to existing markets.

Market development: finding new markets for existing products either by selling abroad or by identifying a new segment of the domestic market.

Business in action

easyJet

easyJet offers car rental, a hotel booking service, travel insurance and airport parking to customers when they book flights online.

Business in action

Electronic Arts

Electronic Arts launches a FIFA series every year for gaming machines and PCs.

Market development

A **market development** strategy involves attracting new customer groups to existing products. The aim is to increase the sales of the current product portfolio. Strategies include:

- targeting a different geographical area, including an overseas market
- developing new sales channels, such as e-commerce, to attract a new audience

■ Activity

What are the risks for UK companies targeting China as part of a market development strategy?

■ targeting a new consumer group with a different profile to existing customers.

This can be quite a risky strategy because the company will have little or no knowledge about the new market. The marketing costs could be high and the time taken to achieve a profit in the new market might be considerable. However, the potential gains make this strategy increasingly attractive, particularly because it helps to spread risk: if one geographical market is suffering from poor economic growth, then another market may well be expanding rapidly, so the impact of economic slowdown on the business is reduced.

■ **Business in action**

Nintendo

Nintendo targeted older female customers with games such as DS Brain Training, Sudoku and Wii Fit.

■ Key terms

Diversification: offering a new product in a new market.

Diversification

A **diversification** strategy is the most risky option because it involves the firm moving into new markets with new products, which may or may not be related to existing products and markets. There is often little opportunity to use existing expertise or achieve significant economies of scale in the short term. Diversification may be:

■ Links

For more information about economic slowdown, see Chapter 21 — The relationship between business and the economic environment, page 164.

The specific issues involved in entering international markets are considered in more depth on the opposite page.

■ related, because it is some form of forward, backward or horizontal integration – the firm becomes involved in the activities of its customers, suppliers or competitors

■ unrelated – the highest risk strategy – because the business has no experience or detailed knowledge of the key success factors in the market, although there is evidence that it can lead to the fastest growth.

Strategies might include:

■ a new technology developed by the R&D department of the business or bought from an inventor – if there is evidence of significant potential, the risk is reduced

■ buying an existing business in a completely different market – if the acquisition is successful, then the risk is reduced

■ targeting existing successful markets – if the business already has a very strong brand, the risk is reduced.

AQA Examiner's tip

Remember that large organisations can use more than one of Ansoff's strategies. This is particularly true of global corporations which may use all of the product and market options included in the matrix.

The main benefit of this strategy is that risk is spread. If demand falls in one market, the business will not suffer too much because it can still achieve profits in its other markets with other products. A company can also gain 'first mover advantage' in an emerging market where there are very large profits to be made. In such circumstances, no company will have expertise or the advantage of economies of scale, so firms are competing on a 'level playing field'.

■ Activity

Using Ansoff's matrix and the information on its website, analyse Marks & Spencer's current marketing strategies. (www.marksandspencer.com)

■ **Business in action**

Virgin and Tesco

Virgin and Tesco have successfully gained share of existing markets, for example insurance and banking, by using their strong brand image to gain market share.

Entering international markets

There are increasing opportunities for UK companies to enter overseas markets. This option will particularly appeal to businesses where:

- the UK market is saturated
- the UK market is very competitive, driving down prices and therefore profits
- there are opportunities to achieve economies of scale
- the firm has excess capacity
- the additional costs involved are relatively small.

Ways of entering overseas markets are analysed in Table 9.1. Deciding how to enter an overseas market will be a crucial part of the marketing strategy.

Link

For more information on location, see Chapter 14 — Operational strategies: location, page 102.

Examiner's tip

Do not assume that the same approach works in all cases. It may also be necessary for a company to use more than one method depending on the product and the target market.

Table 9.1 *The benefits and drawbacks of different methods of entering overseas markets*

Method		Benefits	Drawbacks
Exporting from the UK	Accepting international orders, increasingly on an e-commerce website Making regular visits to the target country to identify customers, build relationships and complete sales negotiations Supported by telephone and email sales	Relatively cheap Not very complicated to set up Can be withdrawn easily if it does not work Existing resources, e.g. the sales force and the website can be used Full control over marketing is retained	Distance may make it difficult to identify potential business opportunities Bureaucracy may be complicated Risk of non-payment or delayed payment for goods, due to export problems causing cash-flow difficulties Language barriers may lead to high recruitment and training costs
Opening an overseas operation	Opening a new branch staffed by your own employees Setting up a registered subsidiary in the new market, using locally recruited employees, covered by local company, employment and tax rules Forming an alliance with a local company establishing a new business which is jointly owned	The chance to identify opportunities in the target market Control of operations and the potential for expansion Developing relationships with clients Providing good after-sales service A joint venture means that the risk is shared The local partner in the alliance provides important knowledge and experience	This is a more expensive option, including the cost of the administration and management Local company, employment and tax laws might be difficult to understand and local specialists may be needed The brand name of the product or company may not be appropriate in the target market

Using an overseas sales agent	Acts on behalf of the business in the overseas market, making sales for which they receive a commission	The agents should have a lot of knowledge of the local market, and should be able to identify business opportunities Recruitment, training and relocation costs are avoided The agent should have local contacts saving a lot of time	The UK company is still responsible for all the transport costs and documentation The standard of customer service is difficult to maintain because the agent may work for many companies
A distributor	Buys the goods and sells them in the target market	The distributor is responsible for the transportation and all the paperwork that goes with this If the distributor has an established reputation and contacts in the new market, the chances of a successful launch are greater The marketing expenditure falls mostly on the distributor	The distributor may expect good discounts on price and generous trade credit terms Control of the marketing mix is passed over to the distributor It is hard to give incentives to sell more of the product Distributors may demand exclusive rights to sell a product which may reduce sales

Activity

How and why has Marks & Spencer developed its overseas market?

AQA Examiner's tip

When making an assessment of marketing strategies, it is useful to consider the corporate objectives, the culture of the organisation, and the financial position of the business.

Assessing the effectiveness of marketing strategies

■ The most important consideration is whether or not the strategy has helped the business to achieve its marketing objectives and therefore its corporate objectives.

■ Secondly, the strategy can be assessed in terms of the quadrants within Ansoff's matrix. Has the strategy achieved market penetration, product development, market development or successful diversification?

Case study

Hilton Hotel Group

The Hilton Hotel Group traditionally appeals to the international business market. Until recently, the Group had a disconnected collection of very exclusive leisure hotels in exotic locations. The aim of the award-winning marketing strategy was to change perceptions and create brand awareness by developing a portfolio of resort hotels with a consistency of standards, generating tourist industry recognition, whilst maintaining the exclusivity of the brand and the links with the family name. Extensive market research established qualitative data that there existed a growing demand among high-spending travellers for the resort experience, but that there was inconsistency of quality between hotels. For the Hilton Worldwide Resorts brand to be successful, the packaging of the properties had to be unique and the quality standards consistent.

The strategy was to:

■ create the ultimate leisure experience through a consistent offering, whilst retaining a resort-specific individuality

- achieve a 'total resort experience'
- develop a new resort identity and launch campaign.

  To enhance the overall offering and to achieve differentiation, some new specific product development was undertaken:
- a new children's club and entertainment
- a new family breakfast experience including a children's buffet table
- a personalised welcome and farewell experience
- the creation of individual resort experiences, such as dive training, romance holidays and spa experiences.

www.businessawardseurope.com

The strategy was very successful with 1.5 billion visits by 2020 being projected. The objectives set by Hilton included:

- To create guest satisfaction levels of over 80 per cent.
- To increase repeat visits by 10 per cent.
- To increase Hilton's brand as a key leisure brand.
- To increase its share of tour operator business.
- To achieve 50,000 website hits per month.

Questions

1 To what extent has the Hilton Group implemented a differentiation strategy?

2 Analyse the influence of the sales forecast for growth in the tourism market on the Hilton Group's marketing strategy.

3 Use Ansoff's matrix to assess the marketing strategies used by the Hilton Group.

4 Using all the information:

  a Analyse the case for using Ansoff's matrix to assess the effectiveness of the Hilton Group's marketing strategy.

  b Analyse the case for using marketing and corporate objectives to assess the effectiveness of the marketing strategy.

  c Make a justified recommendation about the best way for the Hilton Group to assess the effectiveness of the marketing strategy.

5 Research task: Use an online annual report to analyse whether or not the marketing strategies of a large UK business of your choice have been successful.

✓ *In this chapter you will have learned to:*

- describe in detail a range of marketing strategies available to a business
- use Ansoff's matrix to assess marketing strategies in a given context
- analyse the risks and benefits involved in entering international markets
- assess the effectiveness of marketing strategies.

Summary questions

1 Explain the difference between a low-cost strategy and a differentiation strategy. (6 marks)

2 How is Ansoff's matrix useful when setting strategic marketing objectives? (4 marks)

3 Explain the difference between market penetration and market development. (6 marks)

4 What is the relationship between Ansoff's matrix and risk? (2 marks)

5 Explain the difference between product development and diversification. (4 marks)

6 What type of strategy is a business using if it offers its products in a greater range of sizes? (2 marks)

7 Virgin Mobile customers were offered free texts between 9 pm and 10 pm on 'Eviction Fridays' during the 2007 season of *Big Brother*. Analyse this marketing strategy using Ansoff's matrix. (10 marks)

8 Tesco made its first move abroad to Hungary in 1995, before entering **Poland**, **the Czech Republic** and **Slovakia** the following year, then taking a more daring step into **Thailand** and **Taiwan around 1998**. The company has tended to make its moves with little fanfare, preferring to build solid businesses before shouting about success. Its latest international expansion has been into the US, formally announced in February 2006 but coming only after a series of trials. Tesco has prided itself on a flexible approach rather than trying to export its British model. In Thailand, it has used a store layout and format that borrows from traditional **'wet markets'** where customers rummage through piles of produce to pick what they want. Analyse the risks and benefits to Tesco of pursuing this marketing strategy. (10 marks)

9 How can the effectiveness of marketing strategies be assessed by a mass market footwear retailer? (18 marks)

10 Discuss the relationship between effective marketing strategies and marketing objectives in a multinational car manufacturer. (18 marks)

10 Developing and implementing marketing plans

In this chapter you will learn to:

- describe the components of marketing plans for larger businesses

- assess the internal and external influences on marketing plans in specific contexts

- discuss the issues in implementing marketing plans in given situations.

Fig. 10.1 *Microsoft Zune, launched in 2006*

Key terms

Marketing plan: written details of the activities to be used to carry out the marketing strategy.

SWOT analysis: a method of analysing the current situation by examining the internal strengths and weaknesses of the business and the opportunities and threats of the external environment.

Link

See Chapter 7 — Understanding marketing objectives, page 48 for the stages of the marketing planning process.

Setting the scene

Muted welcome for Microsoft Zune in September 2006

The iPod accounts for more than 50 per cent of digital music players sold while iTunes has a 70 per cent share of its market. Experts say Microsoft wanted a share of the growing market for handheld entertainment devices because the market for its core desktop software products has become saturated. The company launched the Zune and its associated download services in direct competition with Apple, but analysts think other MP3 players, for example Sony, are more likely to lose market share. The software giant has a multi-million dollar budget to make Zune a success. Microsoft is optimistic of success because analysis shows that most music kept in iPods is ripped from CDs not downloaded from iTunes.

Adapted from BBC News, 15 September 2006; news.bbc.co.uk

Discussion points

1. Does a business as successful as Microsoft have to worry about competitors such as Apple?

2. Why might Microsoft feel confident that it can gain a share of the digital music player market?

3. Using your knowledge of the marketing mix from AS Business Studies, discuss how Microsoft might achieve its marketing objective of gaining market share.

Marketing plans

The marketing plan is the final stage in the marketing planning process described in Chapter 7. Once the corporate objectives have been decided and the marketing strategy developed, the next stage is to work out the activities needed to actually carry out the strategy. This set of tactics makes up the **marketing plan** and will include:

- a description of all the activities involved, i.e. the marketing mix
- a time frame
- reasons justifying each action.

Marketing objectives

The marketing plan is part of the range of actions taken by a business in order to achieve its goals. The objectives set by the marketing function are designed to fit into this overall company direction and should reflect the objective of other functional areas.

SWOT analysis

SWOT analysis is an assessment of a firm's current position, in terms of:

AQA Examiner's tip

Revise the marketing mix section of your AS work because it can be applied here when discussing specific marketing plans.

Link

Look back at Chapter 1 — Using objectives and strategies, page 2, for a discussion of the relationship between corporate and functional objectives.

Links

For more information about investment, see Chapter 6 — Making investment decisions, page 38.

For more information about workforce skills, see Chapter 16 — Understanding HR objectives and strategies, page 121.

Activity

Using www.marksandspencer.com, find the Chief Executive's Business Report via the Student Information area and use the information to prepare a SWOT analysis for Marks & Spencer.

Key term

Situation analysis: an assessment of the business (see SWOT analysis), its customers, competitors and the market environment.

■ strengths: what the business is good at and why it is successful. This could be:

- a strong brand name
- highly motivated employees
- a dynamic and progressive organisational culture
- a cutting edge R&D department

■ weaknesses: the aspects of the business that could hold back development strategies. This could refer to:

- financial constraints, such as lack of investment
- human resource issues, such as lack of skilled employees
- bad publicity causing a poor customer image
- a reputation for low quality

■ opportunities: what is happening in the market? It could be that:

- a market segment is growing rapidly
- a potential market is emerging overseas due to international political and economic changes
- a long-standing competitor in the market has gone into decline giving an opportunity to increase market share

■ threats: anything that will constrain the activities of the business. This could refer to:

- changes in legislation making trading in a particular market more difficult
- the actions of competitors
- economic or political conditions becoming less favourable to a UK business.

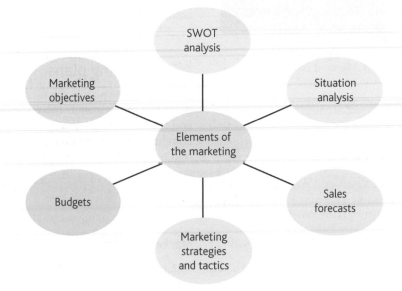

Fig. 10.2 *Elements of a marketing plan*

Situation analysis

Situation analysis builds on SWOT analysis and market research to create a picture of the business situation:

- the business: the internal resources and processes of the company
- customers: demand and behaviour
- competitors' activity and technological developments
- the market environment: the structure of the market, for example competitive and relationships with suppliers and partners.

Budgets

Budgets control the money used for activities such as advertising and market research. It is not always the case that very large companies have unlimited funds to spend on marketing. Organisations will expect spending to be justified and reviewed in relation to SMART targets to ensure that it represents value for money. The size of the marketing budget may depend on:

- how much competitors are spending on marketing: if a major rival increases expenditure on promotion and/or product development, it may be necessary to do the same
- expected returns: past success may lead to increased marketing expenditure in the hope of achieving similar results in the future
- the current financial position of the business: if trading conditions are difficult, then the money allocated to marketing may be reduced.

Sales forecasts

There are ways of analysing markets using data from a range of sources:

- back-data: successful marketing plans from the past can form the basis of future plans, and any mistakes may be identified, analysed and, hopefully, eliminated. Employees can use their expertise which should increase confidence about the success of future marketing plans
- current trends: market analysis provides a picture of the current situation. This will answer questions such as when, why and where products are purchased, and who is the most serious rival in the marketplace
- future expectations: techniques such as extrapolation, moving averages and test marketing and predictions about competitor behaviour, technological developments, social and economic trends. These predictions are not exact, especially if they look too far into the future, but are still valuable.

Marketing strategies

There should clearly be a direct link between the strategies selected by the business to achieve its objectives, and the **marketing tactics** identified in the plan to implement the strategies. The marketing mix should be considered when developing any of the strategies and the most appropriate marketing tactics will become clear from an analysis of all the above components of the marketing plan.

Internal influences on marketing plans

Marketing plans cannot be developed in isolation, and must take into account the other functional areas of the organisation. Internal influences include: the finance available, operational issues and human resources.

Finance available

Obviously a business cannot allocate money that is not actually available. Therefore the success of the company will have an impact on the marketing

---

Link

For SMART targets, see Chapter 1 – Using objectives and strategies, page 2.

Activity

Refer to the Setting the scene case study on page 75. What part do you think sales forecasting played in the launch of Zune?

Links

For more information about market analysis, see Chapter 8 — Analysing markets and marketing, page 54.

For more information about changes in the business environment, see Chapters 21–25, pages 164–216.

Key term

Marketing tactics: the marketing mix activities (price, place, product and promotion) undertaken to achieve a chosen marketing strategy.

Link

For more information on marketing strategies, see Chapter 9 — Selecting marketing strategies, page 66.

budget. There is an irony here, because it suggests that when turnover falls, spending on marketing will be reduced, and vice versa. It could be argued that if the company can raise the finance, spending on marketing should increase in adverse market conditions, so that market share can be maintained or increased or new markets developed. However, many firms are nervous about spending money when turnover and profits are falling.

Operational issues

There are very strong links at the tactical level between the marketing department and the operations function, for example how long is the manufacturing process or how practical is the packaging? If these two areas do not communicate, the marketing plan will be ineffective because the product will not be available in the right quantity for the customer to buy when required. The methods of production used by the organisation are also significant: the capacities available, the flexibility of the system and quality issues. The relationship between operations and marketing does not only apply in the manufacturing sector, of course. There are the same implications for service provision; stocks and equipment must be in place to meet expected demand, for example sufficient parking, camping, medical, security and toilet facilities at a music festival.

Human resources

Developmental strategies such as new markets or new products may require different employee skills, creating recruitment and training issues. Job descriptions and person specifications should give the precise requirements needed so the most suitable candidates are employed. On the other hand, if the strategy is market penetration, it could simply be that the sales force needs to be increased.

■ External influences on marketing plans

The marketing objectives are influenced by external factors including competitors' actions, the market conditions and technological change. At a tactical level, when developing the marketing plan, these familiar external influences should be considered.

Competitors' actions

Competitors' actions may have an impact on the money allocated to the marketing function. If a competitor decides to change one element of the marketing mix, for example launch a large-scale promotional campaign, then the company will have to decide how to respond. A lot will depend on relative market strength, but any firm in a competitive market (which is nearly all of them) should not ignore what rivals are doing. For example, if one company increases product awareness through a promotional campaign, sales for all brands in the market may rise, leading to an unexpected increase in demand, causing shortages and a subsequent loss of business.

Market conditions

Market conditions will also influence the planning decisions taken, and are linked to the sales forecasting discussed earlier in this chapter. Businesses need to be aware of the economic climate so that the marketing plans can take any likely changes into account. For example, if the marketing strategy is product development, and the economic forecast is for a slowdown in growth, then products which offer cost savings and represent improved value for money may be preferable to those aimed at the luxury end of the market.

Technological change

Technological change will also influence the marketing plans and businesses should be aware of the latest developments. This will have an impact on all the aspects of the marketing mix. Firms that are aware of new trends in consumer behaviour and make creative use of technology can gain a competitive advantage over others in the market.

Link

For more information about influences on marketing objectives, see Chapter 7 — Understanding marketing objectives, page 48.

Business in action

Sony and Amazon

Sony and Amazon have made a deal to put the entire Sony catalogue of tracks on the Amazon MP3 store, free of Digital Rights Management (DRM) controls. Amazon becomes the only company to offer tracks from all four big music companies free of DRM, making it a significant rival for market leader Apple iTunes.

Activity

Refer to the Setting the scene case study on page 75. What were the main internal and external influences on the marketing plan for the Microsoft Zune?

Issues in implementing marketing plans

- **Scheduling key tasks** is very important for a business so everyone has an idea of what will be completed and by when. If there is no schedule for completion, it is very difficult to know whether the plan is being implemented. This is particularly important in large organisations where members of the marketing function may be geographically separated and the lines of communication very long.

- **Resources required** must be in place by the time they are needed. This is where communications between functional areas is very important so that raw materials and components can be sourced effectively. In the same way, human resource needs such as additional sales staff or telephone operators can be met.

- **The cost** of the marketing plan needs to be included in a budget, which should be set after all those responsible for the activities making up the plan have been consulted. If not, the employees given responsibility for achieving the key tasks and meeting the targets set out in the marketing plan may not feel any sense of involvement and are less likely to be motivated to achieve their goals. Having said that, the marketing budget needs to be realistic and should not be diverted from other areas of the business leading to shortages of finance elsewhere in the organisation.

- **Control** of the marketing plan should also be established, with responsibility given to an appropriate manager to ensure that the plan stays on schedule. This monitoring role should not be difficult if the planning has been completed effectively and the timescale is realistic. However, if key tasks fall behind schedule, or costs overrun, there should be enough flexibility in the plan to adapt to changing circumstances.

Link

For more information on scheduling, see critical path analysis in Chapter 15 — Operational strategies: lean production, page 114.

Case study

Apple launches ultra-thin laptop

Fig. 10.3 *Apple CEO, Steve Jobs, shows off the MacBook Air during his keynote speech*

Steve Jobs unveiled the Macbook Air, the world's thinnest laptop, and new movies download system. He said Apple's objective was to control the video market with movie rentals and a revamped Apple TV product to stream films direct to television screens.

Until now, iTunes customers have only been able to buy movies outright. Apple TV has struggled to make an impact – but Jobs predicts that a relaunch will mark a significant shift in the film industry; no computer is required, customers rent movies directly on their widescreen TV at DVD or high-definition quality. This links with plans to offer films to rent through its iTunes store. The system will launch with support from every major Hollywood studio, with a thousand new titles and back-catalogue films. Launched in the US, the service should be available worldwide within a year, making downloads watchable on TV, iPods and iPhones.

Adapted from guardian.co.uk

Questions

1 Analyse the impact of technology on Apple's marketing plan.

2 Analyse how internal influences at Apple may have influenced the marketing plans for the MacBook Air.

3 To what extent would external factors have influenced Apple's marketing plans?

4 To what extent will issues in implementing Apple's marketing plans impact on their success?

5 Investigate another major product or market launch to assess the development and implementation of marketing plans.

☑ *In this chapter you will have learned to:*

▧ describe the components of marketing plans for large companies

▧ analyse the internal influences on marketing plans for given scenarios

▧ analyse the external influences on marketing plans for given scenarios

▧ make a judgement about the factors affecting the implementation of marketing plans in given scenarios.

Summary questions

1 Explain what the components of a marketing plan are likely to be. (4 marks)

2 Explain the relationship between corporate objectives and marketing plans. (4 marks)

3 Assess the importance of sales forecasts on marketing plans. (10 marks)

4 Describe the main internal influences on the marketing plan. (6 marks)

5 Following its collapse in 2008, assess the impact of financial constraints on the marketing plans for Northern Rock. (18 marks)

6 How might the marketing plans for a luxury car manufacturer be affected by a predicted global economic slowdown? (18 marks)

7 Describe the issues in implementing marketing plans. (6 marks)

8 Why would the scheduling of tasks be important in a global company such as IBM? (6 marks)

9 Discuss the importance of having resources in place when implementing marketing plans for a nation-wide fast-food retailer, for example Subway. (10 marks)

10 Is cost the most important factor in the implementation of marketing plans? (18 marks)

Introduction

Chapters in this section:

This section examines the range of operational objectives set by large organisations. Operational objectives relate to the core function of a business in either the production of a good or the provision of a service. Having considered the role of operational objectives in allowing a firm to achieve success in their particular market, and the contribution of this function towards corporate goals, this section moves on to look at the operational strategies available to businesses. This builds upon the operations materials studied at AS to take a more strategic, i.e. long-term, view of how a business can alter aspects of its operations to achieve success.

Like the other functional objectives studied at A2, it is as important here to consider the relationship *between* functional areas. If, for example, a business wants to improve cost objectives, an option may be to relocate abroad. Such a strategic decision could not be made without considering the immediate financial implications against future cost savings, the impact upon human resources and any potential effect on the image of the product.

Chapter 11: Understanding operational objectives
This chapter looks at the types of targets a business may set itself, from cost and quality targets to environmental targets. The nature of the targets and the priorities will be directly linked to the nature of the business and the degree of competition within the market. Consideration is therefore given to the internal and external factors influencing the targets set by businesses.

Chapter 12: Operational strategies: scale and resource mix
As organisations grow, it is obvious that the scale of their operation is going to grow, i.e. they will produce more goods or a wider range of goods, provide services to more people in more locations. The result is that these firms can benefit or suffer as a result of the larger scale of their operations. At AS Level only small to medium-sized businesses were being studied and these issues would not have been as relevant as they are now that you are studying large businesses, plcs often with a multinational dimension. This chapter also looks at how businesses aim to maximise their efficiency through altering the mix of human to capital inputs.

Chapter 13: Operational strategies: innovation
This chapter looks at the scientific process of research and development. Large businesses aim to maintain or achieve a competitive advantage by innovation, which is the result of successful R&D. R&D is, however, a very expensive process with no guarantee of success. We therefore look at the costs and risks in relation to the potential rewards. A strategy of innovation will have an influence on the other functional areas, which is considered at the end of this chapter.

Chapter 14: Operational strategies: location

Location is an important decision for business, with the choice of optimal location offering many advantages. This chapter looks at a range of location decisions, including multisite and multinational decisions. It considers why location is so important and the qualitative and quantitative methods a firm uses to aid the decision process. This includes the use of investment appraisal techniques, as examined in Chapter 6 — Making investment decisions.

Chapter 15: Operational strategies: lean production

This chapter looks at a number of operational strategies adopted by firms to help improve efficiency and reduce waste. These involve the effective use of physical and human resources as well as time. The concept of critical path is introduced as a tool which allows managers to plan and better coordinate complex projects.

Understanding operational objectives

In this chapter you will learn to:

- understand the range of operational objectives typically set by larger businesses

- understand how internal and external factors can influence the setting of operational objectives.

Setting the scene

A good day for customers as Severn Trent demonstrates improvements

Severn Trent Water has turned a corner in its journey towards delivering the highest standards of performance and service to its customers. In the published 2007–2008 financial report, the company announced that it outperformed against a tougher leakage reduction target – it had missed the regulator's targets in the previous two years. The company also beat operating efficiency targets and delivered customer service improvements. Tony Wray, Chief Executive of Severn Trent Water, said, 'We can show that we are delivering and investing in a better service for customers. And our financial success means that we are able to deliver further service improvements that our customers expect and deserve.' Severn Trent has invested in an extensive improvement programme to enhance the quality and reliability of their service.

With turnover up 5 per cent to £1,29m, Severn Trent is well placed to aim for even higher standards and achieve higher levels of customer satisfaction, as well as delivering sustainable financial returns to shareholders and better performance against regulatory standards. The company's success in outperforming its leakage reduction target has come through improving measurement and detection, responding more quickly, allocating resources more effectively and better targeting the replacement of its network.

Tony Wray added, 'We still have a lot more work to do as a company to reach our goal of being among the best in the industry for each of our 20 key performance indicators but we are starting to make good progress.'

www.stwater.co.uk

Discussion points

1. What does the word 'quality' mean in the context of Severn Trent Water?
2. What are the operational targets of Severn Trent Water?
3. What factors are likely to influence the targets set by Severn Trent Water?
4. Why might Severn Trent Water set itself 20 key performance indicators?

Key term

Operational objectives: targets set in relation to the production process or provision of a service within a given financial year.

Operational objectives

A wide range of **operational objectives** are set by businesses but, whatever the operational objective, it can always be linked to achieving the corporate objective. Operational objectives will normally look to improve performance with a view to improving competitiveness. At AS, you would have studied operational objectives from a tactical perspective in small to medium-sized firms. At A2, we are looking at how large organisations can set and achieve operational objectives in order to improve competitiveness, and often international competitiveness.

Large companies are seen to compete in the marketplace with one or more competitive priority. These can range from quality, lead time, cost and flexibility to innovation and reliability. Increasingly social responsibility issues are being included within operational objectives to achieve competitive advantage.

Quality, cost and volume targets

Operational objectives focus on setting targets in relation to the production process or provision of a service. Three key criteria within this are **quality, cost and volume**.

Quality targets

Quality can be referred to as 'fitness for purpose' or 'meeting customer expectations'. To consider the role of quality targets in improving competitiveness, it is therefore important to recognise the many guises of quality. These include:

- performance, i.e. the core function of the product or service
- advanced performance, i.e. the actual and augmented functionality of the product or service, which may include aesthetics and serviceability
- predicted life; this can be from either a viewpoint of reliability/resilience, i.e. for how long will it continue to function, or from a durability perspective, i.e. at what point will it become obsolete
- conformance with standards and specification requirements
- the perceived quality; often a USP achieved through reputation and brand loyalty.

Cost targets

Cost targets will focus on keeping costs to a minimum in order to allow for competitive pricing without having a detrimental effect on quality or volume targets. Cost targets will almost inevitably have an effect on selling price, added value and ultimately profit. Costs can include the costs involved in the manufacturing of the product or provision of the service, as well as those involved in keeping the product/service running and the servicing of it. Cost targets are often achieved via the reduction of waste. This is done through the adoption of lean production techniques.

Volume targets

Volume targets relate to not only the number of units a firm is able to process but also its flexibility, i.e. its ability to respond to varying demand volumes. If volume targets are high, this will help a business achieve cost targets through economies of scale which result in a fall in average costs. Both these operational issues are key to achieving volume targets, and the resource mix in particular will influence the degree of flexibility possible.

Innovation

Innovation is when a new product or process is launched on to the market. Firms can achieve a competitive advantage by having new, innovative products or new, innovative processes. The latter, for example, might be a better or more efficient method of production. This, in turn, may reduce costs in the long run and increase the volume and quality of outputs.

Link

For more about social responsibility issues, see Chapter 23 — The relationship between business and the social environment, page 195.

Key term

Quality, cost and volume targets: operational objectives which set a minimum acceptable standard of provision measured by cost, quality or volume.

Innovation: the launch of a new product or process, an invention, onto the market for commercial gain.

Link

Lean production techniques are discussed in more detail in Chapter 15 — Operational strategies: lean production, page 114.

Link

Economies of scale are discussed along with the resource mix in Chapter 12 — Operational strategies: scale and resource mix, page 90.

Activity

At AS Level you studied capacity utilisation. How will a firm's capacity utilisation affect its ability to meet volume targets in terms of both number of units produced and degree of flexibility?

Links

Innovation is studied in more detail in Chapter 13 — Operational strategies: innovation, page 96.

Key terms

Efficiency targets: operational objectives which set a minimum acceptable standard of provision in relation to efficiency.

Environmental targets: operational objectives which set a minimum acceptable standard of provision in relation to the environment.

AQA Examiner's tip

When discussing operational objectives, look for links between the objectives, for example cost, volume and efficiency targets are likely to be interdependent.

Link

Environmental issues are considered in more depth in Chapter 23 — The relationship between business and the social environment, page 195.

Key term

Benchmarking: a management tool which aims to increase performance by identifying, investigating and adopting aspects of best practice from other firms.

Activities

Read Business in action: Morrisons' environmental targets.

1. What are the advantages and costs to Morrisons of pursuing these operational objectives?

2. Look at Morrisons' most recent Corporate Social Responsibility Report to check on their progress and review any new targets set.

Efficiency and environmental targets

At AS, you looked at how entrepreneurs take inputs and process them to achieve an output. Large businesses will measure their efficiency by the added value gap between the input, process and output. An efficient firm will be able to maximise its output whilst minimising the input and process costs. This will involve setting targets for machinery usage, stock wastage and labour productivity. In the same way as costs targets (discussed on page 93) may be achieved through lean production techniques, these will also be fundamental in achieving **efficiency targets**.

Businesses should be aware of the impact of their actions on the environment. For example, a supermarket stocking exotic fruits from around the world should consider the food miles of the product. Many large organisations now set **environmental targets** to reduce their negative impact on the environment. These targets focus on issues such as carbon footprint, pollution, sustainability of resources and food miles. Setting and achieving environmentally friendly targets can gain a business a competitive advantage, particularly as members of society become more aware of, and are likely to act upon, their concern for environmental issues.

■ Business in action

Morrisons' environmental targets

It is common practice for large organisations to produce a Corporate Social Responsibility Report. An aspect of this will normally include the setting of environmental targets. In its 2008 Report Morrisons set the following targets in relation to energy efficiency and performance:

- reduce carbon footprint cumulatively by 36 per cent by 2010 (based on 2005 emissions)
- reduce group energy use by 8 per cent per square metre by 2010 (based on 2005 emissions)
- 10 per cent of energy from renewable sources by 2010
- air freight produce to be labelled for customer choice/information
- carbon labelling to be explored
- end sale of incandescent light bulbs in favour of CFL energy-efficient light bulbs by 2010.

www.morrisons.co.uk

Benchmarking

Benchmarking is a management tool which aims to increase a firm's competitiveness by improving performance. It could be linked to any of the operational objectives discussed above. Benchmarking involves identifying best practice and then adopting aspects of this to improve your own performance. For example, one firm may identify the need to improve its rate of successful innovation. It would then identify a business whose performance outshines its own in this area and work alongside that organisation to identify its strengths and internal processes. Once areas of potential change have been identified, the learning organisation can then look at how these can be applied to its own activities. This process requires time, money and commitment as well as an open relationship between the two organisations. This can be difficult to achieve particularly if the two organisations are in direct competition with each other.

Internal and external influences

Businesses cannot set operational objectives in isolation of other functional objectives or without regard to the corporate objectives. Similarly they cannot ignore other factors that will influence the firm's priorities and capabilities both from within and outside of the business. These influences include:

- competitors' performance
- resources available
- the nature of the product
- demographics.

Although competitors' performance and demographics are clearly external influences, it is less easy to categorise resources and the nature of the product as they might have both internal and external influences. Competitors' performance will influence the operational objectives set whether it is to benchmark against their superior performance, increase environmental targets to maintain competitiveness or focus more on innovation. The resources available may influence a firm's need to increase its operational efficiency or review its cost and volume targets. This may, however, be a direct result of internal resources such as expertise and budgets or external influences such as non-sustainable supply of raw materials.

The nature of the product, and indeed the market it is aimed at, will influence the way in which quality, cost and volume targets are matched together. A technologically advanced product aimed at a niche market, for example, will focus more on the setting of high quality targets, but accept that a target of cost minimisation may be unrealistic given the limited volume targets. From an external perspective, however, the setting of some operational objectives may be enforced by national objectives or standard regulations.

Finally, the demographics of a region, country or wider geographical target market may influence the operational objectives set. Demographics refers to the make-up of the population in terms of characteristics such as age, gender, socio-economic group and ethnic background. Supermarkets such as Waitrose who brand themselves as 'the upmarket supermarket' make strategic operational decisions about the location of their stores based upon average income levels within a town or city.

Fig. 11.1 *One environmental target set by firms may be to reduce carbon footprint*

Fig. 11.2 *Benchmarking involves measuring your performance against a business that is performing better*

Case study

Profit threat for maritime safety

Industry experts report that safety is being compromised in the container shipping industry in the hunt for profits. Tight schedules, larger ship designs and lack of control of cargo have all been identified as problem areas. 'The industry needs to work together,' says Stephen Meyer, head of the UK's Maritime Accident Investigation Branch. Meyer warns that 'whilst there is no safety standard, and companies are in cut-throat competition with each other, then corners will be cut and safety will be compromised.' Meyer says that hazardous contents of containers are not always reported, ships are frequently

Fig. 11.3 *The* Napoli *sank off the coast of Devon in 2007*

overloaded and the development in the design of ships has not kept up with the growth of vessels themselves.

In 2007 Meyer led an inquiry into the beaching of the container ship *Napoli* off the Devon coast. The report showed that more than 15,000 similar ships were screened following the incident, of which 12 unidentified ships required strengthening work 'to bring them up to acceptable safety standards'. The *Napoli* was considered huge when built in 1991, with a capacity to carry 6,000 containers; ships are now being built that can carry almost three times this cargo. The largest container ship operating in 2008 by the Maersk Company is a quarter of a mile long and can carry 15,200 containers.

Richard Meade, news editor for Lloyds list, also has concerns. He blames the increased pressure on shipping lines to deliver their goods with a 'just-in-time mentality'. He says that 'the booming nature of the industry means that ships are being run as hard as possible'.

The deputy director general of the British Chamber of Shipping reports that 'for some time it has been working on guidelines for best practice for the whole of the container industry to draw together all the good practices.'

www.bbc.co.uk

Questions

1. Briefly explain how cut-throat competition may lead to a compromise in setting and meeting operational objectives.

2. Explain how the introduction of the larger ship by the Maersk Company may affect the operational objectives set by other container shipping companies.

3. Analyse the relationship between quality, cost and volume targets in the container shipping industry.

4. The British Chamber of Shipping 'has been working on best practice'. To what extent do you believe that a policy of benchmarking would help avoid another disaster such as *Napoli*? Justify your answer.

✔ *In this chapter you will have learned to:*

- show understanding of the range of operational objectives set by larger businesses

- understand how internal and external factors influence the setting of operational objectives.

Summary questions

1. With the use of an appropriate example, explain what the term 'operational objectives' means to a manufacturer of soft drinks, such as Coca-Cola. (5 marks)

2. Analyse the role of environmental targets within the supermarket industry. (10 marks)

3. What might be the operational targets of an online insurance company such as Direct Line? Justify your answer. (8 marks)

4. Discuss the potential advantages of adopting a policy of benchmarking between NHS hospitals. (10 marks)

5. Identify two industries in which you think innovation will be a priority in the setting of operational targets. Briefly explain why you chose these industries. (8 marks)

6. What are the operational objectives of your school or college? What internal and external factors might have influenced the setting of these objectives? (12 marks)

12 Operational strategies: scale and resource mix

In this chapter you will learn to:

- identify the causes of economies and diseconomies of scale

- assess the importance of economies and diseconomies of scale

- understand the advantages and disadvantages of capital and labour intensive resource mixes.

Setting the scene

World's biggest print plant opens

Fig. 12.1 *Modern printing technology has greatly reduced operating costs for newspapers*

News International, publisher of *The Times*, *Sunday Times* and the *Sun*, relocated from Wapping to Hertfordshire in 2008. The new plant, the largest print plant in the world, is equivalent in size to 23 football pitches and home to twelve state of the art colour printing presses. The presses are quieter and much faster than the previous presses, capable of printing 70,000 full colour papers in just one hour.

The new presses also only require 200 people to operate them compared to 600 at the previous site. It is thought that the advantages associated with this new technology could give the newspaper industry a new lease of life. Despite rumours of popularity of newspapers being in decline, this £650 million investment suggests they may be around for some time to come.

Adapted from www.news.bbc.co.uk

Discussion points

1 What are the advantages enjoyed by News International as a result of operating on such a large scale?

2 How will the opening of the new plant make it more difficult for smaller publishers to compete?

3 What are the advantages and disadvantages associated with moving to machinery that requires fewer staff?

Scale of operation

The size of an organisation will directly influence its ability to operate efficiently. The point at which a firm is operating at its most efficient is known as its optimum output and it is at this point that the average cost of production will be at its lowest. Before a firm reaches its optimum output, it will be benefiting from **economies of scale** as it grows, but once optimum output is reached and then exceeded further growth will start to cause problems, **diseconomies of scale**.

Economies of scale

Economies of scale are the benefits to a firm of operating on a large scale resulting in a fall in average costs. Economies of scale present large businesses with a competitive advantage and, as such, can act as a barrier to entry to smaller firms who cannot manage to compete or achieve sufficiently low average costs.

Purchasing economies

Purchasing economies refer to the ability of large firms to buy in bulk and negotiate better terms with their suppliers. Suppliers will be keen to secure large orders and consequently offer better payment terms and larger discounts, the result being a fall in the variable cost per unit and hence average cost.

Technical economies

Technical economies refer to the ability of large firms to invest in the most up-to-date and technologically advanced equipment. Because the cost of the equipment is spread over a larger number of products, the average cost is lower. The ability to invest in such equipment also allows the firm to operate more efficiently and possibly provide a more advanced and better quality product. Technical economies may also lead to a further saving as new machinery may reduce the number of workers required. This will affect the resource mix as discussed later in this chapter.

Specialisation

Specialisation refers to the ability to employ specialists as a firm grows. Large businesses will have their own legal specialists, for example, or IT specialist who will be an integral part of the business. They will know more about the actual needs of the business and will be cheaper than having to buy in the help of a consultant or services of an external professional.

Specialisation can also refer to the ability to adopt greater division of labour. As the number of employees grows they can focus on one particular task and become more efficient at that task due to specialisation. In smaller organisations workers may have to take on several roles and fail to become a specialist in any of them.

Diseconomies of scale

Diseconomies of scale are the problems encountered by a business when it grows beyond its optimum output level and hence **average costs** start to rise. Diseconomies are often qualitative in nature and it can therefore be difficult to measure their exact impact. A firm suffering from diseconomies will have to look at what actions they can take to minimise their harmful effects and restore the business to a more efficient situation.

Key terms

Economies of scale: the benefits enjoyed by a firm as a result of operating on a large scale, leading to a fall in average costs.

Diseconomies of scale: the disadvantages experienced by a firm as a result of operating beyond optimum output, leading to a rise in average costs.

Purchasing economies: benefit of buying on a large scale leading to lower average costs from suppliers.

Technical economies: ability of larger firms to buy technically advanced equipment and spread the cost over a larger number of units.

Specialisation: the ability to employ specialists, e.g. accountants, and for staff to focus on one particular area or function.

Average cost: total cost divided by the number of units produced to give cost per item.

Communication diseconomy

Communication becomes increasingly difficult as an organisation grows in size and not only does the efficiency of communication start to fall but the cost of it starts to rise. Effective communication is crucial to the smooth running of an organisation so, rather than allow for failures in communications, businesses will normally opt to invest in more sophisticated channels of communication. An additional problem with communication may occur if as this business grows it takes on a multinational dimension. This leads to issues to do with language barriers, cultural differences and time zones.

Coordination diseconomy

Coordination becomes difficult as the number of employees and resources within an organisation grows. It becomes difficult to ensure that all workers are working towards the same objectives and that jobs are being carried out efficiently. Managers may find it increasingly difficult to motivate workers or to delegate responsibility to them. The diseconomy of coordination can be a major factor contributing towards the success or failure of mergers and takeovers. Often, after a merger has taken place, a period of rationalisation is needed in order to reduce duplication of job roles and focus all employees on the new structure, work practices and objectives.

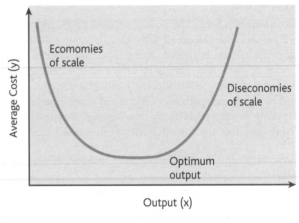

Fig. 12.2 *Average cost curve*

■ Mix of resources

Businesses can aim to improve their performance if they have an understanding of the costs of their operations. These costs include the people, equipment, data and facilities used to meet the quality and delivery requirements of the customer. Performance can hence be improved by optimising the value obtained from the mix of these resources or by altering the **resource mix** in order to optimise the return. Here we are interested in the way that firms combine capital equipment and labour in order to achieve an **optimum resource mix**. The resource mix will, however, have to be achieved with the constraints of a budget.

Capital intensive

A **capital-intensive** industry is one where the weighting of resources used within operations management is biased towards capital equipment as opposed to labour. Historically this has been true of mainly manufacturing industries where heavy investment in automation and robotics has achieved mass production with a minimum of staff input. In modern society, however, we now find many service industries also moving towards greater capital intensity, for example banks and insurance providers.

Table 12.1 *Benefits and drawbacks of operating a capital-intensive industry*

Benefits	Drawbacks
Reduction in human error	High initial capital outlay
Greater speed and uniformity of output	Prone to fluctuations in interest rates (if financed by loans)
Ease of workforce planning	Lack of initiative, i.e. introducing Kaizen ideas
Greater scope for economies of scale	Less flexibility in responding to a fall in demand

Table 12.2 *Benefits and drawbacks of operating a labour-intensive industry*

Benefits	Drawbacks
Provide greater flexibility, especially if staff are multiskilled	Can be prone to labour relation problems, e.g. union action
Creates employment in the economy	Possible workforce shortages
More personal response to consumer needs	High HRM costs
Can offer tailor made goods or services to meet individual consumer needs	
Opportunity for continuous improvement	

Labour intensive

A **labour-intensive** industry is one where the weighting of resources used within operations management is biased towards labour as opposed to capital equipment. Labour-intensive industries are often found in the service sector where customer interaction with employees is key to the service being provided, for example hotels and retail. However, as a result of the growth of e-retail there has been some sway towards more capital-intensive businesses even in the retail sector.

> **Key term**
>
> **Labour intensive:** businesses that rely more heavily upon labour, i.e. the workforce rather than capital equipment.

Business in action

Farming the future

John Deere's CEO says the internet will change agriculture as much as the tractor did 80 years ago. In the 1900s, John Deere was faced with the decision whether to adopt new technology and introduce tractors or stick with the popular horse-drawn equipment it manufactured. Deere & Co wrote in a bulletin, 'There is nothing as yet, we believe, to prove the idea (for tractors), but there is much to substantiate a conclusion that the horse will always be the mainstay of the farmer'. Despite this statement, they eventually moved into tractors. A more outward looking Deere now states, 'We see that, while the move to tractors let farmers go from a work-intensive to a capital-intensive way of doing things, the internet is letting all of

Fig. 12.3 *John Deere continues to be guided by the core values established by its founder; integrity, quality, commitment and innovation*

us move from a capital-intensive to a more efficient, information intensive approach.'

Recognition of the importance of information often leads to talk of knowledge-intensive or knowledge-based industry. This recognises the combined importance of inputs of technology and human capital.

Adapted from Context Magazine, *August/September 2001;*
www.contextmag.com

Case study

Staying in fashion for centuries

Nestled deep in the Derbyshire countryside, knitwear manufacturer John Smedley has survived the test of time. Founded at Lea Bridge in 1784, 13 years after Richard Arkwright established the first water-powered spinning mill just two miles down the road, it claims to be the world's longest running factory manufacturer.

John Smedley has a thriving business manufacturing luxury knitwear favoured by celebrities including Victoria Beckham, Tom Cruise and Madonna. It has 450 employees and made £13m of sales in 2007. It is one of a number of UK manufacturers who have been able to overcome the challenges posed by low-cost countries such as China and India, where the bulk of the world's clothes are now made.

Fig. 12.4 *John Smedley, founded in 1784*

Operating in a low-volume, niche market, the key to John Smedley's survival has been to focus on quality rather than price. The fine-knit Merino wool and sea-island cotton cardigans, sweaters and tops retail for about £100 each. Ms Stubbs, the company's brand manager acknowledges that it is expensive to manufacture in the UK but explains that, 'there would be a huge loss if we didn't manufacture here … the skills we have here, that have been passed through generations of families, are worth keeping and contribute to the product and to our brand.' Smedley's pride themselves on the level of workmanship that goes into each garment. Knitters train for between six months to two years to operate the machines.

However it has not all been smooth sailing for Smedley. In 2002 and 2003 they made a loss, leading to the loss of a substantial number of jobs and left Smedley with a larger site than they required. It used to supply woollen yarn to customers including Marks & Spencer. Ms Stubbs tells of how 'Marks & Spencer walked into all their suppliers and demanded a 20% reduction in costs.' At that time the company thought about moving abroad but decided against it.

In the future John Smedley believes its biggest challenge will be finding the highly skilled staff needed to produce the garments. Unlike many regions in the UK, migrant labour is not readily available and younger people do not view manufacturing as an attractive career option. To partially address the skills shortage, the firm recently introduced new Japanese machines, worth £125,000 each, that can knit a whole garment in about an hour.

Adapted from news.bbc.co.uk

Questions

1. Compare and contrast the business models of John Smedley and Marks & Spencer

2. Explain how Marks & Spencer has benefited from purchasing economies of scale.

3. Do you consider John Smedley to be capital intensive or labour intensive? Justify your answer.

4. What are the key factors that have contributed toward John Smedley's resource mix?

✔ *In this chapter you will have learned to:*

- show understanding of the causes and importance of economies and diseconomies of scale

- discuss the advantages and disadvantages of capital and labour intensive resource mixes

- assess the right scale of production and resource mix for a particular business.

Summary questions

1. Distinguish between economies and diseconomies of scale. (5 marks)

2. What is meant by the term 'optimum level of output'? (3 marks)

3. With the use of appropriate examples, explain how a chain of high quality Indian restaurants may benefit from economies of scale. (8 marks)

4. With the use of appropriate examples, explain how a large distribution business may suffer from diseconomies of scale. (8 marks)

5. Distinguish between capital intensive and labour intensive. (5 marks)

6. What is meant by the term 'optimum resource mix'? (3 marks)

7. Briefly explain two factors that will affect the resource mix chosen by a business. (10 marks)

Operational strategies: innovation

In this chapter you will learn to:

- understand the importance of innovation and research and development to the competitiveness of larger business

- understand the costs and risks of innovation and research and development

- understand the implications of innovation to finance, marketing and human resources.

Designs on Dyson

James Dyson was watching one of his inventions, the ball barrow, being mass produced when he spotted an imperfection in the manufacturing process. The air filter in the spray finishing room often became clogged with powder particles. Dyson solved this by inventing a cyclone that was capable of removing the powder particles by exerting centrifugal forces 100,000 times greater than gravity. From this invention, he started to wonder whether the same scientific principle could be applied to the vacuum cleaner. Five years and 5,127 prototypes later, the first bagless vacuum cleaner was launched. It was originally sold in Japan with a selling price of $2,000.

When it was later launched as the Dyson Dual Cyclone in the UK, it became the fastest selling vacuum cleaner ever to be manufactured in the UK. Dyson had proved that a superior functioning product could be made at a price people could afford. This success prompted the research and development department at Dyson to strive for even greater performance resulting in the launch of the Root Cyclone, a vacuum with 45 per cent greater suction.

The cost of such inventions can be very high, on top of which inventors have to pay substantial annual fees to renew their patents. Dyson was forced to fight to protect his patent when Hoover tried to imitate the Dyson. Fortunately for Dyson, the end result of an 18 month court battle was in his favour.

news.bbc.co.uk

Discussion points

1. Why do you think the price of the original Dyson was so high?

2. How might Dyson have achieved success in launching his invention into a mass market?

3. What were the potential risks and rewards associated with Dyson's investment in R&D?

4. Why was it important for Dyson to patent his invention?

Fig. 13.1 *James Dyson — a man who likes to make things much better*

Key term

Research and development (R&D): the scientific research and technological development of a new product or process.

Research and development

Research and development (R&D) is the scientific research and technological development of new products and processes. R&D can be both expensive and time consuming, but it is the process through which firms are able to develop new products, new materials, improve existing products and improve production processes. It is through this that they can innovate and consequently enjoy the competitive advantage generated by a USP or greater productive efficiency.

R&D is the first stage of the product life cycle, the stage prior to the launch of the product. It is at this point that money is only flowing in one direction, outwards. For this reason, a firm may want to keep the amount of time spent on R&D to a minimum, in order to help cash flow and also to achieve first mover advantage. R&D is, however, an ongoing process as many firms will be looking for continual improvements in product and/or process, as well as how to stop a product from going into decline once at the mature stage of the product life cycle.

The process of R&D

R&D involves heavy investment in both time and money and, therefore, it is not undertaken lightly by businesses. They want to know that when the outcome is launched, it has been thoroughly researched, tested and developed. A scientific process is hence taken which involves a number of stages as outlined in Fig. 13.2.

Idea generation involves the identification of a wide range of possible new ideas. The R&D team is encouraged to think imaginatively, and at this stage no consideration is given to the practicality of the ideas as this may stifle creativity. Organisations that have an enterprising culture may involve employees in this process.

The ideas generated in Step 1 of the process are now narrowed down to a small number of potentially viable ones. **Idea screening** involves considering the practical nature of the idea in terms of resources available and customer needs. Some organisations may choose to involve consumers at this stage in the form of focus groups, but this may be left until the next step in the process.

At the **concept testing** stage, a limited number of ideas are shared with consumer groups to assess their responses and consider further the viability of the concept. Using a combination of words and images, the R&D team will provide information about the basic functions of each concept and the additional features that it offers. These are referred to as the core and actual aspects of the product or service.

Development of ideas

The responses from the consumer panels are used to develop those ideas still seen as potentially viable.

Business analysis

Having identified a small number of potentially viable concepts, **business analysis** involves considering whether or not each one has the potential to make a profit. This means whether they can turn the idea into a marketable good or service, at an affordable price and whether there will be sufficient demand. At this stage, a business should also consider where the new product or service will fit into their current portfolio. One concern here may be cannibalisation, i.e. whether the new product will just attract current customers to switch products and not attract new customers, in which case there may be little benefit.

Product development

At this stage the business should just be left with the ideas which are both feasible to the business and acceptable to the target market. Product development means developing these potentially successful products into working prototypes that can be fully tested.

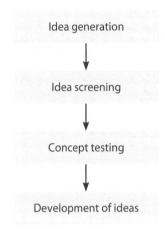

$\mathbb{AQA}$ **Examiner's tip**

Market research may be important in informing R&D, but it is not the same as it. Market research may identify a niche or find what customers want, but it is then the R&D department's job to find out how this can be made, what materials are needed and what design is needed.

Fig. 13.2 *The process of R&D*

Key terms

Idea generation: the process of identifying a wide range of possible new ideas.

Idea screening: the process of streamlining all the ideas generated to shortlist those worthy of further consideration.

Concept testing: the process of pitching potential ideas to consumer panels to assess their reactions.

Test marketing

Test marketing involves launching the product to a small target market, normally geographically defined, to identify any final adjustments necessary before rolling the product out fully. Care must be taken here as this is not only the first time the market will have access to the product but it will also be the first time that competitors see the product.

Business in action

Involve shoppers in new product development from the start

Mr Scamell-Katz, founder of TNS Magasin, a market intelligence organisation which focuses on retail and shopper insights believes that the poor performance of most new products in the UK is down to a fundamental error – the failure to involve shoppers. He explains that the standard model for bringing products to market has traditional consumer research at its heart, i.e. the market research/focus group model. The fundamental flaw he believes is that this may indicate how a consumer will react to a product, but it is unable to predict how a shopper will behave. As the shopper and the consumer have different needs and may be different people, he states that the shopper must be included from the outset.

Including the shopper, however, is not an easy task as this can only be achieved through objective research. Respondents cannot accurately describe their shopping behaviour as some 80 per cent of in-store decisions are made subconsciously. Mr Scamall-Katz concludes by saying, 'True insight into shopper decision-making, choice systems and category roles, spread throughout the organisation, drives NPD that works with appropriate packaging, marketing and distribution.'

The Grocer, March 2008

The purpose and costs of R&D

The purpose of R&D is to keep your product or service at the cutting edge. This allows for a competitive advantage and the charging of premium pricing. It is through successful R&D, leading to the implementation of new products and processes, that businesses either maintain their position as market leader or gain market share.

The costs of R&D must also be considered. Large sums of money are invested in R&D without the guarantee of a successful outcome. With any expenditure, there is always the opportunity cost to be considered. For example, the money invested in R&D could have been used to train staff, buy new machinery, launch a promotional campaign or invested in expansion.

However effective or creative R&D is this in itself, it will not satisfy the operational objectives of a business. It is only when the outcome of R&D is used for economic gain that it leads to competitive advantage. The practical implementation of the results of R&D is the launch of a new product or process so that it becomes an innovation.

Business in action

Top spenders in R&D

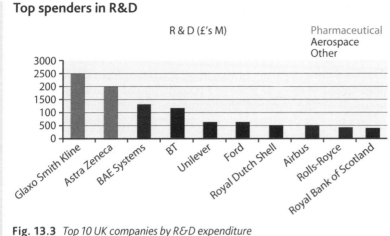

Fig. 13.3 *Top 10 UK companies by R&D expenditure*

www.innovation.gov.uk

Innovation

When a new product or process (an invention) is launched onto the market it becomes an **innovation**. Normally an invention will be patented because, when a company launches a new product or process, it wants to be able to recoup the cost of this by being a market leader. It does not want to have invested heavily in R&D to find that its competitors copy the idea and reap the rewards without having taken the risks by being able to undercut on price because they do not have the high R&D costs associated with an innovation.

Risks and rewards

It is only through taking risks in investing in R&D and launching new innovative products that businesses can access the potential rewards that success can bring.

The possible risks of innovation include:

- heavy time and resource commitment with no guarantee of success
- potential loss of focus on core function of business
- competitors' reaction
- company image and reputation if new product fails or detracts from brand image.

The potential rewards of innovation include:

- development of a USP leading to a competitive advantage
- ability to charge premium prices
- improvements in the efficiency of production processes
- reputation as being innovative in an industry.

Activity

Look at Fig. 13.3. Why is investment in R&D so high within the pharmaceutical and aerospace industry?

Link

See Chapter 11 — Understanding operational objectives, page 84 for more on operational objectives.

Key term

Innovation: the launch of a new product or process, an invention, onto the market for commercial gain.

Activities

1. What new products have been launched onto the market in recent years?

2. How have these influenced the lives of consumers?

3. How have competitors reacted to the launch of these new products?

Link

One way of assessing the risks and rewards of strategic decisions to develop new products is the force-field analysis, covered in Chapter 31 — Implementing and managing change, page 258.

Impact of innovation on marketing, finance and human resources

The actions of functional areas of a business will have some effect on others and R&D is no exception to this.

Marketing

The marketing department may have acted to inform the R&D department in the first place of a potential niche or of consumer opinions. In this instance, the business is taking a market-led approach to new product development. The marketing department is also going to have a major role to play in getting the product to the customer and designing an effective marketing mix in order to achieve sales targets.

Finance

Finance will be involved from the outset in setting and monitoring budgets for R&D. During the business analysis stage of the R&D process, they are also likely to be involved in costing the new products and, along with marketing, looking at possible pricing structures and potential profit levels.

Human Resources

Equally the HR department will have to be informed of the work of R&D and have an opportunity to contribute to the decision-making process. R&D is likely to have workforce planning issues. These could be the need for new skilled workers to manufacture an innovative product or the need to reduce staffing numbers due to innovations in the production process.

In all these situations, it is going to be important that all the functions have an input and an integrated approach from the outset and not just after a product has reached the development stage. The adoption of simultaneous engineering from the beginning can save a lot of time, money and expensive reworking of a project.

Case study

The science of innovation

Each year, visitors to the annual Food and Drink Expo at the NEC are amongst the first to discover many new brands. In 2008, the emphasis was on healthy, organic and additive-free versions of traditional lines – with exhibitors ranging from the giants behind the sector's big brands to specialist independent producers.

The food innovation team from Sheffield Hallam University were there reinforcing their message that 'the future of tomorrow's food and drink companies rides on the ability to innovate faster, more consistently and with greater understanding of consumer needs'. The team are aware of the fact that companies will be under increasing pressure to measure the carbon footprint or the GM credentials of products. The team discussed how 'research and development can drive innovation and competitiveness in any size or type of company'. Project manager, David Johnson, explained that 'although the UK food industry has a strong reputation for R&D, there is often a lack of research, which hampers genuine innovation. This is one reason for our food innovation programme, which is based on a multidisciplinary approach ...'

Among the exhibitors at the Expo were:

- Steenbergs Organic Pepper & Spices, launching a home bakery range to add to its portfolio of organic and fair-trade teas and spices

- The Premium Food Company, launching the mulberry super juice drink Mul-Be

- Xtazy Energy, showing its range of drinks aimed at the younger market containing herbs and nutrients based on the guarana seed

- Wensleydale Creameries, unveiling a new version of Wensleydale cheese with ocean spray cranberries

- Really Garlicky, unveiling a ciabatta bread to join its recently launched baguette.

Adapted from The Grocer, *March 2008*

Questions

1 Why do so many businesses choose to launch new products at a trade fair such as the annual Food and Drink Expo?

2 To what extent do you agree with the innovation team from Sheffield Hallam University that the future depends upon the ability to innovate faster, more consistently and with greater understanding of consumer needs? Justify your answer.

3 What does David Johnson mean by 'a multidisciplinary approach' and why might this be important?

4 How important do you think R&D is to the UK's food and drink industry? Justify your answer.

☑ *In this chapter you will have learned to:*

- show understanding of the importance of innovation and research and development to the competitiveness of larger businesses

- understand the costs and risks of innovation and research and development

- analyse the implications of innovation to finance, marketing and human resources.

Summary questions

1 What is meant by the term 'innovation'? (3 marks)

2 Why are patents often associated with investment in R&D? (4 marks)

3 Explain two potential benefits to a firm of investment in R&D. (8 marks)

4 Explain two potential drawbacks to a firm of investment in R&D. (8 marks)

5 If R&D is a high risk activity, why do firms still undertake it? (8 marks)

6 Why do you think the top two spenders on R&D in the UK are in the pharmaceutical industry? (8 marks)

7 Explain how the R&D department interrelates with other functions in order to meet corporate objectives. (8 marks)

14 Operational strategies: location

In this chapter you will learn to:

- analyse the importance of an optimal location to the success of a business
- apply quantitative decision-making techniques to location decisions
- apply qualitative decision-making techniques to location decisions
- evaluate the advantages and disadvantages of multisite locations
- analyse and discuss important issues relating to international location.

Setting the scene

Business location in the UK – you win some, you lose some

Indo European Foods to manufacture ethnic foods in the UK

'There is a huge potential market for our authentic Indian spices, sauces, pastes and chutneys in the UK and the rest of Europe,' said Dave Roberts, the Operations Director of Indo European Foods. By locating a factory in eastern England, the company will be able to supply this market more quickly, efficiently and profitably than importing directly from India. Felixstowe offers the business a suitable site of over 9,000 square metres, close proximity to ports, excellent rail links and east–west road connections via the A14. 'This area also gives us a good base for finding a suitably skilled multicultural workforce,' added Mr Roberts.

Electrolux factory to close in Durham with loss of 500 jobs

An Electrolux cooker factory in Durham is to close with the loss of 500 jobs. It has been making increased losses. Only three years ago, the company believed this was still the best location for manufacturing cookers and invested £7m in the plant with the aid of a government grant of £1.6m. Now, the company believes that the £ exchange rate and wage and other cost pressures make it uncompetitive and have decided to switch production to a factory in Poland. It has been estimated that the break-even level of production at this new plant will be less than half that of the UK factory.

Adapted from www.bbc.co.uk

Discussion points

1. Why do you think a good location is important to both of these businesses?
2. List as many factors as you find that influenced these two location decisions.
3. Why might the 'best' location for a business change over time?
4. What might be some of the problems for Electrolux resulting from its decision to switch production to Poland?

The benefits of an optimal location

Location decisions for existing firms – choosing new sites for expansion or relocation of the business – are some of the most important decisions made by management teams. Selecting the best site will have a significant effect on many departments of the business and, ultimately, on the profitability and chances of success of the whole firm. Location decisions have three key characteristics:

- strategic in nature – as they are long term and have an impact on the whole business

- difficult to reverse if an error of judgement is made – due to the costs of relocation
- taken at the highest management levels – they are not delegated to subordinates.

An **optimal location** decision is one that selects the best site for expansion of the business or for its relocation, given current information. This best site should maximise the long-term profits of the business. This is not as easy to achieve in practice as it sounds, because the optimal site is nearly always a compromise between conflicting benefits and drawbacks. For example:

- A well-positioned high-street shop will have the potential for high sales, but will have higher rental charges than a similar sized shop out of town.
- A factory location which is relatively cheap to purchase, due to its distance from major towns, might have problems recruiting staff due to lack of a suitably large and trained working population.

So an optimal location is likely to be a compromise one that balances:

- high fixed costs of site and building with convenience for customers and potential sales revenue
- the low costs of a remote site with supply of suitably qualified labour
- quantitative factors with qualitative ones (see below)
- the opportunities of receiving government grants in areas of high unemployment with the risks of low sales as average incomes in the area may be low.

Key terms

Optimal location: a business location that gives the best combination of quantitative and qualitative factors.

Quantitative factors: these are measurable in financial terms and will have a direct impact on either the costs of a site or the revenues from it and its profitability.

Table 14.1 *Some potential drawbacks of poor, non-optimal location decisions*

Problem	Impact on business
High fixed site costs	High break-even level of production
	Low profits – or even losses
	If operating at low capacity utilisation, unit fixed costs will be high
High variable costs, e.g. labour	Low contribution per unit produced or sold
	Low profits – or even losses
	High unit variable costs reduce competitiveness
Low unemployment rate	Problems with recruiting suitable staff
	Staff turnover likely to be a problem
	Pay levels may have to be raised to attract and retain staff
High unemployment rate	Average consumer disposable incomes may be low – leading to relatively low demand for income elastic products
Poor transport infrastructure	Raises transport costs for both materials and finished products
	Relatively inaccessible to customers
	Difficult to operate a just-in-time stock management system (see page 114) due to unreliable deliveries

Methods of making location decisions

Quantitative methods

These techniques of taking location decisions depend on accurate estimation of **quantitative factors**.

■ Site and other capital costs, such as building or shop fitting: These costs vary greatly from region to region within a country and between countries too. Prime office and retail sites may be so expensive that the cost of them is beyond the resources of all but the largest companies. The cost of building on a 'greenfield' site – one that has never previously been developed – must be compared with the costs of adapting existing buildings on a developed site.

■ Labour costs: The relative importance of labour costs as a locational factor depends on whether the business is capital- or labour-intensive. An insurance company call centre will need many staff, but labour costs of a nuclear power station will be a very small proportion of its total costs. The attraction of much lower wage rates overseas has encouraged many UK businesses to set up operations in other countries, for example bank and insurance company call centres.

■ Transport costs: Businesses that use heavy and bulky raw materials, such as steel making, will incur high transport costs if suppliers are at a great distance from the steel plant. Goods that increase in bulk during production will, traditionally, reduce transport costs by locating close to the market. Service industries, such as hotels and retailing, need to be conveniently located for customers and transport costs will be of less significance.

■ Sales revenue potential: The level of sales made by a business can depend directly on location. Confectionery shops and convenience stores have to be just that – convenient to potential customers. In addition to this, certain locations can add status and image to a business and this may allow value to be added to the product in the eyes of the consumers. This is true for high-class retailers situated in London's Bond Street, but also for medical specialists operating in Harley Street.

■ Government grants: Governments across the world are very keen to attract new businesses to locate in their country. Grants may be offered to act as an incentive. Existing businesses operating in a country can also be provided with financial assistance to retain existing jobs or attract new employment to deprived areas of high unemployment.

Business in action

Nissan

Senior management at Nissan were initially reluctant to build the new Micra at their Sunderland factory. However, a UK government grant of £3.26m helped to clinch the decision to invest a total of £95m into the new production facilities at this factory in the north of the UK. It secured 250 jobs in this area of high unemployment.

Once these quantitative factors have been identified and costs and revenues estimated, the following techniques can be used to assist in the location decision: profit estimates, investment appraisal and break-even analysis.

Profit estimates

By comparing the estimated revenues and costs of each location, the site with the highest annual potential profit may be identified.

The limitation of this technique is that annual profit forecasts alone are of limited use. They need to be compared with the capital cost of buying and developing the site. A site offering 10 per cent higher annual profits than an alternative location is unlikely to be chosen if the capital cost is 50 per cent higher.

Activities

1   Using Table 14.2, calculate the estimated annual profit from the two possible locations for a mobile phone shop.

2   In future years, why might the annual profits made from each location change?

Table 14.2 *Two possible locations for a mobile phone shop*

	Site A City centre location	Site B Shopping arcade out of the city
Fixed rental and other property costs	£225,000	£98,000
Estimated annual variable costs	£750,000	£400,000
Expected annual sales (units)	25,000	17,000
Forecast selling price per unit	£50	£45

Investment appraisal

Location decisions often involve a substantial capital investment. Investment appraisal methods, such as the average rate of return and net present value, can be used to identify locations with the highest potential returns over a number of years. The payback method can be used to estimate the location most likely to return the original investment quickest. This could be of particular benefit to a business with a capital shortage or in times of economic uncertainty.

Link

Average rate of return, net present value and payback are discussed in Chapter 6 — Making investment decisions, page 38.

Activity

TLC Cosmetics is planning to open a new branch selling upmarket cosmetics. The company has expanded rapidly and it has substantial loans. Some economists are predicting an increase in interest rates by the Bank of England.

Using the investment appraisal results in Table 14.3 and any other information, which of these two sites would you recommend the company should choose for the new shop?

Table 14.3 *Investment appraisal results for new branches of TLC Cosmetics*

	Site X Capital cost of £2m	Site Y Capital cost of £3m
Payback period	2.5 years	3.8 years
Average rate of return (over first 5 years)	12%	14%
Net present value (over first 5 years) at 10% discount rate	£1.5m	£2.5m

The limitations are that these methods require estimates of costs and revenues for several years for each potential location. This introduces a considerable degree of inaccuracy and uncertainty into this form of quantitative decision-making.

Break-even analysis

This is a relatively straightforward method of comparing two or more possible locations. It calculates which sites will break even at the lowest level of production and the estimated profits to be earned at the expected output level. This information might be particularly important for businesses that face high levels of fixed costs and which may benefit from a location with lower overheads.

Break-even analysis should be used with caution and the normal limitations of this technique apply when using it to help make location decisions.

Activity

ICT Chemicals Ltd plans to open a new paint factory with a maximum capacity of 10 million litres per year. It has narrowed the choice of sites down to Site C in the UK, located 5 miles away from a large city and Site D in a less economically developed country with very low labour wage rates and few health and safety controls.

1. Recommend to the business which location should be selected by analysing the data in Table 14.4. The expected annual production level is 6 million litres.

2. Why do you think that the results from break-even analysis may be unreliable?

3. What other factors do you think the business should consider before taking the final location decision?

Table 14.4 *Site comparison for ICT Chemicals*

	Site C	Site D
Annual fixed costs	£2m	£1m
Estimated contribution per litre (including the transport costs from Site D to UK)	£0.40	£0.75

Qualitative factors

Clearly potential profit is a major consideration when choosing an optimal location, but there are other important factors that cannot be measured in financial terms. These are called **qualitative factors**.

■ Safety: To avoid potential risk to the public and damage to the company's reputation as a consequence of an accident that risked public safety, some industrial plants will be located in remote areas even though these may increase transport and other costs.

■ Room for further expansion: It is expensive to relocate if a site proves to be too small to accommodate an expanding business. If a location has space for further expansion of the business, this might be an important long-term consideration.

■ Managers' preferences: In small businesses, managers' personal preferences regarding desirable work and home environments could

Key term

Qualitative factors: non-measurable factors that may influence business decisions.

influence location decisions of the business. In larger organisations, such as plcs, this is unlikely to be a factor as earning profits and increasing returns to shareholders will be key objectives that will take priority in location decisions.

- Ethical considerations: A business deciding to relocate from the UK is likely to make workers redundant. This will cause bad publicity and could also be contrary to the ethical code of the business and may be viewed by **stakeholders** as being immoral. In addition, if the relocation is to a country with much weaker controls over worker welfare and the environment there could be further claims that the business is acting unethically.

- IT infrastructure: The quality of IT infrastructure varies considerably around the world and this is an important consideration for companies that need quick communication with its different sites or customers, for example call centres or selling via the internet. The growing popularity of online shopping in developed countries may lead to some retailers opening fewer high street stores and more 'warehouse' operations to supply consumers directly.

Key terms

Stakeholder: any person or group that has an interest in the activities of a business, e.g. community, workers, suppliers, customers, government.

Multisite locations: a business that operates from more than one location.

Business in action

Rolls-Royce goes for a quality location

Choosing the lowest cost location for the Rolls-Royce factory was not a priority. When BMW moved production from the industrial northern town of Crewe, it chose one of the most crowded and expensive parts of the country – the south-east of England. The Goodwood factory has many advantages, but low cost is not one of them. One of its main benefits is its proximity to a small airport where the helicopters and executive jets of intending purchasers of Rolls-Royce cars can arrive in style. Potential buyers are identified by the company and invited to visit the factory and attend events held at the nearby exclusive marina and horse race and motor race courses. The area has been termed a 'playground for the wealthy' and future customers often spend a day or two at the races or a morning at the marina before browsing the cars – and more often than not, signing an order form!

Adapted from business.timesonline.co.uk

Link

Look again at the activity on ICT Chemicals on page 106. How important should qualitative factors be in the final location decision?

Advantages and disadvantages of multisite locations

Most relatively large businesses operate on more than one site, i.e. they have **multisite locations**. This is clearly true of the major retailing companies that expand mainly by opening new sites in new locations. It would be pointless trying to serve the whole of the UK from one shop, unless of course the business sold only over the internet, such as Amazon and until the opening of a second depot in 2008 one giant warehouse was adequate to provide supplies to consumers throughout the country!

Banks, building societies, hotels, hairdressers and other tertiary service providers must operate from more than one site if they wish to expand beyond a certain size by offering convenient customer services in several locations. Primary producers such as oil exploration companies and mining businesses will operate in more than one location to avoid the risks of exhaustion of supplies from just one site. Very large secondary manufacturing businesses also operate from more than one location, despite the potential gains from technical economies of scale on one site.

Fig. 14.1 *Amazon's two UK warehouses supply the whole of the UK*

■ **Business in action**

Toyota

Toyota is one of the best examples of a multisite business with 52 manufacturing facilities in 26 different countries. In a typical recent 12-month period, it opened its first factory in Mexico and opened its 13th manufacturing facility in the USA – in Mississippi. In 2007, concerns were expressed by the company that its production capacity in the USA was starting to outstrip demand for vehicles so this could be the last new factory the company builds there for some time.

Adapted from reuters.com

Table 14.5 *Advantages and disadvantages of multisite locations*

Advantages of multisite locations	Disadvantages of multisite locations
Greater convenience for consumers, e.g. McDonalds restaurants in every town	Coordination problems between the locations – excellent two-way communication systems will be essential
Lower transport costs, e.g. breweries can supply large cities from regional breweries rather than transport from one national brewery	Potential lack of control and direction from senior management based at head office
Production-based companies reduce the risk of supply disruption if there are technical or industrial relations problems in one factory	Different cultural standards and legal systems in different countries – the business must adapt to these differences
Opportunities for delegation of authority to regional managers from head office – helps to develop staff skills and improves motivation	If sites are too close to each other there may be a danger of 'cannibalism' where one restaurant or store takes sales away from another owned by the same business
Cost advantages of multisites in different countries – see next section	

International location decisions

One of the main features of globalisation is the growing trend for businesses to relocate completely to another country or to set up new operating bases abroad. Electrolux is a typical example (see page 102).

This process is often referred to as **off-shoring**. The world's largest corporations are now virtually all **multinationals**.

Reasons for international location decisions

International location decisions are made to reduce costs, access global markets, avoid protectionist trade barriers and for other reasons.

Cost reduction

This is undoubtedly the major reason for most company moves abroad. With labour wage rates in India, Malaysia, China and Eastern Europe being a fraction of those in Western Europe and the USA, it is not surprising that businesses that wish to remain competitive have to seriously consider relocation to low wage economies. Examples include:

- Norwich Union call centres to India
- Panasonic TV production to the Czech Republic
- Hornby Trains to China
- Dyson vacuum cleaners to Malaysia.

Business in action

German labour costs

Look at the data in Table 14.6 for labour costs in different countries compared to German labour costs, which are some of the highest in the world. It is easy to see what cost advantages multinational companies have when they operate in countries such as Bulgaria, Hungary, India and China.

Table 14.6 *International labour costs in comparison with Germany*

Country	Weekly (Euros)	Compared to Germany (= 100%)
India	25	3
China	41	6
Bulgaria	43	6
Brazil	60	8
Hungary	159	22

Federation of European Employers. January 2008

Access to global (world) markets

Rapid economic growth in less developed countries has created huge market potential for most consumer products. Access to these markets is often best achieved by direct operation in the countries concerned. Markets for some products in Western Europe have reached saturation point and further sales growth can only be achieved by expanding abroad. Some businesses have reached the limit of their internal domestic expansion as there are threats from government regulatory bodies about increasing monopoly power.

All of these reasons help explain Tesco's recent international expansion. Tesco shops are now common sights in Thailand and Eastern Europe. It has also become the only major UK-based retail business to expand successfully into the USA. The 'Fresh 'n Easy' convenience stores opened

Key terms

Off-shoring: the relocation of a business process done in one country to the same or another company in another country.

Multinational: a business with operations or production bases in more than one country.

AQA Examiner's tip

Do not confuse off-shoring with outsourcing, although they may be linked. Outsourcing is transferring a business function such as HR to another company. It is only off-shoring if this company is based in another country.

Fig. 14.2 *This traditional British toy is now manufactured in China*

by Tesco in California have quickly become established and profitable, helping to make up for slow growth in the UK grocery market.

Avoidance of protectionist trade barriers

Barriers to free international trade are rapidly being reduced but some still exist, notably between the large trading blocs such as the EU and the North American Free Trade Association (NAFTA). To avoid **trade barriers** on imported goods into most countries or trading blocs, it is necessary to set up operations *within* the country or trading bloc concerned. Examples include Honda's factory in Swindon that produces cars for the EU market and Toyota's new factory in Mexico that gives tariff-free access to that country's car market.

Other reasons

These include substantial government financial support to relocating businesses, good educational standards (as in India and China) and highly qualified staff and avoidance of problems resulting from exchange rate fluctuations. This last point makes pricing decisions very difficult with products that are not made within the country, but are imported, when its currency fluctuates considerably. One way around this problem is to locate production in the country.

Issues and potential problems with international location

International locations have potential for success, but they also add to the number of drawbacks that might result from an inappropriate location decision. Here are some of the major additional issues that need to be weighed up carefully before going off-shore:

■ Language and other communication barriers: Distance is often a problem for effective communication, for example direct face-to-face contact is less likely. This problem is made worse when some operations are abroad and when company employees, suppliers or customers use another language altogether. This is one of the reasons for India's success in attracting off-shoring companies – English is one of the official languages.

■ **Key term**

Trade barriers: taxes (tariffs) or other limitations on the free international movement of goods and services.

AQA Examiner's tip

Do your own research during the A2 course on major location decisions, both at home and abroad, of UK-owned businesses.

◻ Cultural differences: These are important for the marketing department if products are being sold in the country concerned – consumer tastes and religious factors will play a significant role in determining what goods should be stocked. Cultural differences also exist in the workplace. Toyota found that the typical Mexican worker is self-reliant and independent, yet the Toyota manufacturing system depends greatly on team work and cooperation! Effective staff training may be necessary to ensure that cultural differences do not prevent successful overseas expansion.

◼ Business in action

Toyota staff training

Oscar Rodriguez was only 20 when he was employed by Toyota's new Tijuana factory. 'I was self reliant and I would conceal production problems and try and fix them myself,' he said. 'But I was taught how to communicate and I have learned that there is never a stupid question. The company supervisors teach us well and they are patient.'

www.detnews.com

◻ Level of service concerns: This applies particularly to the off-shoring of call centres, technical support centres and functions such as accounting. Some consumer groups argue that off-shoring of these services has led to inferior customer service due·to time difference problems, time delays in phone messages, language barriers and different practices and conventions, for example with accounting systems.

◻ Supply chain concerns: There may be some loss of control over quality and reliability of delivery with overseas manufacturing plants. This reason is always cited by Zara, the clothing company, for their decision to not off-shore clothing production to cheaper countries, as 'fast fashion' requires very close contact with suppliers. Using just-in-time manufacturing may become much riskier if important supplies have to be shipped thousands of miles to an assembly plant.

◻ Ethical considerations: There may be a loss of jobs when a company locates all or some of its operations abroad and this may, as in the case of Burberry clothing, lead to a consumer boycott as there were claims that the company's decision to close its Welsh factory was not 'the right thing to do'. In addition, there are several reports of high street clothing retailers sourcing supplies from Asian factories using child labour and very low wage labour. Could this negative publicity cancel out the competitive advantage of low cost supplies? This important consideration is just another reason why the important location decisions should be taken at the highest management level.

Fig. 14.3 *Is it right to sell clothing in European shops that has been made by low wage labour in Asian countries?*

◼ Case study

Is off-shoring best for HiSonic Ltd?

HiSonic manufactures some of the highest quality hi-fi systems in the world. They are not cheap – some systems cost up to £50,000, but the company's products have an excellent reputation for both sound quality and reliability. Currently, all systems are assembled

Table 14.7 *Comparison of Malaysian site with expansion of existing UK site*

	Malaysian site	Expansion of UK site
Capital cost	£5m	£3m
Payback	2 years	1.5 years
ARR for first 5 years	20%	15%
NPV for first 5 years @ 10%	£6m	£4m
Break-even level of production	40% of expected output	60% of expected output

from components in the company's factory in the south-east of England. The workforce is loyal and skilled. The components are not made in-house, but are imported from the best suppliers all over the world. The company is experiencing increasing demand and the factory has reached capacity. One option being considered is to establish an assembly plant in Malaysia. Rents and wage rates are only 25 per cent of the levels in the UK. The Chief Executive has asked an external consulting firm to undertake an appraisal of this project, based on sales forecasts for the next five years. These quantitative results could then be compared with those estimated from expanding the existing UK facility. One of the potential benefits of a Malaysian site, according to the Chief Executive, is the access to the expanding Asian markets and the opportunity in the future to transfer all production to this site, if quality proves to be up to standard.

Questions

1. Differentiate between quantitative and qualitative factors involved in location decisions.

2. Explain how the sales revenue forecasts for the expansion of the business might have been obtained.

3. Analyse problems that might result from this business transferring all production in the future from the UK to Malaysia.

4. Using the information provided, recommend to the Chief Executive whether the business should expand its UK factory or open a new operating plant in Malaysia.

5. Choose a well-known multinational corporation and investigate:

   - the number of countries it operates in

   - what it produces in each country

   - its latest overseas expansion projects.

6. Is the pace of its foreign expansion slowing or accelerating, do you think? Why is this?

✔️ *In this chapter you will have learned to:*

- understand the importance of location decisions to the competitiveness of a business

- analyse the key quantitative and qualitative factors involved in a location decision

- apply quantitative techniques to location decisions such as break-even analysis and investment appraisal

- evaluate the advantages and disadvantages of multisite locations

- understand why there is a growing trend towards international locations and the advantages and issues that result from this trend.

Summary questions

1. What would be meant by the term 'optimal location' for a new Tesco supermarket? (5 marks)

2. Outline possible reasons why Tesco chose the USA as a country in which to expand. (8 marks)

3. Analyse the problems that Tesco had to overcome before deciding to locate new convenience stores in the USA. (8 marks)

4. Explain how a location decision might influence the break-even level of output of a business. (6 marks)

5. Analyse two reasons why a car manufacturer such as Toyota has chosen to operate as a multinational. (6 marks)

6. Analyse two ways in which the location of a retail shop could affect its competitiveness. (6 marks)

7. Examine the quantitative factors that a hairdressing business might take into account when deciding whether to relocate. (8 marks)

8. Why might a high technology business decide to locate in Germany despite the huge labour cost advantages that some developing countries have? (6 marks)

9. Do you think that a decision to locate a new clothing factory for a European high street store should be taken by senior management? Explain your answer. (6 marks)

10. How might the increasing use of internet shopping have an impact on the location decisions of businesses that sell to final consumers? (8 marks)

Operational strategies: lean production

In this chapter you will learn to:

- identify a range of techniques associated with lean production

- understand the benefits to larger businesses of adopting lean production techniques

- interpret and complete critical path networks

- assess the benefits and limitations of critical path analysis

- describe the effective management of other resources through methods of lean production.

Fig. 15.1 *Work is carried out on a 'just-in-time' Toyota Prius*

Key terms

Lean production: the adoption of techniques that help to reduce waste.

Just-in-time (JIT): a lean production technique which aims to minimise stock holdings.

Setting the scene

The triumph of lean production

On the assembly line at Toyota's giant plant, Laura Wilshire is not happy. There is something wrong with a seatbelt fitting on the Camry she is working on. Laura pulls a cord, stopping the production line – and prompting her five fellow workers on trim line three to crowd round. They soon see why it is not screwed in properly and fix the problem. 'I don't like to let something like that go,' she says. 'That's really important for people who buy our cars.' Pulling the cord, called 'andan', is part of Toyota's 'lean' production system, which means that it has been able to produce cars much more cheaply, and to a higher quality, than its US rivals.

Toyota also pioneered the 'just-in-time' manufacturing system, in which suppliers send parts daily – or several times a day – and are notified electronically when the assembly line is running out. More than 400 trucks a day come in and out of Toyota's Georgetown plant, with a separate logistics company organising the shipments from Toyota's 300 suppliers – most located in neighbouring states within half a day's drive of the plant. Toyota aims to build long-term relationships with its suppliers, many of whom it has taken a stake in, and says it now produces 80 per cent of its parts within North America.

news.bbc.co.uk

Discussion points

1. What are the advantages to Toyota of having staff in the production line committed to ensuring quality?

2. What are the potential advantages and disadvantages to Toyota of having parts delivered on a daily basis?

3. How might both the commitment of staff and relationship with suppliers help Toyota achieve operational objectives?

Lean production techniques

Productive efficiency comes about as a result of making quality products at the lowest cost possible. One way in which firms aim to achieve this is by the adoption of **lean production** techniques. These are techniques which aim to reduce waste within the business. There are a range of techniques available and businesses will need to assess the technique or range of techniques which will allow them to act at optimum efficiency. These techniques include just-in-time, kaizen and time-based management.

Just-in-time (JIT)

Just-in-time is a philosophy that aims to reduce waste by limiting the stock holding at each stage of the production process. Materials are delivered as required, for example, in manufacturing to be taken straight to the production process, in retail directly to the shop floor or in catering ready for that day's service. Similarly, the time stock spends as work in progress is minimised as is the holding of finished product. The result is a reduction in costs due to less physical need to hold and handle stock, less wastage due to obsolete or ruined stock and lower associated costs such as insurance. However, the introduction of JIT is a strategic decision as, although it should in the long run lead to a competitive advantage, in the short run it takes time and money to introduce. Systems have to be reviewed, new systems introduced, possible staff trained and often investment in better IT systems. JIT also carries with it risk, particularly if the supply chain is long, complex or susceptible to interruptions, for example if importing from abroad.

Kaizen

Kaizen is an approach to improving the efficiency and performance of a business through continual improvement.

For continual improvement to be achievable within a business, it requires the commitment and involvement of all staff as the improvement can come from any stage or level within a business's operations. This means that all employees must be empowered with the ability to spot opportunities and make recommendations for improvement.

Kaizen recognises that employees are often best placed to make suggestions for small-scale improvements. This provides motivation for the employee who is consulted more and given the opportunity to improve the efficiency of not only their own working practices but potentially the organisation as a whole.

Small but regular improvements generated through a culture of enterprise and initiatives are easier to implement than large irregular changes. The overall result, however, is the same or greater in terms of overall efficiency and competitiveness.

Time-based management

Like the other approaches to lean production, **time-based management** aims to reduce waste. The focus here, however, is on reducing time wasted or unproductive time to improve efficiency. In order for time-based management to be effective, staff must be trained and able to perform a number of tasks, as flexibility in the production process is key. The resulting benefits of time-based management include quicker time to market for new products, shorter lead times and an improved ability to respond to changes in market conditions and consumer tastes.

Critical path analysis (CPA)

Critical path analysis is the use of network diagrams (**critical path network**) to help plan and complete complex projects in the shortest time possible by identifying those activities that can be carried out simultaneously. CPA has a wide range of possible applications within business, including:

- a marketing campaign
- launch of a new product
- opening a new store
- relocating a business
- automating the production process.

Key terms

Kaizen: a lean production technique which aims to improve efficiency by making small but frequent improvements, also known as continual improvement.

Time-based management: managing resources effectively to ensure products are fit for market in the shortest time possible.

Critical path analysis (CPA): a technique for planning complex projects to allow them to be completed in the shortest time possible by identifying activities that can be carried out simultaneously.

Critical path network: a visual representation of the sequencing and timing of all the activities involved in completing a complex project.

Activity

The Manufacturing Institute says that many businesses start down the lean business improvement route but that 90 per cent fail to complete the course. The Head of Training and Education explained that, 'After the initial buzz of enthusiasm for lean, the momentum often fizzles out with many failing to appreciate that it is an ongoing process of continuous improvement.'

What action could firms adopt to maintain the initial 'buzz'?

Key terms

Earliest start time (EST): the earliest time an activity can start in a project based upon the completion of a preceding activity.

Latest finish time (LFT): the latest time an activity must be completed by to avoid any delay to the project.

Critical path: the route which outlines all those activities that cannot be delayed, i.e. have zero float time, if the project is to be completed on time.

Critical activities: those activities with zero float time, i.e. if it takes four weeks to complete, there is only four weeks between the EST and LFT.

Float time: the amount of time by which a non-critical activity could be delayed without having an effect on the whole project.

Non-critical activities: those activities with float time, i.e. if it takes four weeks to complete, there may be six weeks between the EST and LFT.

AQA Examiner's tip

You may be asked to complete a critical path by calculating ESTs and LFTs, or to interpret one, but you will not be asked to draw a critical path network diagram.

CPA is a visual technique which shows all the activities needed to complete a project placed in the order in which they can be completed. Activities are shown as lines with the activity description or letter above the line and the duration (length of time) to complete it below the line. The key to critical path is for managers to be able to identify which activities are dependent upon the completion of an earlier activity. For example, if opening a new retail store you could not accept delivery of stock before placing the order, but you could place an advert in the paper for staff. This allows for the planning of activities to be carried out simultaneously. Circles, known as nodes, are drawn to show the earliest each activity can be started and the latest it must be completed by in order not to delay the completion of the whole project. Each node shows three numbers:

- the number of the node – represents the order in which it was drawn
- the **earliest start time (EST)** – the earliest the next activity can start
- the **latest finish time (LFT)** – the time by which the previous activity must be completed.

The best way to demonstrate this is through the example shown in Fig. 15.2.

The **critical path** is identified as those activities that must be finished at an exact time to allow for the next activity to be started on time. Activities along the critical path, known as **critical activities**, are said to have no **float time**, i.e. there is no spare time in which they could be completed. Other activities, known as **non-critical activities**, do have float time. Float time is calculated as:

Float time = LFT – Duration – EST

Benefits of critical path analysis

The very nature of the technique is in itself a benefit as it forces management to fully think through and plan for a complex project before undertaking it. This process allows the firm to identify the shortest time period in which a project can be completed, shortening the time from conception to implementation.

CPA can be used as a planning and monitoring tool as well as to aid decision-making. If, for example, it is necessary to choose between two new stores or two new products, a business may consider which one can

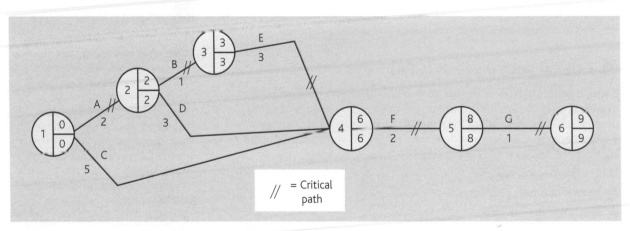

Fig. 15.2 *An example of a critical path network*

be launched quicker in order to start generating cash inflows. CPA also helps with the implementation of JIT as the EST of an activity would indicate when any materials associated with that activity will be needed. A manufacturer building a new factory, for example, would not want to order the windows when it first starts laying the foundations, but would want to know when the project would need the windows to be delivered.

CPA also allows managers to allocate resources more effectively. Staff can be allocated to set tasks and, if necessary, redeployed to focus on critical activities in order to ensure that a project is not delayed. This can be motivational as employees will be given clear targets to work towards. It also gives managers a clear understanding of the whole project and a tool with which they can monitor and review progress. CPA can also help in financial planning as it will indicate when money will be needed to fund certain parts of a project allowing for more accurate budgeting and cash-flow forecasting.

Limitations of critical path analysis

Like any planning tool, its main limitation comes from the fact that it is based on estimates and so its reliability is dependent to an extent on the accuracy of those estimates. This said, however, if the estimates do prove inaccurate, it is still useful if closely monitored and appropriate corrective action taken as necessary. CPA should not be seen as a static or one-off process as it may need to be altered and updated on an ongoing basis as a project develops.

> **AQA Examiner's tip**
>
> When reading the case study in the examination, consider the source of the estimates and skill of the managers.

Case study

Premier Fuels Ltd

Premier Fuels Ltd operates 23 petrol service stations in the south-east and employs 210 staff. Gill Tree is the recently appointed Managing Director of Premier Fuels Ltd. On her appointment, she had been told by the outgoing boss of the family firm, Ray

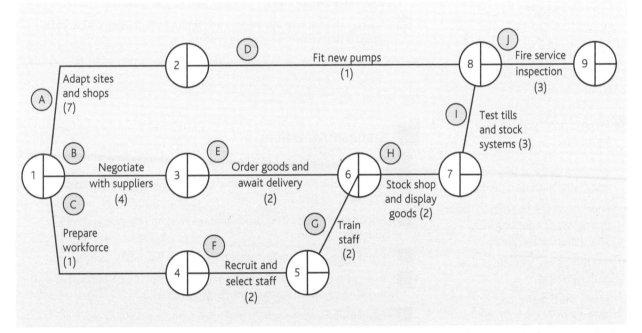

Fig. 15.3 *Network diagram for new convenience stores and petrol stations*

Peacock, 'I retain a controlling share of the business and I expect my dividends to grow by 15 per cent a year.' Gill had quickly realised that this would be achieved only with a continual expansion programme in high profit margin markets.

Gill was proposing that the company should buy leases on three large petrol stations sites on main roads used by commuters driving into a large city in the Midlands. Unlike all of the company's existing sites, these locations would be developed into high-class convenience stores as well as petrol stations. The focus would be on high quality, ready-to-eat meals, branded groceries, wines and spirits.

The location of the new sites would be crucial to their success. The consultants had used quantitative decision-making techniques, as well as considering qualitative factors, before making their proposals for the three locations. Timing is important for the company's cash flow, as the sooner these service stations and high-quality convenience stores open, the faster the payback would be on the project. The consultants produced a network diagram (Fig. 15.3) to help determine the duration for the redevelopment of the site.

AQA, June 2006

Questions

1. Make a copy of Fig. 15.3.
   a Complete the network diagram to show ESTs and LFTs at each node.
   b Calculate the total float times on activities D and F.
   c Identify the critical path.

2. Assume that there is a delay of two weeks in completing activity F. Analyse one action that the operations manager could take to avoid exceeding the current length of the critical path.

3. Analyse the qualitative factors that the consultant should have considered before making the proposals for the locations.

4. Analyse the possible advantages and limitations of using critical path analysis to the decision-making process.

☑ *In this chapter you will have learned to:*

- explain a range of techniques associated with lean production

- understand the benefits to larger businesses of adopting lean production techniques

- interpret and complete critical path networks

- assess the benefits and limitations of critical path analysis.

Summary questions

1. What is meant by the term 'lean production'? (3 marks)

2. What are the financial benefits to a firm of operating a JIT system? (6 marks)

3. Briefly explain why JIT is dependent upon a good relationship with suppliers (9 marks)

4. Explain the terms 'earliest start time', 'latest finish time' and 'float time'.

5. Assess the benefits and limitations of using critical path analysis when planning to launch a new product. (10 marks)

6. Explain why a house builder might fail to meet a building deadline despite constructing a critical path prior to starting a project. (10 marks)

Human resource strategies

Introduction

Chapters in this section:

There are strong links between the operational section and the human resource section at A2. In both cases, there is an emphasis on using resources as efficiently as possible. As the pace of technological change increases, the demands on employees for new skills also increase. At the same time, employees are looking to improve their work–life balance, which gives a business the opportunity to develop a more flexible workforce to meet the changing needs of the market. Further elements in the mix are the continued growth of legislation to protect employees and the pressure on businesses to trade fairly.

It is also important to understand the need for good industrial relations to be maintained, particularly when terms and conditions of service are changing. The issue of company pension schemes is of concern to many employees who see ending such programmes as a threat to their long-term security. Senior managers, on the other hand, may see this as an effective cost-cutting measure. It would be a mistake to assume that pay is the only issue of concern to employees and their representatives. In an atmosphere of constant change and in a drive to maximise efficiency, the non-financial needs of employees can be overlooked or undervalued.

Before starting this section, it would be a good idea to revisit the AS Human Resources content, as much of what follows builds on the topics introduced in the earlier section of the syllabus.

Chapter 16: Understanding HR objectives and strategies

In any organisation, the objectives of the other functional areas will have a direct impact on the objectives of the human resources function. The size, skills and location of the workforce may be determined by financial, marketing and operational decisions, and the HR function should reflect these decisions in its objectives and strategies. This chapter investigates possible HR objectives. Consideration is given to different HR strategies and their strengths and weaknesses.

Chapter 17: Developing and implementing workforce plans

To be most effective, the HR function needs to anticipate changes to the workforce needs of the organisation rather than reacting to change. This has been a major change in the role of the function once known as 'Personnel'. Today, the HR department is likely to view the workforce as a resource to be employed as efficiently as possible. In this chapter, the concept of a planned workforce strategy is discussed and the internal and external influences on such an approach are analysed. The value of workforce planning and issues of implementation, both positive and negative, are evaluated.

Chapter 18: Competitive organisational structures

This chapter investigates the issues facing a business as it grows, improving its competitiveness through adapting its organisational structures. This could involve moving from a centralised structure, very common amongst small, entrepreneurial businesses, to a decentralised structure, where decision-making is devolved and communication becomes more complex. Implementing and operating a range of methods of structural change is analysed, including the development of a flexible workforce offering a range of contracts to employees.

Chapter 19: Effective employer–employee relations

As businesses grow, the importance of managing communication in employer–employee relations becomes more significant; industrial disputes are likely to be public and potentially very damaging. Methods of enabling employee representation are analysed in terms of their advantages and disadvantages. Ways of avoiding and resolving industrial disputes are also considered.

Chaos on the opening day of the new Terminal 5 building at Heathrow in March 2008. Many employees and union representatives said that British Airways management did not listen to the concerns of their employees prior to opening. There were also claims that not enough staff were employed in the terminal building. Some experienced workers were concerned about the lack of training and of low morale among BA workers at Heathrow

16 Understanding HR objectives and strategies

In this chapter you will learn to:

- identify the range of HR objectives typically set by larger businesses
- explain how internal and external factors can influence the setting of HR objectives
- understand the difference between 'hard' and 'soft' approaches to HR
- evaluate the relative strengths and weaknesses of 'hard' and 'soft' HR strategies.

Advanced Subsea Engineering

Fig. 16.1 *The MCS logo*

Links

For more information about lean production, see Chapter 15 — Operational strategies: lean production, page 114.

Key terms

Human resource management (HRM): making the best use of all employees to achieve corporate goals.

HR objectives: targets the HR management hopes to achieve by implementing HR strategies, so that the business can achieve its corporate objectives.

Setting the scene

MCS Group

The MCS Group provides advanced engineering solutions for the offshore oil and gas industry. The MCS mission is to continue to be a best-in-class company at integrating and supporting engineering expertise with state-of-the-art analysis, to provide high value solutions for clients. HR for MCS assists in maintaining that vision by ensuring that they employ and develop high calibre and highly motivated individuals, who can deliver the very best engineering expertise. This includes a scheme for the professional development for all graduate engineers within the company to ensure that their training and development focuses upon the core engineering competencies required to achieve Chartered status.

WorkforcePotential.com

Discussion points

1. Why is it important for MCS to retain the graduate engineers they recruit?

2. How does the HR objective of recruiting and developing high calibre and highly motivated individuals support the MCS corporate objective?

3. What other objectives might the HR function have?

Human resource objectives

As a business grows, the need to manage the workforce increases. In large companies, there is normally a dedicated functional area, the Personnel Department, or, increasingly, the Human Resources (HR) Department. HR is based on the principle that employees are the most valuable asset of a firm and must be managed to yield maximum efficiency for the business. This fits in with total quality management (TQM) and lean production strategies.

The objectives of **human resource management (HRM)** should contribute to achieving corporate objectives. By setting **HR objectives**, detailed planning can occur, enabling the company to be proactive in its business environment rather than reactive. This could give the organisation a competitive advantage to ensure it retains or increases market share. Typical human resource objectives include:

- matching workforce skills to business needs
- matching workforce size to business needs
- matching workforce location to business needs
- minimising labour costs
- making full use of the workforce's potential
- maintaining good employer–employee relations.

Matching workforce skills to business needs

There are many reasons why the skills of a workforce may have to change if a business is to remain competitive: changes in technology, new product development, international growth. Part of the HR planning process is to identify future business needs so that recruitment, selection and training programmes reflect these requirements.

■ Business in action

Toyoda Gosei Fluid Systems

Toyoda Gosei Fluid Systems UK Ltd is a leading manufacturer of automotive fluid handling systems. Reorganisation, including the promotion of operational staff to managerial positions, made the company more competitive. Unfortunately these managers had not developed the necessary management skills so Skillspoint, a specialist workforce development team, was employed to find training providers who matched what Toyoda needed.

Matching workforce size to business needs

Lean production techniques, technological change, expansion or retrenchment can all lead to a change in the size of the workforce a company needs. In terms of HRM, this may mean that employees who leave or retire are not replaced (natural wastage) or that staff are given more opportunity to change their working hours to suit their individual circumstances. The key is flexibility and an awareness of the impact of corporate strategy on workforce numbers.

Links

For more information about flexibility, see Chapter 18 — Competitive organisational structures, page 138.

■ Business in action

Rolls-Royce

In January 2008, Rolls-Royce announced plans to cut its global workforce of nearly 40,000 by just under 6 per cent to boost efficiency and competitiveness. The 2,300 job losses were confined to the company's managerial, professional and clerical staff. Rolls-Royce said it would continue to recruit graduates, apprentices and those 'required directly to deliver growth'.

Activity

Read the 'Rolls-Royce' Business in action. Why did Rolls-Royce believe that reducing its workforce would make the business more efficient and competitive?

Matching workforce location to business needs

More and more businesses are operating in the global market and can be defined as multinational. This may mean that existing employees have to relocate or local staff must be recruited. The same situation could arise if a UK business decides to move to an area of high unemployment because the Government is offering financial incentives.

■ Business in action

Dyson

In 2002, Dyson relocated production to Malaysia. Eight hundred semi-skilled UK assembly workers lost their jobs, although 1,200

Fig. 16.2 *Products in the Dyson range*

head office and research employees remained at the Wiltshire headquarters. This move was heavily criticised. However, record profit of £102.9m – representing a 137 per cent increase on previous figures – seemed to support the relocation. Dyson has even overtaken Hoover to become the best-seller in the US. It appears the new location strategy is working!

Minimising labour costs

This is illustrated by Rolls-Royce and Dyson outlined above: Rolls-Royce targeted indirect labour costs because it had become more efficient from productivity initiatives and needed to employ fewer administrative and support staff. For Dyson direct labour costs (UK workers cost three times more than Malaysian workers) were part of the rationale, although planning difficulties in the UK and an established supply chain in the Far East were equally important factors in making the decision.

Making full use of the workforce's potential

It would be inefficient for a business to under-utilise the skills of its employees, in just the same way that it should make full use of its productive capacity. This strategy can begin with a workforce audit and continue through the appraisal system. It may also involve offering existing employees more flexible working arrangements to reduce labour turnover and retain valuable members of staff whose personal circumstances change.

Maintaining good employer–employee relations

When the relationship between workers and management breaks down, there is often press coverage which causes bad publicity for a business. There are many strategies that the HR function can use to try to ensure that channels of communication are effective and good industrial relations are maintained. The European Union has also become involved through the Worker Information and Consultation Directive.

▉ Internal and external influences on HR objectives

The objectives selected by the HR function cannot be chosen in isolation and must take into account influences from within and outside the organisation.

Internal influences

- Corporate objectives may include growth in market share or through the development of new markets, new product development, improved returns to shareholders and increased competitiveness. In all cases, there will be an impact on the workforce. As shown at the beginning of this chapter, new skills may be required, employees may have to relocate or jobs may be lost as part of a rationalisation programme.
- Production strategies will have an impact on the workforce: loss of jobs through a capital-intensive strategy, new skill development for innovation, relocation or lean production needing teamwork training and improved communication skills.
- Marketing strategies such as product development and market development may have an impact on future recruitment and selection, as well as training for existing employees.

Link

For more information about lower costs, see Chapter 5—Selecting financial strategies, page 32, and Chapter 14—Operational strategies: location, page 102.

Link

For details of the Worker Information and Consultation Directive, go to www.hrmguide.co.uk

Links

For more information on production strategies, see Chapters 12–15, pages 90–118, on operational strategies.

■ **Link**

For more information on marketing strategies, see Chapter 9 — Selecting marketing strategies, page 66.

For more information on financial strategies, see Chapter 5 — Selecting financial strategies, page 32.

■ **Activity**

Refer to the Setting the scene case study on page 121. What would you consider to be the most important internal influences on the MSC Group's HR objectives?

■ Financial strategies such as the introduction of profit centres, cost minimisation and the allocation of capital expenditure will influence the training programmes offered by a business. In some cases, this could mean that the training budget is cut or out-sourced, or that the training and development programme is reviewed and adapted to changing needs (as illustrated by the Toyoda Gosei Fluid Systems example above).

External influences

■ Market/economic changes can have an impact on HR objectives. If a recession is forecast, the plan might be to reduce the workforce by either natural wastage or voluntary redundancy. If the buying habits of consumers change, for example more internet purchasing, the sales force could be reduced in size and more technical support staff employed.

■ Technological change continues to have a big impact on the skills required by employees at all levels within an organisation. Consideration should also be given to the impact of new technology on the motivation of the workforce, and how the HR function can address this issue.

■ Competition for skilled employees can influence HR objectives as this may cause problems of staff retention. In many sectors, there are severe shortages of suitably qualified workers so a company may have to consider improving financial and non-financial incentives or look to recruit overseas.

■ Population changes will have an impact on a business in several ways. As the UK population ages, there are fewer school leavers to fill vacancies, which can lead to higher wage costs. Alternatively, firms can actively recruit older workers or encourage mothers to return to work.

■ Government, both national and increasingly European, can have an influence on the HR objectives of all businesses. EU directives covering a wide range of HR issues have to be incorporated into UK law and become custom and practice in UK organisations. In October 2006, for example, it became illegal to discriminate against anyone at work on the basis of their age. HR departments must incorporate forthcoming changes into their strategies.

AQA **Examiner's tip**

Do not forget your AS work and remember that HR management has to be integrated into the plans of all the other functional areas in the organisation.

■ Approaches to HR management

There is no single approach to HR management that can be used by every organisation. It is possible to categorise types of HR management into 'soft' and 'hard' policies, although there is evidence to suggest that many companies use a mixture of methods which reflect their culture and management style.

'Soft' HR management

'**Soft' HR management** is concerned with how employees are managed, based on the belief that they are the most important asset of the business. Each member of staff will be seen as a long-term investment opportunity with a personal training and development plan enabling them to achieve their potential, in relation to corporate goals.

Features common to the 'soft' HR approach include:

■ training and development opportunities

■ internal promotion

■ **Key term**

'**Soft' HR management:** concerned with communication and motivation. People are led rather than managed. They are involved in determining and realising strategic objectives.

- developmental appraisal systems
- consultation and empowerment
- a flat organisational structure.

Strengths of this approach

- Reward systems are designed to encourage employees to be creative and work at a consistently high standard.
- Training, development and appraisal allow the employee to fulfil their individual needs as well as the needs of the organisation, which should lead to improved motivation.
- Recruitment costs should be reduced because retention rates should be high, labour turnover below average and absenteeism should not be a significant problem.

Weaknesses of this approach

- The role of trade unions is unclear and this could lead to tension where there is an established system of collective bargaining.
- It relies on an organisational culture which embraces a commitment to long-term training and development and an acceptance of the need to delegate responsibility. This may not be easy to implement in practice, without time-consuming and expensive training for senior management.

'Hard' HR management

'Hard' HR management considers employees to be a resource of the organisation to be used as necessary to achieve organisational objectives. The purpose of HR management is to plan the number and type of employees needed by analysing future workforce needs and ensuring that workers are recruited and released as necessary.

Features of 'hard' HRM include:

- fixed-term contracts
- external recruitment
- judgemental appraisal systems
- limited delegation of authority for decision-making
- a tall organisational structure
- minimum wage levels.

Strengths of this approach

- There are lower training and development costs.
- Competitive advantage can be achieved through cost minimisation – lean production methods and minimum wages.
- Reward systems are linked to output so it is possible to achieve a positive correlation between quantity produced and pay.

Weaknesses of this approach

- Little attention is paid to the needs of the employees. They are a resource to be used as necessary to achieve corporate objectives. This can lead to high labour turnover and absenteeism, which are costs to the business.
- It may be difficult to recruit new employees if the company has a reputation for 'hiring and firing'. This has been a particular problem in the UK construction industry where 'hard' HRM principles have been applied.

> ### Key term
>
> **'Hard' HR management:** emphasises costs and places control firmly in the hands of management. Their role is to manage numbers effectively, keeping the workforce closely matched with requirements in terms of both bodies and behaviour.

■ The limited delegation and lack of empowerment can demotivate employees and reduce the quality of work. The tall organisational structure which supports this can cause communication problems, particularly in large organisations, where bureaucracy slows down the decision-making process.

Case study

Penguin Books

The Penguin Group is about finding the best authors and ideas, giving them superb editorial support and producing the best books with marketing to match. The company hopes that developing better work–life policies will ensure employees deliver 'the best' in a competitive environment. Penguin is a creative environment with a high percentage of female employees.

Table 16.1 *Penguin Books: some statistics*

No. of employees	1,200
% female	67%
% ethnic minorities	8%
% turnover (labour)	11%
% women returning after maternity leave	99%

Penguin continues to develop a work–life strategy by expanding and improving the range of available benefits. Some have been in place for over 20 years, while others such as counselling have recently been added. All benefits have now been extended to temporary employees. Work–life policies include:

■ up to one year's maternity leave with 26 weeks at full pay (including Statutory Maternity Pay)

■ four weeks' paid paternity leave for fathers over the first four years of a child's life

■ childcare allowance

■ career breaks

■ counselling: 24/7 telephone access and up to six free, face-to-face counselling sessions via a counselling company

■ up to 15 days' compassionate leave for family or domestic problems

■ on-site occupational health centre

■ up to three days' fully paid leave for employees engaged in charitable or community work

■ private healthcare.

Penguin provides an intranet with information about benefits, employee news and charity work to support a positive work–life culture. Training courses are available to employees at all levels to support career and skills development.

The Workforce Foundation

Fig. 16.3 *Penguin Books worked towards developing a successful work–life strategy*

Questions

1 To what extent will Penguin achieve the objective of 'employees delivering the best in a competitive market' through its work–life policies?

2 Analyse the external influences that might have influenced Penguin's HR objectives.

3 To what extent will using 'soft' HR strategies be beneficial to Penguin?

4 Using all the information available:

a Analyse the case for Penguin introducing better work–life policies to achieve a competitive advantage in its market.

b Analyse the case for the use of 'hard' HR strategies at Penguin to achieve a competitive advantage.

c Make a justified recommendation about the option most likely to achieve the objective of achieving a competitive advantage for Penguin in its competitive market.

5 Find out why there may be HR management problems in the UK construction industry. Use a search engine and type in the phrase 'lean construction' as a starting point. What initiatives are in place to try to resolve the issues facing this industry? (Hint: Search for the Construction Industry Council.)

✔ *In this chapter you will have learned to:*

▪ explain the range of HR objectives typically set by larger businesses

▪ assess internal and external influences on HR objectives

▪ explain the difference between 'hard' and 'soft' approaches to HR

▪ evaluate the strengths and weaknesses of 'hard' and 'soft' HR strategies.

Summary questions

1 Explain why matching workforce skills, size and location are important HR objectives in large organisations. (4 marks)

2 How can making full use of the workforce's potential make a business more competitive? (6 marks)

3 Distinguish between 'hard' and 'soft' HR management. (4 marks)

4 It is claimed that more and more businesses are 'spying' on employees who claim to be sick. The aim is to reduce absenteeism which costs firms in the UK millions of pounds every year. What are the benefits and disadvantages of Next using this strategy at its stores? (10 marks)

5 The Widdowson Group is a logistics company with 500,000 square feet of warehouse facilities minutes from the M1/M69 near Leicester. In this fast-moving and demanding business, Widdowson's wants to take advantage of the latest barcode and scanning technology, allowing a more efficient and flexible solution for its customers. Staff need to be trained in these modern warehousing techniques, efficiency and high levels of service. Discuss the internal and external influences on the HR objective of matching workforce skills to business needs. www.euskills.com (18 marks)

Developing and implementing workforce plans

In this chapter you will learn to:

- describe the components of a workforce plan

- explain how internal and external factors influence workforce plans

- analyse the issues involved in implementing a workforce plan

- evaluate the value of using workforce plans.

Wales outlines NHS workforce plans, May 2008

Nurses in Wales could have new specialist roles and pass lesser tasks to health care assistants, according to a workforce review. Following a period of consolidation after registration, nurses will support 'innovative service development' delivered by the management of lower band workers, including assistant practitioners and other health care support workers (HCSW).

The development of a strategic approach to creating a more flexible and sustainable workforce for NHS Wales was carried out to consider how and when changes should be made, because, according to the report, the NHS can not afford to continue to provide or staff the service the way it currently does. Its recommendations will be piloted in four NHS organisations before being rolled out across the rest of Wales.

Adapted from Nursingtimes.net, published 13 May 2008

Discussion points

1. Why is it important for the NHS to use its labour force as efficiently as possible?

2. How can a workforce review help to ensure that the NHS workforce is used effectively?

3. Why are the recommendations to be piloted in four NHS organisations before being launched across Wales?

Key terms

Workforce planning: getting 'the right number of people with the right skills, experiences, and competencies in the right jobs at the right time.' A comprehensive process that provides managers with a framework for making staffing decisions based on an organisation's corporate objectives, strategic plan, budgetary resources, and a set of desired workforce skills.

Workforce plans: details of how the business will implement its HR management policies.

Workforce plans

Workforce planning is a key task for HR management and begins, inevitably, with the corporate objectives (see Fig. 17.1). The second stage is to develop HR objectives and strategies. In terms of the information required to make these decisions, the most important is a forecast about the size, skills and location of the future workforce, which can then be compared to the current provision. This workforce planning enables decisions to be taken about how to achieve the required workforce as and when it is needed. These decisions form the basis of the **workforce plans**, which require detailed information if they are to be effective.

Components of a workforce plan

The typical factors to take into account when drawing up a workforce plan are:

- a skills audit of the current workforce to identify the qualities and abilities of existing employees. It is quite possible that managers might be unaware of the potential of their staff. New qualifications and relevant experience may have been achieved outside the workplace, for example through voluntary work or a trade union

Fig. 17.1 *The workforce planning cycle*

Links

For more information about developing HR strategies, see Chapter 16 — Understanding HR objectives and strategies, page 121.

- data about labour turnover, wage rates, trend analysis of workforce demographics such as the level of entrants into the market (school leavers, apprentices, university graduates), statistical forecasts about the impact of economic migrants

- market research data and sales forecasts which will indicate the number of employees needed. If this is combined with technological developments, the quality of workers required and their productivity can be estimated

- EU directives and government initiatives relating to working conditions and practices.

From all this information, the workforce plan can be formulated. The main components (as shown in Fig. 17.2) are:

- recruitment requirements: new job descriptions and person specifications, specialist recruitment consultants

- training and development programmes: the acquisition of new technical skills to meet future business needs and the development of employee potential

Activity

Why might it be difficult for very large multinational organisations to conduct effective workforce planning?

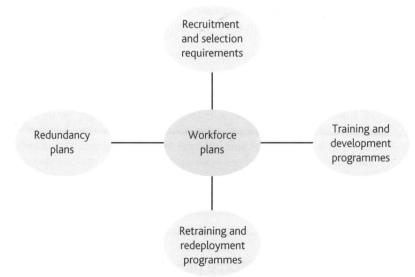

Fig. 17.2 *The main components of a workforce plan*

■ retraining and redeployment: when skills become redundant as a result of technological change, employees can be encouraged to acquire new ones which will be in demand in the future. If the business plans to relocate its manufacturing facility, this may involve the redeployment of some workers

■ redundancy: if the forecasts suggest that a smaller workforce is needed then planned redundancies must be included in the workforce plans. This should begin with natural wastage and then move on to voluntary redundancy before compulsory redundancy is considered. The aim is to ensure that people of future value to the business are not encouraged to leave, because this would be counter-productive.

■ Benefits of workforce plans

■ Workforce plans provide a strategic basis for making human resource decisions and facilitating solutions to current and future workforce issues. This allows managers to anticipate change and therefore be proactive, rather than reacting to events that take everyone by surprise.

■ Managers can plan replacements and changes in workforce skill levels by focusing on components such as workforce demographics and retirement forecasts. Gathering detailed information on anticipated change, the skills retirees will take from the workforce and key positions that may need filling will assist with this.

■ Organisational success depends on having the right employees with the right skills at the right time. Workforce plans enable managers to identify the skills needed in the workforce in the present and in the future, and then select and develop that workforce.

■ Managers can identify ways in which technology may change the skills required in the workforce, which can then be addressed through recruitment, training and retraining.

■ Workforce plans facilitate the introduction of flexible working arrangements. Training to make employees multiskilled helps to create job enlargement and therefore improves motivation. Creating a better work–life balance for employees can ensure that high calibre staff are retained, which is particularly important in areas of skill shortage.

■ The efficient use of current and future employees will help the company to reduce costs in the longer term.

Business in action

Inland Revenue

The Inland Revenue needed to extend its public opening hours to provide a more accessible service whilst at the same time helping staff to have a good work–life balance. Working together, unions and management explored ways to give employees more options about their working hours while allowing the business to open beyond the core hours of 9–5 and at weekends.

The Work Foundation

■ Influences on workforce plans

There are a range of factors that will have an impact on the workforce plans of a company.

Internal influences on workforce plans

■ Corporate objectives:

- A growth objective could mean that direct labour recruitment is increased.

- Earning higher returns for shareholders might be achieved by delayering, causing an increase in managerial redundancies.

■ Production objectives:

- The development of TQM would involve training in team-working.

- The introduction of new technology could lead to new skill requirements or the loss of low skilled jobs.

■ Marketing objectives:

- The development of new markets overseas could lead to redeployment and the recruitment of a local sales force.

- The introduction of innovative new goods and services to the product portfolio would have implications for retraining, as existing knowledge and skills may no longer be sufficient.

■ Finance is likely to have a significant impact on workforce plans, and there is evidence to suggest that many organisations are unwilling to pay for the training and development costs associated with 'soft' HR management. Similarly, redundancy proposals may prove to be too expensive even for large organisations. The current financial position of the business and whether or not it takes a short-term or long-term view of planning are likely to have a significant influence on the availability of funding for workforce plans.

■ Business in action

Staff training

A study of 500 companies and over 1,000 employees indicates that multinational companies continue to lead in staff training with expenditure of just over 4 per cent of total employee costs, slightly below the EU average of 4.15 per cent.

Cipd in Ireland

External influences on workforce plans

■ The market and trends in buyer behaviour: The growth in fairly-traded goods may lead to the relocation of manufacturing, and the need to establish the ethical credentials of suppliers. In the construction industry, there is growing demand for environmentally friendly features and recycled materials. Workers will need to retrain to use new materials and techniques.

■ Business in action

Alliance Boots

Alliance Boots employs ethical auditors whose role is to ensure that all suppliers meet the company's strict code of practice.

■ New technology: The need to retrain employees may have a negative impact on motivation as well as a direct financial cost. This may lead to the need for better customer support services which may result in changes to recruitment and selection. In retailing more products are being bought via the internet, so fewer sales staff may be needed, but after-sales service is more important to ensure customer satisfaction. There is evidence to suggest that the impact of technology is not always positive in terms of the relationship between a business and its customers. Some of this may be due to lack of job-specific training.

Business in action

Call centres

Problems with call centres have become one of the UK's most popular national moans. According to a recent survey, only 4 per cent of people had a positive experience when dealing with a call centre.

■ Competition: If there is a skills shortage, then competitors might attempt to attract high quality employees with attractive reward packages. This can lead to higher labour costs or encourage the business to explore the possibility of attracting skilled workers from other countries or introducing an apprenticeship scheme or in-house training programme. It will depend on the type of skilled labour required, for example how long does training take? Similarly if major competitors are moving towards a more capital-intensive approach, a company may decide to follow the trend or look for a competitive advantage by retaining a more 'personal' approach by retaining a highly skilled workforce.

■ Labour market trends: They will give an indication of the availability of suitable workers in the future. In recent years, for example, the ageing population has encouraged businesses to re-evaluate their attitude towards older employees who may be motivated by non-financial factors and who have a wealth of experience to offer. Similarly, the expansion of the European Union has led to an increase in economic migrants from Eastern Europe. This has changed the skill-pool available to employers which should be reflected in future workforce planning.

Business in action

B&Q

B&Q is well known for its policy of recruiting older staff. An example of its commitment to older workers is shown by the policy of offering term-time contracts not only to parents, but also to grandparents, in recognition of the supportive, caring role that many of them have.

■ UK government legislation and European Union directives: Changes in working practices such as minimum wage legislation, limits to working hours, compulsory breaks and equal opportunities will all impact on future human resource plans. Changes in education and training in the UK will have an impact on the supply of skilled workers: The City Academy programme has been supported by several large organisations, as has the Modern Apprenticeship scheme. More recently Foundation degrees and the Diploma programme have been designed to meet future business labour needs.

■ Trade unions are part of the negotiation process in many large organisations and any workforce plans should involve union representatives to ensure that there is minimum disruption and reduce the likelihood of industrial unrest. In many organisations trade unions represent an official channel of communication between managers and employees which should not be ignored, particularly if significant changes in working arrangements are proposed.

Implementation issues

Employer–employee relations

The development of workforce plans can have a positive or negative impact on the relationships between employers and employees: good communications may be the key to resolving differences. When workforce plans involve the possibility of redundancy or the introduction of flexible working practices, it is likely that employees may be concerned about the future. 'Soft' HR management involves negotiating with individual employees which is obviously a potential problem if the workforce is unionised. Many organisations have tried to introduce a single union agreement to reduce the complexity of the negotiation process, with varied degrees of success. It is worth noting that the current state of relations between employers and employees will also have had an impact on the type of plan drawn up in the first place.

Positive effects

These include improved communications because a good workforce plan should involve all areas of the business, including the employees. By conducting a workforce audit, for example, staff may feel that they are part of the decision-making process which should improve motivation. The introduction of flexible working could solve issues about work–life balance and may give workers the opportunity to meet outside commitments as well as continue with their chosen career.

Activity

What impact might the UK government's Train to Gain initiative have on a large organisation's workforce plan? (www.traintogain.gov.uk)

AQA Examiner's tip

Do not fall into the trap of assuming that all employee organisations, for example trade unions, will resist workforce plans. The key to success is usually effective communication, and industrial action over changing working practices is generally the last resort option.

Business in action

Unilever

Unilever employs 12,500 people in the UK across 30 sites. It developed a harmonised policy for flexible working and communicated this widely across the business. Flexible working options are now available to all employees. Benefits to the business have included the retention of skilled staff: over 90 per cent of employees now return from maternity leave. Research among managers working part-time suggests that 60 per cent would have left had they not been able to work flexibly. Scores for satisfaction with work–life balance in the company's regular employee surveys have improved and there is a new 'can do' attitude across the business: colleagues and managers are very supportive of team members who want to work flexibly. Absenteeism rates have fallen at sites where employees feel most in control of their working hours. This is particularly evident at manufacturing sites, where employees can job-share on shifts or swap shifts to meet emergency needs.

The Work Foundation

Link

Use www.bbc.co.uk for to find coverage of recent examples of industrial disputes.

Negative effects

Workforce plans may be the cause of fear and unrest, particularly where the channels of communication are complicated and long. Workforce audits, redeployment and, of course, redundancies can all cause uncertainty amongst workers who see them as threats to their job security. There have been well publicised examples in the UK where such plans have led to protracted industrial disputes involving postal workers, fire fighters and airline staff.

Cost

There will be cost implications for any workforce plan. Even if the objective is to reduce labour costs by streamlining the workforce, there will be short-term expenses such as redundancy payments. For recruitment and selection or training, the issue may be whether or not to manage these plans in-house or sub-contract the work to specialist organisations.

Positive effects

This will require a longer-term view of business performance. Inevitably there are short-term costs to achieve longer-term gains. As the examples in this chapter and Chapter 16 indicate, improved retention rates and falling absenteeism are features of good HR plans. As a result, future labour costs should be reduced through the implementation of comprehensive workforce plans.

Negative effects

In some large organisations, the role of HR is still seen as peripheral to strategic decision-making. To spend a significant amount of the overall budget on recruitment and training may bring opposition from budget holders in marketing and operations, who may see a cut in their allocation. In the short term, it is also very difficult to measure the success of workforce plans which may take several years to fully implement.

Corporate image

The way that potential employees, customers and investors view the business can be influenced by how successfully workforce plans are implemented.

Positive effects

The organisation may be seen as caring for its employees and their individual needs which may encourage high calibre potential employees to apply for positions with the company. It should also have a positive impact on the service given to customers.

Link

For more information about negative effects of workforce plans, see Chapter 16 — Understanding HR objectives and strategies, page 121, the Business in action: Dyson.

Negative effects

The decisions taken by organisations may be unpopular and cause criticism, particularly if the workforce plans involve redundancies. As a result, it may be more difficult for the company to attract the best employees in the future.

Training

Throughout this chapter, reference has been made to the importance of training and development in any workforce plan. It has also been noted that spending on training tends to be limited and, in fact, it is often the first casualty of cost reduction when a firm faces difficult trading conditions.

Positive effects

There is a wealth of evidence to suggest that good training, whether it is in-house or provided by outside specialists, can have a beneficial impact on a business in terms of motivation and competitive advantage. Companies that invest time and money in developing their employees are likely to be able to respond better to changes in market conditions because their workforce should be more highly motivated and have a greater range of skills.

Negative effects

Training can be very expensive in the short term and there is no guarantee that employees will remain with the company once their development programme is complete. There is evidence to suggest that in the health sector, for example, practitioners train in the UK National Health Service then move abroad or into the private sector to earn higher salaries.

■ The value of workforce plans

There is academic discussion and disagreement about the value of workforce planning and plans. However, in the context of strategies for success, there can be little doubt that if the planning process is carried out effectively, workforce plans play a significant part in the achievement of corporate objectives. They enable managers to be more effective and for strategic objectives across the organisation to be achieved. Finally, workforce plans allow managers to address in a systematic way, the issues that are driving workforce change within the company and the market. Without clear plans, the firm will always be reacting to change which is disruptive and ultimately expensive.

■ Case study

HBOS

HBOS banking was having problems with consistency of service at its call centres. At peak times there was a 26 per cent higher volume of calls but the same staffing as at all other times. Research suggested that demand for HBOS's services would increase in the future and the workforce needed to grow, but it was difficult to recruit additional talented staff because unemployment was very low. The company wanted to achieve the following improvements:

■ handle more calls with fewer people

■ staff to work more hours at busy times

■ introduce flexible working practices for its staff

■ reduce sickness from 10 per cent.

They hoped to achieve all this with the agreement of the unions within six months.

The first stage of the workforce plan was to introduce sustainable working patterns and encourage employees to work more hours at busy times. The second phase was called 'The New World Model' and included:

■ recruitment of three senior managers with experience of workforce planning in call centres

■ recruitment of part-time employees who were both talented and motivated to work. This was a real change of policy for HBOS and gave the company access to a new market of people who wanted to work in the contact centre

■ a system called FLEXTRA to manage the new full-time and part-time flexible working patterns, including time-off arrangements.

The plans, which depended on intensive communications between employers, employees and unions, were such a success that the company received the Call Centre Innovation of the Year Award. The company believes that the new workforce arrangements will give them a competitive edge in the financial services market.

QPC.com

Questions

1 Analyse the main components of HBOS's workforce plan.

2 To what extent will internal and external factors influence HBOS's workforce plan?

3 Analyse the possible advantages and disadvantages to HBOS of introducing its workforce plans.

4 Using all the information:

a Analyse the case for using a workforce plan to help HBOS achieve its objective of improving the consistency of its service to customers.

b Analyse the case against using a workforce plan.

c Make a justified recommendation about the value of implementing a workforce plan to achieve the objective of improving the consistency of customer service.

5 Use the internet to investigate workforce planning in a large organisation.

✔ *In this chapter you will have learned to:*

■ identify and explain the components of a workforce plan

■ assess the internal and external factors influencing workforce plans

■ analyse positive and negative effects that the issues involved in implementing a workforce plan may have

■ assess the value of using workforce plans.

Summary questions

1 Identify the main components of a workforce plan. (4 marks)

2 Explain what a workforce plan for a DIY retail business wanting to improve its customer service in the face of fierce competition from online catalogue rivals might include. (6 marks)

3 Explain why a skills audit is an essential part of workforce planning for a business formed by the merger of two pharmaceutical companies. (4 marks)

4 Analyse the internal influences on the workforce plan of a mobile phone manufacturer. (10 marks)

5 A major high street retail chain has a corporate objective of survival in a very competitive market. How might this impact on workforce planning? (6 marks)

6 Analyse the possible influence of age discrimination legislation on the workforce plans of UK businesses. (10 marks)

7 A major double glazing manufacturing and installation company is finding it difficult to recruit skilled technical staff. How might this influence its workforce plans? (6 marks)

8 Shareholders are putting pressure on a large manufacturing company to increase profits. This has led to a workforce plan designed to reduce direct and indirect labour cost by multiskilling the workforce and delayering the organisational structure. Analyse the positive and negative effects of this approach. (10 marks)

9 A UK bank plans to relocate its call centre back to the UK and prepares an appropriate workforce plan. Evaluate the possible impact on its corporate image of this approach. (18 marks)

10 Following an assessment by the Learning and Skills Council, Dolland & Aitchison identified literacy and numeracy as key issues affecting the productivity of its staff. Consequently, these core skills are now assessed as part of the overall NVQ training programme for existing employees, while new staff are assessed at interview stage, so that training needs can be identified at the outset. Discuss the costs and benefits to the business of implementing this plan. (10 marks)

Competitive organisational structures

In this chapter you will learn to:

- explain the factors influencing the choice of organisational structure in larger businesses

- explain how larger businesses adapt their organisational structures to improve competitiveness

- evaluate the issues involved with implementing and operating an adapted organisational structure.

Setting the scene

BP

BP chief executive Tony Hayward criticised the management structure of BP as fundamentally flawed. Mr Hayward described BP, Britain's second largest company, as a complex and fragmented business and indicated the need for a major shake-up of the business. 'There is massive duplication and lack of clarity of who does what,' Mr Hayward is quoted as saying. A process of simplification of BP is the solution, he says. 'We will reduce the number or organisation units [and] reduce the number of layers from workers up to chief executive officer from eleven to about seven.'

Adapted from the London Evening Standard, *27 March 2008*

Discussion points

1 What are the advantages to BP of reducing the number of layers from eleven to about seven?

2 Are there any possible disadvantages to this restructuring?

3 What issues might be involved in implementing this delayering and restructuring?

Organisational structures in larger businesses

It would be very misleading to assume that organisations develop a single structure which never changes, or that there is a perfect organisational structure which can best meet the needs of all businesses. The reality of modern business life is that the organisation of the company probably will and should change on a regular basis as it adapts to changes in the marketplace. There are three types of organisational structure appropriate to larger organisations and it is quite likely that within a large company more than one type will appear:

- A traditional hierarchical structure may be appropriate in the financial and administration function where confidential or sensitive data is involved, processes are important and a consistency of service is expected.

- A matrix structure, which is project-based, may be appropriate for the marketing function. If the market is divided up geographically or by type of customer, sales teams will have different goals. On the other hand, each product within the portfolio could have a dedicated marketing team.

- An informal structure has no obvious 'organisation', although a support system will be in place. This approach may be the best way to operate a research and development function where creativity is very important.

AQA Examiner's tip

Revisit your AS Business Studies notes to refresh your memory about organisational structures.

When deciding on the best structures to use within the company, senior executives may take the following factors into consideration:

■ If there are a lot of highly skilled, specialised employees, the structure is likely to be less formal than if the majority of employees are semi-skilled or unskilled.

■ The business environment will also have an impact on the organisational structure. If the market is very competitive and market conditions are difficult, there will be pressure to reduce costs by streamlining the structure and speeding up the decision-making process and responsiveness of the business to changes in the market.

■ If the company wishes to move away from a risk-taking culture as it grows and wishes to become a more established force in the market emphasising quality rather than innovation, then a more formal structure may be introduced.

■ The leadership style of the senior executives will affect the structure: those who wish to retain control of decision-making are likely to prefer a tall, hierarchical structure with narrow spans of control. Leaders who prefer to delegate decision-making are more likely to favour a wider span of control or a matrix structure.

■ Impact on competitiveness

However the organisation is structured, its effectiveness will be judged in terms of how efficiently the business performs.

■ How quickly are strategic decisions made? If the company is struggling to maintain its market share or losing out to rivals in the market, this would suggest that the strategic decision-making is too slow.

■ Does the business operate efficiently at minimum cost? The structure of the organisation may be inefficient with unnecessary levels of management. This is particularly relevant where there have been significant advances in technology and tasks can be completed more quickly and efficiently than in the past.

■ How effective are the channels of communication within the organisation? If the channels of communication are too long and complicated, then there is a good chance that communications will be poor and as a result important information may not reach decision-makers quickly enough for the company to respond to change.

■ Who is involved in the decision-making process and are they the most appropriate people? As a business grows, the entrepreneur(s) who initially made all the decisions will have to relinquish some control. Those with the most knowledge about the market, customers, suppliers and competitors, need to be included in strategic decisions.

Business in action

C&A

In 2000, the C&A chain, which has 577 stores in 12 European countries, withdrew from the UK market. A number of UK high street retailers had suffered sharp falls in profits including Marks & Spencer, Arcadia Group, Storehouse and Littlewoods. What united them is that they were in the mid-market, with centralised, hierarchical organisational structures. They had been squeezed on all fronts by growing competition from more dynamic, responsive

Link

For more information on diseconomies of scale, see Chapter 12 — Operational strategies: scale and resource mix, page 90.

businesses such as Next. C&A UK said that it had suffered £250m losses in the UK in the previous five years. 'C&A has been part of the British high street for over 75 years and was determined to remain so. Unfortunately, business conditions did not allow this to happen.'

Adapting to improve competitiveness

As has already been noted, large organisations are prepared to adapt the structure in order to become more competitive. This can be achieved by a number of methods.

Centralisation

Centralisation is a strategy which limits the number of people involved in the decision-making process to a few senior executives. Authority to make strategic decisions is returned to the top or centre of the organisational structure. It is most likely to be the chosen strategy in times of crisis when the survival of the business is at stake. There are benefits achieved by implementing this option including:

- Strategic decisions can be taken quickly as few very experienced people will be involved in the process.
- There is tighter control over the day-to-day running of the business and in particular financial control such as budgets. This should ensure that available funds are allocated appropriately given the situation the business finds itself in.
- Procedures can be standardised throughout the organisation which should mean that buying economies of scale can be achieved.
- Strong leadership can be very effective at a time of crisis.

However, there are also drawbacks to this approach:

- bureaucracy
- diseconomies of scale.

The drawbacks to the implementation of centralisation are best illustrated by considering the opposite approach: decentralisation.

Decentralisation

Decentralisation is in some respects inevitable as a business grows because the entrepreneur(s) cannot physically retain total control of the day-to-day running of the organisation. Decentralisation that occurs in order to increase the competitiveness of a business is most likely to happen when a company has become too bureaucratic and diseconomies of scale have set in. The purpose is to delegate decision-making to people lower down the organisational hierarchy. It involves training issues, because middle and junior managers may not have the expertise required to make strategic decisions. There are advantages to implementing this approach:

- Senior managers can concentrate on making longer term corporate decisions concerned with the overall direction of the business.
- Subordinates are likely to have increased motivation because their jobs are being enriched, which has a positive effect on productivity and quality.
- Day-to-day problems and issues should be resolved more quickly because those closest are making the decisions.

- Delegation increases flexibility and means that the business should adapt to changing market conditions more quickly because decisions can be made faster, without reference to senior managers.

- Middle and junior managers are better prepared for more senior roles within the organisation and employees have more opportunities to demonstrate their potential. This should improve the training and development within the organisation, and reduce the need to recruit externally, thereby cutting costs.

However, there are disadvantages to decentralisation:

- slower strategic decision-making
- more difficult to control the business on a day-to-day basis; in particular the finances
- more difficult to achieve economies of scale
- leadership and direction in the company is more difficult to maintain.

Delayering

Delayering is the process of removing levels in the hierarchical structure in order to create a leaner and more efficient organisation. The development of technology and the competitive pressure from China and India have encouraged UK businesses to reduce indirect costs. This has happened alongside the growth of management techniques which emphasise team-working, empowerment and TQM, all of which reduce the need for direct supervision. Organisational structures have become flatter and the span of control has widened. There are positive and negative issues involved in the implementation of this approach.

> **Key term**
>
> **Delayering:** removing levels in the organisational structure.

Table 18.1 *Benefits and drawbacks of delayering*

Benefits	Drawbacks
Indirect costs are reduced when permanent, full-time salaried staff are removed.	Valuable market knowledge and experience may be lost, and loss of job security may reduce the levels of motivation amongst employees.
The motivation of workers throughout the organisation should improve because they have more responsibility and control over their working environment.	Recent legislation makes it illegal to discriminate by age, which could make this approach more complicated to administer.
Those at the bottom of the organisational structure may have good ideas on how to improve business performance and a better understanding of customer needs than those at the very top. By delegating authority the company may be better able to respond to changes in the market and gain a competitive advantage.	The workload of the managers remaining is likely to increase as the span of control widens, increasing stress levels and possibly absenteeism. Those given additional responsibilities may require training which can be very expensive in a large organisation.

Flexible workforces

The idea behind this approach is that firms are less able to respond to changes in the market if they have a largely permanent, full-time staff. If, on the other hand, more of the workforce are part-time, on temporary contracts or have no set contracted hours, the business is able to use its employee resources more effectively and efficiently. Along the same lines, if some aspects of work can be outsourced or completed at home by employees, then indirect/overhead costs are reduced. In the past, lack of employment protection for these **peripheral workers** made them an attractive proposition because rights to sick pay, holiday pay and pensions were not protected. However, this has changed in recent years and it is likely that all employees will enjoy the same rights at work in the

> **Activity**
>
> Refer to the Setting the scene case study on page 138. Why has BP chosen to delayer its business?

> **Key term**
>
> **Peripheral workers:** part-time, temporary and self-employed workers brought into the businesses as and when needed.

Key terms

Flexible workforce: where a significant percentage of employees are on part-time and temporary contracts rather than the vast majority being on permanent, full-time contracts, and/or where employees are multiskilled and work wherever needed in the organisation.

Core workers: full time, permanent employees, with business-specific skills and knowledge, performing tasks key to the success of the business, often rewarded with high salaries and excellent working conditions.

future, which reduces the cost-cutting attraction of introducing a **flexible workforce**.

Core workers are those considered to be essential to the ongoing operation and success of the business. These employees are given permanent full-time contracts and are offered financial and non-financial incentives to stay loyal to the company. Typically, core workers are managers and specialist technical staff.

Peripheral workers are the other employees of the business who are seen as less significant to the ongoing success of the business. They are likely to be part-time workers or on temporary or fixed-term contracts. In some cases they may have zero hour contracts which means that they do not have regular hours but may be asked to work at short notice. This approach is commonly used in the hotel and catering industry, where demand can change significantly within a short space of time. In many instances, these employees are semi-skilled or unskilled.

Business in action

Part-time and temporary workers in the UK

People are increasingly choosing to work fewer hours and the level of part-time working has grown. As a result, the average hours worked by individuals has had a downwards trend since a peak at the end of 1994.

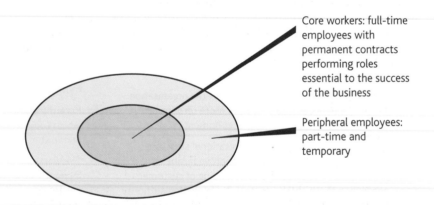

Core workers: full-time employees with permanent contracts performing roles essential to the success of the business

Peripheral employees: part-time and temporary

Fig. 18.1 *The organisation of a flexible workforce*

Key term

Outsourcing: where business functions are provided by external specialist organisations rather than provided in house.

Outsourcing

Outsourcing is part of creating a flexible workforce because it involves employing another business to perform a specialist function required by the organisation. This could be recruitment and selection, technical support services or advertising. Rather than employ specialists within the company (in house), it may be more cost effective to outsource and pay for such expertise as and when required. These external workers may be operating within the business, but are either self-employed or working for another company. The most obvious examples of this option are cleaning, security and catering.

Homeworking

Homeworking is a growing option for many UK employees, largely due to advances in technology making it possible to communicate with 'head office' very easily. There are also a number of unskilled or semi-skilled administrative and manufacturing jobs done by homeworkers, which do not rely on the availability of technology, for example 'hand' knitted garments and home-delivery services.

Key term

Homeworking: where employees can perform their job from home, increasingly linked to their employer via the internet.

Business in action

Siemens

Siemens IT Solutions and Services successfully designed, built and installed a tapeless Digital Production System for ITV Productions, the programme production arm of ITV plc, the biggest commercial television network in the UK. Siemens will support and maintain the system for three years after installation.

Creating a more flexible workforce is not just about reducing costs. There is growing evidence that an increasing number of employees would like the opportunity to work more flexible hours to fit in with other commitments, and improve their work–life balance. If a business can create a more flexible approach to its organisational structure, there are motivational benefits to be gained. Furthermore, it should be possible to retain a larger percentage of employees and reduce absenteeism, both of which should create cost savings and increase efficiency. The success of adapting the organisational structure to improve competitiveness may ultimately depend upon how it is managed: is there sufficient consultation with all groups involved, and is it part of a long-term plan for the organisation or a knee-jerk reaction to unexpected changes in the market?

AQA Examiner's tip

In evaluating the effectiveness of adapting organisational structures, it is very important to assess the context of the scenario you are given. There is never one correct answer to a problem facing a business, and therefore the particular circumstances outlined should always guide your thinking.

Case study

Citigroup

The US bank, Citigroup, announced that it would be axing or relocating 26,500 jobs in a move to improve its performance. Citigroup announced that it was eliminating 17,000 positions – equivalent to 5 per cent of its 327,000-strong workforce. A further 9,500 jobs will be shifted from expensive centres such as London and New York to smaller cities or developing countries, including India and the Philippines. The cuts are intended to yield savings of $4.6bn (£2.3bn) a year by 2009. As part of the reorganisation, Citi will centralise global functions, including finance, information technology (IT), legal, human resources and branding. By centralising these global functions, particularly IT, Citi will reduce unnecessary complexity and accelerate innovation.

Citigroup's chief executive, Chuck Prince, said a review had examined ways to rationalise technology, reduce administration costs and weed out duplication. Among Citigroup's biggest operations outside the US is in Britain, where the company has 11,500 staff. Of these, 9,000 work at the bank's Canary Wharf office, which is the headquarters for Europe, the Middle East and

Africa. Although job losses were not broken down by country, 55 per cent of the cost savings will be in the US because American workers tend to be more 'expensive'. London staff had been informed of the restructuring: notifications of individual job losses began immediately. Citigroup has faced criticism from investors about a lack of cost control. Profits rose 7 per cent in 2006 but it was outshone by its rival JP Morgan, which enjoyed a 70 per cent jump. Analysts believe Mr Prince's own job depends on whether the cuts yield a swift improvement. Initiatives under the plan, which will cost $1.38bn, will include eliminating layers of management, consolidating administration between countries and regions, centralising procurement and standardising technology.

The Guardian, *12 April 2007*

Questions

1. To what extent will centralising global functions such as finance and human resources help to improve Citibank's competitiveness?

2. Analyse the factors that might have determined the organisational structure of a global business such as Citibank.

3. Analyse the advantages of delayering and centralisation in improving the competitiveness of Citibank.

4. To what extent will adapting its organisational structure improve Citibank's competitiveness?

5. Use the internet to find out how the BBC and ITV have adapted their organisational structures to become more efficient and competitive.

☑ *In this chapter you will have learned to:*

- analyse the factors determining the choice of organisational structure in larger businesses

- explain how larger businesses can adapt their organisational structures to improve competitiveness

- evaluate the effectiveness of adapting organisational structures to improve competitiveness.

Summary questions

1. Describe the main factors determining the choice of organisational structure. (4 marks)

2. Explain why a matrix structure might be the most appropriate structure for the R&D department of a pharmaceutical company. (6 marks)

3. How can the organisational structure of a large organisation lead to inefficiency? (4 marks)

4. Examine the benefits to a national chain of estate agents of decentralising decision-making from its London headquarters to regional offices. (10 marks)

5 An international haulage company has noticed that, since delayering its organisational structure, there has been an increase in stress-related absenteeism. Discuss whether or not delayering always lead to improved competitiveness. (18 marks)

6 Unilever developed a harmonised policy for flexible working and communicated this widely across the business. Flexible working options are available to all employees. To what extent will this help to improve the competitiveness of the business? (18 marks)

7 Analyse the disadvantages to a business of only retaining a small percentage of core employees in its workforce. (10 marks)

8 Pattinson offered the opportunity to become part of the north-east's largest independent estate agency through its successful network of self-employed agents working from home. Benefits included potential for high earnings, flexible working hours, the opportunity to meet new people and an increased knowledge of the property market. All home-workers would receive comprehensive training covering sales, lettings, auction, commercial, mortgages, property inspections and surveys, which would equip them with the knowledge and business skills required to reach their full potential. Discuss whether or not this policy was likely to make Pattinson's a more competitive business. (18 marks)

Effective employer–employee relations

- explain the importance of communication in employer–employee relations

- discuss the methods used by employees to represent themselves

- analyse the methods used to avoid and resolve industrial disputes

- discuss whether or not methods used to avoid or resolve industrial disputes are going to be successful.

Setting the scene

ITV redundancies: 25 PR jobs face axe

The majority of staff at ITV's 75-strong programme publicity department have been told to reapply for about 50 positions in a shakeup of the broadcaster's PR operation. It is understood that ITV is restructuring following a benchmarking process of PR practices across the British TV industry, to better focus on flagship programmes such as *Coronation Street* and *I'm a Celebrity... Get Me Out of Here!* Staff in London, Manchester and Leeds were informed of the restructure at a series of meetings and PR staff were given less than two weeks to apply for the new positions, according to ITV insiders.

The ITV Group Director of Corporate Affairs said that significant savings were needed and there would be just one head of department. However, one insider argued that ITV's programme publicity office is already a 'very lean operation'. ITV confirmed a restructure of the programme publicity department and a consultation process with staff has begun.

Adapted from guardian.co.uk, 11 June 2008

Discussion points

1 Why is a period of consultation important in the restructuring of ITV's programme publicity department?

2 Why are communications important in employer–employee relations at ITV?

3 What difficulties might ITV face in communicating the restructure to its employees?

The importance of communication

Effective communication is vital for creating a successful organisation. In a business environment characterised by uncertainty and change, high quality internal communication should be a priority. Organisational change, whether large or small, should be supported by consistent and frequent communication between employers and employees.

As part of the AS syllabus, you looked at the structure of organisations and how communication flows can affect business performance. At A2, the emphasis is on the importance of communications in the relationship between employers and employees. Effective communication can have a beneficial impact on employees: positive, constructive feedback on performance can improve motivation, as can greater involvement in decision-making. In large organisations, it is often difficult to ensure that every area is focused on achieving the corporate objectives, and poor communication can leave employees with no sense of direction or purpose: they do not know why they are doing what they are doing. For example, a lack of information can make the people furthest away from the centre of decision-making feel vulnerable when dealing with customer enquiries.

There is, therefore, a strong link between effective communication and motivation, which managers should see as a priority, particularly during times of change. If the organisational structure is being adapted, good communication with all employees is vital so that the informal 'grapevine' does not create an atmosphere of mistrust and fear, which may be unfounded, and will almost certainly lead to declining motivation and productivity. This could then have a negative impact on the competitiveness of the business, by increasing costs.

■ **Business in action**

Effective internal communication

A recent report by Deloitte & Touche Human Capital asked CEOs: 'Which human resource issues are very important to the success of the organisation?' While 95 per cent identified 'effective internal communication', only 22 per cent thought it was being delivered effectively.

Advantages to effective internal communication include:

- All areas of the business are pursuing the same corporate objectives.
- Change can be introduced more successfully.
- Employees identify with the culture of the organisation and have more loyalty to it.

How can internal communications be improved?

There is a big difference between effective communication and increased communication. It may be tempting to use technology to pass more information around a business. However, this does not guarantee that the communication will be good; it may just lead to information overload. There are ways to improve communications between employers and employees, and the best combination of these should be found.

- Establish the needs of the employees before changing existing methods of communication. There is no need to use high technology equipment if it is not necessary. Employees may see it as intrusive rather than supportive. The use of mobile phones is a good example of this situation; being able to contact employees 24 hours a day may be a benefit to managers, but not to their subordinates. On the other hand, receiving important information from head office very quickly may be a benefit to mobile workers.
- Improving employee skills in all areas of communication from reading and writing to using the latest technology is very important. Employees are likely to resist change and employers cannot assume that this will be different in the case of communication.
- Cultural and language differences can be particular barriers to effective communications in the largest organisations. There has been a lot of research, but the impact on employees is still underestimated.

■ Links

For more information about corporate objectives, see Chapter 1 – Using objectives and strategies, page 2.

Research at Napier University

Students at Napier University, Edinburgh, conducted a survey of corporate communication managers from organisations across Scotland. This showed that internal communication is regarded as vital to the success of the business by senior management in all sectors. It also showed that large private and public sector organisations see money spent on internal communications as an essential investment. However, most of those surveyed still thought that external communications were more important than internal communications.

Activity

Look again at the Setting the scene case study on page 146. Why is effective consultation important to a company such as ITV?

Are there any costs to improved communication?

Effective consultation is said to increase loyalty to the business, help to reduce staff turnover, keep recruitment costs down and keep expertise within the business. However, if there has not been the appropriate training, there is the possibility that employee representatives may slow down the business decision-making process and create discontent within the workforce by ineffectual feedback processes.

Employee representation

As businesses grow, the need for employee representation, even where communication is very efficient, will be necessary. Decision-making would be almost impossible if every member of the organisation was consulted directly before a choice was made. Therefore, to make communications with employees really effective, some form of representation needs to be put in place, with a clear remit about what can and cannot be discussed. It is important to stress here that whichever system is chosen, the purpose should be to encourage constructive dialogue between employers and employees and not simply pay 'lip service' to the principles of good communication. Workers will know whether they actually have a voice within the organisation, so it makes sense for senior managers to ensure that the process works properly from the outset. This process will in itself involve effective communication so everyone is aware of the structure and objectives of the system.

Methods of employee representation

Employee groups

Key term

Employee groups: forums made up of employee representatives from selected areas of the business and representatives of the employers.

Employee groups (also known as staff representative forums) are joint consultative committees made up of management, HR and staff representatives from selected parts of the business. They meet to discuss and raise issues that affect or are likely to affect employees.

Staff representatives are employees who have been elected by their colleagues to represent them at meetings with the employer. They can benefit the business by bridging the gap between management and the workforce and assist in two-way communications between employer and employee.

Trade unions

Trade unions are national organisations that negotiate on behalf of a group of employees in a place of work or organisation. It may be that there are several unions within one establishment, representing the interests of specific groups of workers, or that there is a Single Union Agreement in place, where one union represents all employees in negotiating terms and conditions of employment.

Works councils

This system of employee representation has been very successful in several European countries, and has become the default provision in the UK if businesses resist the trend towards improved communication with employees. A **works council** has to be introduced by law, if requested by employees in organisations employing 50 staff or over. The following features are the minimum requirement:

- An election of representatives must take place.
- One representative must be elected for every 50 employees.

Information must be provided for discussion on recent and probable developments in the company's activities; the economic situation; the situation, structure and probable development of employment within the organisation, especially where there is a threat to employment; decisions that are likely to lead to major changes in working conditions including change of business ownership and collective redundancies.

Key terms

Trade union: an organisation of employees, which acts collectively in dealings with management for mutual protection and assistance and is often concerned with wages and conditions of employment.

Works council: a committee representing the employer and elected employee representatives of a plant or business meeting to discuss working conditions, grievances and pay.

Business in action

Current legislation

The European Directive of September 1994 established the right of employees in organisations with at least 1,500 employees within the European Union member states and at least 150 employees in each of two member states to request a European Works Council.

Following a European Parliament and Council Directive establishing a general framework for informing and consulting employees, on 6 April 2005 the UK Information and Consultation Regulations came into force. This provided employees in businesses with more than 150 staff the right to require the setting up of a staff representative body. The legislation subsequently applied to businesses with 100+ staff from April 2007, and 50+ staff from April 2008.

The advantages and disadvantages of employee representation

Advantages

- Managers seem less remote because employees have easier access to them at all levels.
- Employees are encouraged to 'voice' their views frankly and freely, which they may be reluctant to do if there were not representatives to

speak for them. This should reduce tension and clear up uncertainty and misunderstandings.

■ The range of the subjects over which information is given and consultation takes place should increase. Managers should find that it is easier to maintain confidentiality with small numbers of representatives.

■ It provides an opportunity to discuss and order priorities, which increases employees' sense of involvement and considerably improves effectiveness and efficiency. Discussion of major matters affecting employees in general is practically very difficult to organise on an individual basis; if there are as many opinions as employees, it does not help managers very much.

■ It enables managers to gauge the likely reaction of employees at an early stage in decision-making.

■ The quality of employee input into decision-making is improved: being involved in an ongoing dialogue means that employee representatives are more likely to develop the knowledge and expertise to make a meaningful contribution.

■ The skills of managers, as well as employee representatives, are developed in such areas as listening, diplomacy, making presentations and problem-solving.

■ Trust and cooperation should improve, thereby contributing to better understanding of the need for change, increased acceptability of decisions and improved business performance.

Disadvantages

■ Managers feel undermined in that their actions are scrutinised by employees.

■ Representatives may want to discuss sensitive issues and there is more likelihood of breaches of confidentiality.

■ Employees may try to determine the order of priorities within the organisation which may be to further their own interests, rather than those of the business.

■ More time is spent in discussion, and the decision-making process becomes longer and slower. This could result in the business missing the opportunity to gain a competitive advantage over rivals.

■ If managers do not take the input of representatives seriously, this could lead to resentment and mistrust, which could undermine attempts to improve business performance.

■ Avoiding and resolving industrial disputes

Industrial disputes arise when employers and employees or their representatives fail to reach an agreement about how to resolve an issue which has an impact on the workforce. As you have already seen in this section, workforce plans and adapting organisational structures may have a direct impact on employees, for example redundancy or changes to working conditions and practices. The aim should always be to reach agreements about the way forward, and it would be misleading to assume that either employers or employees deliberately set out to instigate industrial unrest.

Methods for avoiding industrial disputes

■ Consultation and involvement by creating channels of communication to keep employees informed and involved. This could include a staff forum or working group to collect ideas from workers, an employee consultative body to discuss major issues as they arise, regular consultation with a recognised trade union, and team or group meetings and feedback sessions.

Also important is an effective grievance procedure that has been agreed by employees or their representatives, which allows employees to voice their concerns before they develop into major disputes.

Acas, an independent statutory body, offers advice and help to prevent disputes arising in the first place. It helps employers and employees to work together to resolve problems in the workplace before they develop into disputes.

No-strike agreements between employers and unions mean that in return for an enhanced pay and working conditions, the unions agree not to take **industrial action** for a stipulated amount of time.

Methods for resolving industrial disputes

Resolution normally occurs without the need for industrial action, if those involved are prepared to explore all the options available. However, if negotiations become deadlocked, then it may be necessary to get outside help, probably from Acas.

Conciliation/mediation is an attempt by Acas negotiators to resolve disputes by helping both parties discuss their differences and reach a settlement, without recommending or imposing a settlement.

Arbitration is different from conciliation, but can be very effective. Use of Acas arbitration is voluntary, but the parties accept in advance to be bound by the arbitrator's award, made within agreed terms of reference for the arbitrator. The decision to go to arbitration may be an agreed stage in the parties' dispute resolution procedure, although this is not always the case.

Businesses can also build into employment contracts a provision for using alternative means to resolve disputes rather than through legal action. Using a less antagonistic process than the court or industrial tribunal system may allow an acceptable compromise to be reached. Larger firms of solicitors now have specialists who act as mediators under such arrangements.

Key terms

Acas: an independent and impartial organisation established to avoid and resolve industrial disputes and build harmonious relationships at work.

Industrial action: sanctions imposed by workers to put pressure on a business during an industrial dispute, including overtime ban, work to rule, go slow and ultimately strike action.

Conciliation: an independent third party encourages continued discussion between those in disagreement to reach a compromise and resolve their dispute.

Arbitration: where no agreement can be found between parties in dispute, they agree to accept the judgement of an independent third party.

Case study

British Airways

The Easter travel plans of at least 100,000 British Airways passengers face severe disruption unless conciliation talks avert strike action by the airline's pilots. BA and the British Air Line Pilots Association (BALPA) have agreed to take their dispute to a mediator after 3,000 BA pilots voted for a walk-out. Industrial action can take place any time over the next 28 days provided pilots give seven days' notice, which could disrupt Easter and threatens to overshadow preparations for the launch of Heathrow's Terminal 5 on 27 March. Strike action would ground around 100,000 BA passengers a day, when the airline is attempting to banish the tarnished reputation of its Heathrow operations by the move into Terminal 5. The latest PR blow came yesterday when baggage handling facilities at Terminal 4 broke down, forcing BA to ask thousands of passengers to leave their hold baggage at home or reschedule their flights.

AQA Examiner's tip

Do not assume that employees go on strike at the first sign of an industrial dispute. Acas can be used to settle differences between employers and individual employees, as well as groups of workers and their representatives.

The BALPA general secretary offered some hope to BA customers in a joint statement with the airline this afternoon. He said, 'The ballot result (86% voted for a strike on a 90% turnout) shows the strength of feeling of our members about the implications of the creation of OpenSkies. We have no quarrel with the travelling public and have always maintained that these issues could be resolved through negotiation rather than confrontation.'

BA's chief executive, Willie Walsh, said he was 'confident' that a settlement would be reached. He went on, 'We are proud of the professionalism and high reputation of our pilots and have never sought conflict with them.' The dispute centres on the launch of subsidiary airline OpenSkies, which BALPA fears will be used to undermine pay and conditions for all BA pilots. OpenSkies will operate flights between continental Europe and the US, but BALPA fears it will offer lower pay to its pilots, which would be retained if those staff transfer to BA's mainline operations. BA says its CityFlyer service, which operates out of London's City airport, operates under similar principles with no objections from BALPA members.

Walsh will be hoping for a swift and successful conclusion to talks after counting the cost of a cabin crew dispute last year, which was resolved at the 11th hour but too late to allow customers to reschedule their plans. The lost business cost BA an estimated £80m.

Adapted from the Guardian, *21 February 2008*

Questions

1   To what extent will good communication between employers and employees be important when a new subsidiary like OpenSkies is proposed?

2   Pilots at British Airways are represented by a trade union, BALPA. Analyse other forms of employee representation that British Airways might introduce.

3   Analyse the advantages to British Airways of using a mediator to resolve its dispute with the pilots.

4   Using all the information available:

a   Analyse the case for using a mediator to resolve the dispute between British Airways and BALPA.

b   Analyse the case for using arbitration to resolve the dispute between British Airways and BALPA.

c   Analyse the case against using a workforce plan.

5   Use online news archives (BBC, *Guardian*, *Times*, *Telegraph*, *Independent*) to investigate another recent industrial dispute.

☑ *In this chapter you will have learned to:*

- explain the importance of communication in employer–employee relations

- analyse how employers might manage communications with employees

- describe the different types of employee representation including works councils, employee groups and trade unions

- explain the methods of avoiding and resolving industrial disputes

- analyse the advantages and disadvantages of different types of employee representation

- evaluate the extent to which methods of avoiding and resolving industrial disputes are likely to be successful.

Summary questions

1 Explain the importance of communication in the relationship between employers and employees. (4 marks)

2 Why might effective internal communications be important in a business planning to move operations to a new location in the UK? (10 marks)

3 Why might improving the communication skills of employees help with overall communications within a large organisation like Tesco? (10 marks)

4 Why might a staff forum be beneficial to a business planning to introduce new technology into its manufacturing process? (6 marks)

5 Describe the methods of employee representation. (4 marks)

6 What are the advantages and disadvantages of employee representation? (10 marks)

7 Explain how industrial disputes may be avoided in a large organisation. (6 marks)

8 Analyse the benefits of using Acas to resolve industrial disputes. (10 marks)

9 To what extent are industrial disputes a sign of poor communications? (18 marks)

10 Evaluate whether or not industrial disputes can be resolved. (18 marks)

Introduction

Chapters in this section:

20 Understanding mission, aims and objectives

Find out how and why Shell has grown and changed since its foundation in 1897

Unit 4 of the AQA A Level specification is designed to be synoptic. Do not worry about this word – it just means that examination questions can lead to answers that cover the whole of the course! Clearly the BUSS4 examination paper will focus on the main themes contained in the chapters that follow, but your answers can draw upon all other information learned throughout the specification, including the AS units.

For example, if an essay question on the BUSS4 paper asks: 'Discuss the factors a business should consider when opening new markets abroad', any relevant knowledge or decision-making methods covered in the marketing sections of the specification can be included in the answer – but they will not make a complete response to the question. It would also be important, for example, to consider financial and operations management issues too.

Unit 4 looks at business in its broadest context, and brings together all the elements of the specification, including the AS units. It considers the external factors which have an impact on organisations and the strategies that can be deployed in response to changes in the business environment.

The skills you will develop throughout this unit are:

- the ability to use the concepts learned to build a logical and balanced argument
- the ability to take a holistic approach to business problem-solving, including both internal and external factors
- the ability to evaluate strategy options open to businesses managing change.

When a business grows so large that it becomes a truly global organisation, with turnover greater than the GDP of some small countries, how hard is it to maintain this position? Even when a company is apparently very powerful, it must still be aware of its business environment and changes that may occur. The need for a focus for decision-making is still important and there are plenty of examples of organisations that feel the need to reinvent themselves with a new name or image as market conditions change.

This short opening section looks at the long-term goals of business: what it is that a company ultimately wants to achieve.

Chapter 20: Understanding mission, aims and objectives

This chapter gives a general introduction to Unit 4 and the themes that will permeate all the chapters that follow. The purpose and nature of corporate objectives are discussed and linked clearly to the overarching purpose of the business as expressed in the mission statement. Stakeholder perspectives, and the influence these groups can have on corporate decision-making, are considered.

Understanding mission, aims and objectives

In this chapter you will learn to:

- understand the purpose and nature of corporate objectives

- understand the relationship between corporate strategies and corporate aims and objectives

- understand differing stakeholder perspectives and the potential for conflict

- understand the ways in which stakeholders can influence corporate decision-making.

Setting the scene

Virgin stands for value for money, quality, innovation, fun and a sense of competitive challenge

An independent research study conducted in February–April 2007 from a nationally representative survey of 2,000 adults has shown that the UK public vote Virgin as their most admired brand.

Virgin was conceived in 1970 by Sir Richard Branson, and has gone on to grow very successful businesses in sectors ranging from mobile telephones, to transportation, travel, financial services, leisure, music, holidays, publishing and retailing. Virgin has created more than 200 branded companies worldwide, employing approximately 50,000 people, in 29 countries. Revenues around the world in 2006 exceeded £10 billion.

'We deliver a quality service by empowering our employees and we facilitate and monitor customer feedback to continually improve the customer's experience through innovation. When we start a new venture, we base it on hard research and analysis. Typically, we review the industry and put ourselves in the customer's shoes to see what could make it better. We ask fundamental questions: is this an opportunity for restructuring a market and creating competitive advantage? What are the competitors doing? Is the customer confused or badly served? Is this an opportunity for building the Virgin brand? Can we add value? Will it interact with our other businesses? Is there an appropriate trade-off between risk and reward?'

Virgin.com

Discussion points

1. How does the opening statement about what Virgin stands for assist when deciding how the business should grow?

2. What strategies does Virgin use to achieve the growth of a new business venture?

3. Why is public opinion important to a company like Virgin?

4. Does the opening statement help you to work out what Virgin's long-term aims are?

Fig. 20.1 *The Virgin brand*

Key term

Corporate aims: long-term targets that will enable the business to fulfil its mission.

Corporate aims

Corporate aims are the long-term goals of a business which express the ways in which the organisation intends to develop. They are useful because they focus on the direction of the business and provide a framework within which objectives and strategies can be drawn up. The other benefit of corporate aims is that they are a point of reference against which the progress of the company can be judged: to what extent has the business achieved its aims in the last five years?

■ Mission statement

■ Key term

Mission statement: a declaration of the organisation's purpose, principle business aims, identity, policies and values.

The **mission statement** communicates the corporate aims to all the stakeholders in a business and outlines the reasons why the company exists. A good mission statement should form a link between corporate aims and corporate objectives. By stating the broad goals and purposes of the business, it should be relevant to employees who can therefore identify with the vision and values expressed in the mission statement. Other stakeholders should be able to match it to their own perceptions of the company.

■ Corporate objectives

Corporate objectives are a statement of the quantifiable goals of a business, which should enable it to achieve its long-term aims. Typical corporate objectives include profit maximisation, growth, maximum returns to shareholders, increased market share, to focus on business strengths. They are determined by a range of factors, including:

■ the culture of the organisation, i.e. the norms and values which determine the way in which the company is run, for example whether it is entrepreneurial and risk-taking or traditional and risk-averse

■ whether it is a private sector or public sector organisation. It is likely that private sector businesses will have the interests of the owners and investors at the heart of their objectives, whereas public sector organisations may be more concerned about the public in general and taxpayers in particular

the age of the business. Newly formed companies which may be the result of a merger or takeover are more likely to have survival as an objective, whereas well-established businesses may have more profit-centred objectives.

Business in action

Alliance Boots: corporate objectives

Alliance Boots' corporate objectives include growth: 'Building on the expertise, internationally recognised brands and balance sheet strength of the merged Group, our attractive pipeline of growth opportunities will be further enhanced. It will enable us to expand our retail pharmacy network and wholesale and distribution activities in existing markets as well as new geographical territories.'

AllianceBoots.com

Corporate strategies

These are the medium to long-term plans detailing how the company intends to achieve its corporate objectives. These plans will inform strategies across all functional areas, and are often based on the outcome of a SWOT analysis. **Corporate strategies** are also likely to involve a significant investment in terms of time and resources, which makes them difficult to change.

There are four main types of strategy:

- Operational strategies are designed to increase the efficiency of the business through achieving economies of scale or the best mix of capital and labour. Other options include introducing a flexible workforce, improving market research and the introduction of profit centres.
- Corporate strategies are aimed at securing the long-term future of the business through acquisitions and mergers, by forming alliances or taking part in collaborative/joint ventures.
- Generic strategies focus on gaining competitive advantage by making the most of the strengths of the business. This could lead to the disposal of peripheral parts of the company to concentrate on the core business.
- Global strategies involve establishing operations in more than one country in order to take advantage of different economic conditions. This may be to lower costs, or reduce the impact of changes in exchange rates.

There are three ways of achieving strategic development, and a company may use any combination to achieve its corporate aims and objectives:

- internal development: increasing sales and profit through the organic growth of the business. This is the safest option, but may take a long time. It is an approach that Tesco has used very successfully
- external growth: takeovers, mergers and acquisitions to develop the business. This can achieve results much more quickly and may be the preferred option for international development. However, it can be quite risky and many famous firms have encountered great difficulties with this approach

Links

For more information on corporate objectives, see Chapter 1 — Using objectives and strategies, page 2.

For more information on organisational culture, see Chapter 29 — Key influences on the change process: culture, page 244.

Key term

Corporate strategy: a plan based on the corporate aims and objectives which defines the overall scope and direction of the business by identifying its choice of business, markets and activities.

Link

For more information on SWOT analysis, see Chapter 10 — Developing and implementing marketing plans, page 75.

Activity

Look again at Setting the scene. Which type/types of strategy does the Virgin Group favour?

■ synergy: collaborating with other companies through alliances and joint ventures to achieve greater benefits than they could achieve independently.

Fig. 20.2 *The relationship between corporate aims, the mission statement, corporate objectives and corporate strategies*

Business in action

Alliance Boots: corporate strategy

To mark the formation of the 50:50 joint venture between Alliance Boots and its Chinese partner Guangzhou Pharmaceutical Company Ltd, a two-day celebratory opening ceremony was held on 26 and 27 February 2008 in Guangzhou, China. 'Our aim is to further develop our international presence in new areas and this is a significant step towards meeting our ambition of becoming a global leader,' Stefano Pessina (Executive Chairman of Alliance Boots) commented.

AllianceBoots.com

Fig. 20.3 *The main stakeholder groups having an influence on corporate objectives*

Stakeholder influences

Stakeholder groups are of growing importance to businesses. There is evidence that companies which ignore the interests of stakeholders do so at their peril (think Tesco and small farmers or Nike and child labour accusations). In the past, the shareholders were the most important stakeholder group and in many cases this is still true. However, the activities of businesses are under increasing scrutiny and they need to take the perspectives of all stakeholders into account when establishing corporate aims, objectives and strategies.

Stakeholder perspectives

Although all the groups identified in Fig. 20.3 have an interest in the business, that does not mean that their interests are the same. Each group will have its own objectives for the company:

- Shareholders will expect the business to maximise profits so that they get the best possible return on their investment.
- Managers will expect promotion opportunities, status and financial rewards.
- Employees will look for higher pay awards.
- Customers will look for value for money – low prices and high quality.
- Suppliers will expect regular and increasing purchases.
- The government will anticipate high tax revenues and legal compliance.
- Creditors will look for a healthy cash flow.
- Investors will look for a healthy balance sheet.
- Society will expect the business to demonstrate a responsible attitude to job creation, the environment and ethical issues.

Potential conflict of interest

It is easy to see why a business may find it difficult to meet the needs of all its stakeholders at the same time. For example, by maximising profits for shareholders, it may not be possible to increase pay awards to employees. Managers might believe that profits should be retained and invested in new technology or refurbishment, rather than distributed to shareholders. Similarly, the government or pressure groups may want a more expensive 'green' approach to recycling, which may have an impact on profits and upset shareholders.

In fact, there is disagreement about whether or not a business should be responsible to all its stakeholders. One school of thought suggests the sole responsibility of a company is to its shareholders as owners of the business. Any attempt to consider other stakeholders will make the business less efficient leading to job losses because the firm is unable to compete.

AQA Examiner's tip

Make sure that you are very clear about the difference between stakeholder and shareholder. It is very easy to get the terms mixed up, which may make your exam answer confused. Furthermore, do not assume that all stakeholder groups have the same amount of importance. A lot will depend on market conditions. However, it is safe to assume that in the UK, shareholders are the most powerful group in the long term.

Business in action

Mars

In 2007, the makers of Mars bars did a swift U-turn over plans to use animal products in their chocolate, to avoid a public backlash. It appears the parent company Masterfoods underestimated the UK's vegetarians and their supporters.

bbc.co.uk

Stakeholders and decision-making

As part of corporate decision-making, senior managers may consider the views of one or more of its stakeholders. In fact, it would make sense to anticipate the potential reaction of interested parties as part of the planning process so as not to be taken by surprise. We have already seen how this can be achieved internally through clear channels of communication and by establishing forums through which the views of employees can be expressed. It is more complicated to gain the views of outside stakeholders although the perspective of some groups can be easily anticipated:

- The government is likely to discourage the relocation of operations overseas because it will increase unemployment. It will support training and development initiatives to improve the skill level of UK workers, increase productivity and reduce absenteeism as they will attract inward investment to the UK.

- Customers may put pressure on a business to improve its environmental or ethical responsibility by boycotting products, thereby reducing sales.

- The relative size of the business to its suppliers and/or customers will have an impact on the amount of pressure that can be exerted, with the larger organisation normally having the most influence.

- Creditors and investors can have a significant influence on decision-making if funds are required; investors will need assurance of a good financial return and creditors will want to be paid on time.

- Society can also put pressure on business decisions through the media as well as via pressure groups. This generally refers to issues of social responsibility, such as environmental damage or unethical trading.

A business is under no obligation to take into account the views of stakeholders as long as it is operating within the law. For example, Dyson carried out its relocation plans in the face of widespread criticism and has suffered no apparent loss of popularity.

Activity

Investigate organisations that have underestimated the power of social criticism to their cost.

Links

For more information on the Dyson case, see Chapter 16 — Understanding HR objectives and strategies, page 121.

Case study

Virgin biofuels

Richard Branson's promotion of biofuels is a PR stunt and green taxes on aviation are pure opportunism according to the chief executive of British Airways. Willie Walsh warned there was no credible alternative to carbon-based fuels for airlines and insisted that taxing the industry would not help curb climate change. 'I recognise that we are a polluter. I recognise equally that we don't have an alternative to kerosene and carbon-based fuels at this point.' Asked about Branson's embrace of biofuels – last month flying a Virgin Airways 747 to Amsterdam with one of four main tanks carrying a 20 per cent mix of coconut and babassu oil – Walsh said, 'Saying there is a biofuel available is, to me, a bit of a PR stunt. I won't say biofuels are the answer because I don't believe it's true.' Walsh, who became BA chief in 2005, said the industry's target of using 10 per cent biofuel by 2017 was 'a reasonable ambition' but echoed green campaigners in questioning the implications of a widespread move to biofuel. He also criticised Gordon Brown for doubling air passenger duty (APD) when he was chancellor and failing to invest this green tax windfall in finding alternative fuel sources for aviation.

Adapted from The Guardian, *15 March 2008*

Questions

1 Analyse the relationship between corporate strategies and corporate aims and objectives at British Airways.

2 To what extent might the stakeholders of British Airways have differing perspectives about the decisions the company should make regarding fuel usage?

3 Analyse the corporate strategies British Airways could use to achieve the objective of 'using 10 per cent biofuel by 2017'.

4 Using all the information:

   a Analyse the case for the government and other external stakeholder groups influencing the decisions made by British Airways about environmental concerns.

   b Analyse the case against external stakeholder groups influencing British Airways decisions about environmental concerns.

   c Make a justified recommendation about the role government should play in deciding a company's corporate aims.

5 Discover the corporate aims, mission statement, objectives and strategies of a multinational corporation such as Nike, McDonalds, Disney or Microsoft.

☑ *In this chapter you will have learned to:*

- explain the purpose and nature of corporate objectives

- explain and analyse the relationship between corporate strategies and corporate aims and objectives

- analyse the significance of possible conflict between stakeholder groups to the decision-making of a business

- evaluate the extent to which stakeholders can influence corporate decision-making.

Summary questions

1 Explain the difference between corporate aims and corporate objectives. (4 marks)

2 What is the purpose of a mission statement? (2 marks)

3 Explain the relationship between corporate strategies and corporate objectives. (6 marks)

4 Why might customers and employees have very different perspectives about the objectives of a business? (10 marks)

5 A number of leading cosmetic brands use significant amounts of lead in their lipstick formulations. Examine the pressure that stakeholders might bring to bear on the company concerning this policy. (8 marks)

SECTION 4.2

Assessing changes in the business environment

Introduction

Chapters in this section:

Section 4.2 examines the important impact that the external environment can have on business organisations. This includes the economic condition of the country, legal and political pressures, social and technological changes and the competitive environment. It is important to be able to analyse the potential opportunities that changes in external conditions can offer a business – it is too easy just to consider the threats that they represent. Controlling a business effectively during substantial changes in the business environment requires managers to obtain and manage information and to communicate it clearly – these are continuing themes throughout this unit.

Chapter 21: The relationship between business and the economic environment

All businesses are affected by changes in the wider economy – the 'macro-economy'. Economic growth or recession, rising or falling exchange rates, higher or lower interest rates – these are just some of the economic variables that can have a dramatic impact on a business's performance and on the strategies it decides to follow. Beyond the events within just one country's economy, there are major economic developments that are changing our world forever and, with it, business opportunities and threats. Globalisation and the growing influence of the so-called emerging economies of India and China have had and will continue to have a huge effect on European businesses and the decisions that they take for the future. This chapter analyses these economic influences and considers how businesses might respond to them.

Chapter 22: The relationship between business and the political and legal environment

Government policies aim to improve the state of the macro-economy and new laws can limit various business activities. The power of modern governments is substantial and far reaching, and changes in government policies can create additional constraints on businesses *or* can create new business opportunities. Similarly, the government's involvement in international political and economic developments, such as the European Union, can have both positive and negative effects on UK businesses. This chapter provides an overview of how government decisions influence business performance and strategies.

Chapter 23: The relationship between business and the social environment

The social environment is an increasingly important factor for managers to consider when taking strategic business decisions. Should businesses accept their responsibilities towards stakeholders beyond legal limits? The significance of 'green consumerism' and ethical policies is discussed in this chapter – as well as the risks faced by firms that adopt socially responsible policies for public relations purposes.

Morgan Cars has developed a zero emissions sports car run on hydrogen in response to technical advances and increasing legal controls on traditional cars

Chapter 24: The relationship between business and the technological environment

The impact of technological change in different business situations is assessed in this chapter. The marketing opportunities it can create are analysed, together with some of the potential negative effects. There is a detailed evaluation of the response of businesses to technological change.

Chapter 25: The relationship between business and the competitive environment

The markets in which firms operate can vary greatly in terms of the degree of competitiveness with rival firms. Changes in the level of competitiveness can be caused by new entrants to the market or the integration of two of the existing businesses within it. The key issues dealt with focus on evaluating the response of businesses to these changes in the competitive environment.

The relationship between business and the economic environment

In this chapter you will learn to:

- identify the main economic factors that influence business activity

- identify and explain the key economic variables and trends in them

- assess the impact of globalisation on business activity

- evaluate developments in emerging markets

- assess the strategies businesses might deploy in response to economic changes.

Setting the scene

BMW battles against economic forces

BMW, the world's biggest maker of premium cars, is on course to meet its target of selling 1.8 million cars in 2012. Sales of all three brands owned by the German car maker, BMW, Mini and Rolls-Royce, are expected to continue growing despite dark clouds on the economic horizon. The company is concerned about three main problems:

- the large fall in the US $ exchange rate – this makes exports from German factories more expensive in the USA

- higher materials and components prices driven by more expensive oil and steel costs

- weakness of consumer spending in the USA as a result of the 2008 slowdown in GDP growth.

How is the company, which made a profit before tax of £3.0bn in 2007, battling against these economic forces?

- Firstly, it is cutting back its German-based workforce and increasing production by 60 per cent at its US factory.

- It is buying many more materials and components from US-based suppliers.

- It is expanding sales in non-US markets such as China and the UK.

- It is cutting prices paid to suppliers.

Mr Reithofer, BMW Chief Executive, is worried about the US slowdown but thinks that mass market car manufacturers will be affected most. 'A recession takes some time to hit premium car makers. Will it affect us? It depends on how deep the crisis will be,' he said, rather ominously.

Adapted from BBC Business News; news.bbc.co.uk

Discussion points

1 Explain why BMW is badly affected by a fall in the $ exchange rate.

2 How does BMW benefit by selling in many markets around the world?

3 Do you agree that 'premium car makers' might be less affected by a recession than 'mass market car producers'?

The main economic factors influencing business activity

Even the most successful and efficient business organisation is influenced by external economic factors. External economic factors can be divided into two groups: those operating within the business organisation's *market* and those operating in the whole *economy*.

Economic factors operating within the business organisation's market

These are often referred to as micro-economic factors. For example, the price of diamonds sold by a diamond mining company could be affected by:

- the prices of alternative gemstones – if these fall, then the demand for diamonds might be reduced and the price of them too
- supply problems in other diamond-producing areas – this might lead to higher prices
- reduced demand from industry for diamond-tipped drills.

Economic factors operating in the whole economy

These are often referred to as **macro-economic factors**. This chapter will focus on this second type of external economic influence on business activity.

The importance of the state of the wider economy on business strategy and business success should not be underestimated. The impact of the so-called 'credit crunch' in 2008/2009 on world economic prosperity and the reaction of governments and central banks to the threats that it posed is a good example of how all firms can be affected by economic developments beyond their control.

Our analysis of the impact of macro-economic factors on business strategies begins with a study of the trends in the most important indicators of a country's economic performance.

■ The key economic variables that influence business activity

The economic environment in which organisations operate has a very important influence on business success and failure. The state of the economy can be measured in a number of different ways – often called 'macro-economic indicators' as they measure the performance of the whole economy, not just one industry or one market. These indicators are gross domestic product, economic growth, the rate of inflation, interest rates, unemployment and exchange rates.

Gross domestic product (GDP)

Gross domestic product (GDP) represents the value of a country's national income in one year. It is usually adjusted for inflation (producing 'real GDP') – so any increase in GDP is caused by a real increase in output, not just inflation. An increase in real GDP almost always means that the population's standard of living is increasing – and this means they have more money to spend. Changes in the growth rate of GDP occur frequently. When they are recorded over time, with the inevitable ups and downs of economic activity, the pattern shown is called the **business cycle**. In the next section, we look at recent UK economic data – Fig. 21.1 shows a theoretical business cycle graph.

The four key stages are:

1 Boom: A period of very fast economic growth with rising incomes and profits. However, a boom often sows the seeds of its own destruction. Inflation rises due to very high demand for goods and services, and shortages of key skilled workers leads to high wage increases. High inflation makes this economy's goods uncompetitive and business

confidence falls as profits are hit by higher costs. The government or central bank often increases interest rates to reduce inflationary pressure. A downturn often results.

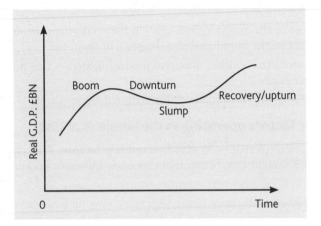

Fig. 21.1 *The business cycle*

2   Downturn leading to recession: The effect of falling demand and higher interest rates start to bite. Real GDP growth slows and may even start to fall. When GDP falls for six months or more, this is technically called a recession. Incomes and total demand for products fall and profits are much reduced – some firms will record losses and some will go out of business.

3   Slump: A very serious and prolonged downturn can lead to a slump where real GDP falls substantially and house and asset prices fall. This is much more likely to occur if the government fails to take corrective economic action. Since the great slump of the 1920s, most governments have taken the necessary action to prevent downturns becoming serious slumps.

4   Recovery: All downturns eventually lead to a recovery when real GDP starts to increase again. This is either because corrective government action starts to take effect or the rate of inflation falls so that this country's products become competitive once more and demand for them starts to increase.

Business strategies during two important phases of the business cycle

Business in action

Vodafone boss upbeat in global slump

Despite the credit crunch and the threat of global recession, Arun Sarin, the boss of Vodafone, is keen to continue expanding the range of services offered by his company's mobile phone network as well as expand the business across the world. Vodafone believe that the demand for existing and new services will not be much affected by any world economic downturn. In any case, as Mr Sarin explained, even while the US and Western Europe markets reach saturation point, there will continue to be huge opportunities in the growing economies of India and China.

Adapted from http://newsvote.bbc.co.uk

Table 21.1 *Business strategies during economic downturn or recession*

Possible business strategies	Evaluation
Close facilities as demand falls and excess capacity increases	▪ Job losses will damage employee relationships and reduce job security for staff remaining ▪ If downturn is short lived, then reducing excess capacity could result in a problem of inadequate capacity – how long will downturn last and how serious is it likely to be?
Develop new products that will appeal more to customers as their disposable incomes fall	▪ May damage the firm's reputation and brand image ▪ Not all consumers will experience a fall in their income
Lower prices to attempt to maintain sales	▪ Could lead to price wars which reduce profits for all firms in the market ▪ May damage brand image ▪ Demand may be price inelastic – revenue will fall
Buy up assets cheaply from other businesses – or even takeover whole businesses at prices much lower than during boom periods	▪ These purchases will need to be financed – this could be risky with borrowed capital ▪ No one can be sure when a downturn/recession will end
Continue with expansion plans and be best prepared for the expansion when it comes	▪ This is perhaps the bravest option of all. It might only be considered by cash-rich businesses or by those that sell products that may not be much affected by changes in consumer incomes – income inelastic products

Table 21.2 *Business strategies during economic recovery, upturn or growth*

Possible business strategies	Evaluation
Use existing capacity and increase output to meet expected increase in demand	▪ This is a low-risk strategy as no additional capital investment is required
Expansion of capacity to cope with expected increase in demand	This is a potentially risky strategy: ▪ It requires substantial capital investment – loans might have to increase ▪ How long will the recovery and growth period last for? ▪ If other firms take the same decision there is no guarantee that sales will increase for every business
Develop new products that will be in greater demand as consumer incomes rise – these are called income elastic products	▪ Research and development takes time and this investment needs to lead to new products before the recovery period ends

Economic growth

All recent UK governments have attempted to adopt policies designed to achieve **economic growth**.

Trend in UK economic growth

The UK economy achieved economic growth every year from 1992 to 2007. In 2007, real GDP rose by 3.2 per cent – the latest forecast for 2008 is for growth to nearly halve to 1.8 per cent. All economists forecast a continued recession – falling real GDP – in 2009.

Key term

Economic growth: an increase in a country's annual GDP, after adjusting for inflation. This is known as a 'real' increase in GDP.

■ Key terms

Inflation: a sustained increase in average prices of goods and services resulting in a fall in the value of money.

Retail Prices Index (RPI): the monthly record of inflation, starting from a base period = 100, calculated by recording price movements in hundreds of consumer goods and services.

Consumer Price Index (CPI): a measure of inflation based on the RPI but excluding housing costs. It is used by the Government and the Bank of England as the UK inflation target. This target is 2% annual CPI inflation.

Demand pull inflation: price rises resulting from excess demand for products allowing firms to increase profit margins.

Cost push inflation: price increases resulting from higher costs of production that are passed on to the consumers.

Interest rates: the cost of borrowing capital.

Table 21.3 *The benefits and drawbacks of economic growth to business*

Potential benefits	Potential drawbacks
■ Most consumers will have higher living standards – increasing demand for income elastic goods, e.g. foreign holidays	■ Rapid economic growth may lead to supply shortages, e.g. of resources such as labour, and this could lead to inflation caused by higher costs
■ Business investment in expansion projects is likely to be more profitable	■ If inflation rises, corrective action such as higher interest rates will have a negative impact on most businesses, especially those with high gearing ratios
■ Higher profits from increased sales and new market opportunities provide finance for expansion projects	■ Economic growth often leads to greater inequality – between regions of the country and between high/low income groups. Business strategies should respond to these changes as to assume that the benefits of growth are evenly distributed could lead to poor business decisions, e.g. trying to sell expensive products in regions benefiting little from economic growth
■ Higher chance of new business startups being successful	
■ Government tax revenue is likely to increase leading to increased spending on education, transport and health services – if these improvements are made, they will improve the competitiveness of the country's industries	

■ Activities

The economic downturn in the USA in March 2008 contributed to mixed fortunes for some of the nation's retailers. Kohl's stores that are aimed at middle-income America experienced a 15.5 per cent fall in sales compared to the previous year. Gap's sales fell by 18 per cent. But Wal-Mart, famous for mass discounting of prices, saw sales rise by 0.9 per cent. However, Target, an upmarket competitor to Wal-Mart, experienced a 4.4 per cent sales drop.

1. Why would you expect an economic downturn to reduce consumer demand?

2. Explain possible reasons why Wal-Mart saw sales increase during an economic downturn, yet other retailers' sales fell.

3. Discuss two strategies that Gap might introduce to counter the effects of the economic downturn.

The rate of inflation

Inflation is measured by recording average price rises. The term 'average' is important. For example, in 2008, UK shoe prices fell on average by 2 per cent but petrol prices rose by 15 per cent. The two most widely used measures of **inflation** are the **Retail Prices Index (RPI)** and the **Consumer Price Index (CPI)**. These both measure average price changes over a range of 600 goods and services each month. Prices rise either because there is higher demand for products than supply to meet it – **demand pull inflation** – or because firms' costs are increasing and they must increase prices to protect profit margins – **cost push inflation**.

Interest rates

The level of **interest rates** in an economy is closely linked to the rate of inflation. In general terms, the higher the rate of inflation, the higher the

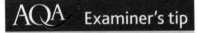

AQA Examiner's tip

Rising inflation may be a sign of a booming economy which means that businesses could more easily raise prices to increase their profit margins. Before assessing the impact of inflation on business strategy, it is important to discuss the most likely cause of the rising prices.

level of interest rates used to try to control and reduce it. Determining the appropriate level of interest rates is the responsibility, in the UK, of the Monetary Policy Committee of the Bank of England.

Table 21.4 *Evaluation of business strategies in response to higher inflation*

Strategy	Evaluation
Cut internal costs to keep price rises down	▪ This rationalisation might be painful in terms of job losses or restructuring
	▪ If improvements in productivity are made, this might come at the cost of investing in capital equipment
Source from cheaper suppliers	▪ Will the source of supplies be as reliable as existing suppliers?
	▪ Will the quality be lower – and could this be identified by consumers with a potential risk of lost reputation?
Cut profit margins by not raising prices as much as costs	▪ The impact of this strategy may depend on price elasticity of demand for the products
	▪ Lower profits may hit future investment plans
Raise profit margins if inflation is largely caused by 'demand pull' pressure – increase prices by more than cost increases	▪ The impact of this strategy may depend on price elasticity of demand for the products
	▪ Will consumers resent firms taking advantage of economic conditions?

 Activities

Cadbury Schweppes has reported a 7 per cent growth in the value of confectionery sales over the past three months. The two main reasons are the huge success of its new chewing gum brand, Trident, and the higher prices for most products. These higher prices were necessary to cover higher raw material costs caused by world inflation and the depreciation of the £ sterling exchange rate.

1. Would you classify Cadbury's decision to raise prices as being led by cost push or demand pull factors?

2. What can you say about the price elasticity of demand for Cadbury's confectionery products from the information above?

3. Would you describe the demand for confectionery products as being 'recession proof'? Explain your answer.

Fig. 21.2 *Will the demand for confectionery be much affected by rising inflation and interest rates?*

 Link

For more information on the Monetary Policy Committee of the Bank of England, see Chapter 22 — The relationship between business and the political and legal environment, page 179.

Link

For information on gearing, see Chapter 4 — Interpreting published accounts, page 22.

The cost of borrowing capital is a vital consideration for nearly all businesses, for a number of reasons:

▪ Most firms have loans or overdrafts – the cost of these increases when interest rates rise. This adds to overhead costs and reduces net profit – having most impact on highly geared firms.

▪ High interest rates will reduce the amount that many consumers will have to spend on goods and services after the monthly costs of mortgage payments and loan interest. This is called discretionary income. When consumers' discretionary incomes fall, then demand will fall for income elastic products.

▪ The £ exchange rate will tend to appreciate in value when UK interest rates are raised.

Table 21.5 *Evaluation of business strategies in response to higher interest rates*

Strategy	Evaluation
Reduce gearing ratio by selling assets	■ Will asset prices be falling during a period of high interest rates? ■ Will the assets be needed when the economy starts to grow again?
Reduce gearing ratio by raising capital from sale of shares	■ Is a period of increasing interest rates a good time to sell shares? The Stock Exchange index could be falling ■ Risk of loss of control
Offer favourable credit terms to customers, e.g. four years to pay for furniture from DFS stores	■ Only feasible for goods usually sold on credit ■ How will the business finance this credit period? It may have problems in financing these deals
Market products to appeal to customers with less disposable income	■ This may mean reducing the 'premium status' of some products and brand image could be damaged
Postpone expansion projects needing big investments	■ Opportunities for growth might be missed ■ Asset prices might be falling – good time to invest by buying land and buildings?

AQA Examiner's tip

A small change in interest rates may not be that influential on business strategy – but a series of small changes in the same direction could start to have a significant impact.

Business in action

BAA in debt crisis

When Ferrovial took over BAA in 2006, and with it the ownership of Britain's biggest airports, it borrowed £9bn. Credit was cheap and plentiful then – but things have now changed drastically. Debt is not cheap now – interest rates are higher. BAA faces a crisis in paying back the debt or arranging new loans. There are rumours that it is planning to sell off one of the airports to cut back on its huge loans.

Activities

1. Describe the apparent relationship between the recent UK trend in interest rates and inflation.

2. Analyse the potential problems for UK businesses if CPI inflation continued to rise in future months.

3. Assess the impact of lower interest rates on a rapidly expanding chain of clothes shops selling top branded products.

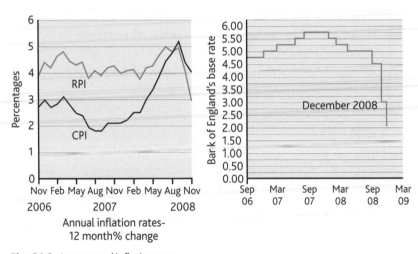

Fig. 21.3 *Interest and inflation rates*

Key terms

Unemployment: the number of people willing and able to work but unable to find employment.

Unemployment

Unemployment is measured monthly by government statisticians. It is often measured in total numbers or as a percentage of the working population. The most reliable data for unemployment is based on the internationally recognised Labour Force Survey.

There are many causes of unemployment. The three most widely recognised are **structural**, **frictional** and **cyclical** causes.

An increase in unemployment could have a double impact on business:

■ Demand for most goods will fall as average incomes will be falling with more people out of work. This might lead to rationalisation and increased redundancies.

■ There will be less pressure on employers to increase wages in line with inflation as workers will be less willing to take industrial action for fear of losing their jobs. They would find it very hard to get alternative employment.

Possible Human Resource strategies in response to falling unemployment (this was the UK trend from 2001 to 2008) include:

■ increasing provision for internal training programmes to ensure sufficient qualified workers are available as they will be difficult to recruit externally. However, this might lead to increased poaching from other firms with less effective training programmes

■ outsourcing or offshoring labour-intensive operations to low labour cost locations – low unemployment tends to drive up wage costs. However, customer service could suffer as a consequence

■ encouraging older staff to work beyond retirement – B&Q has made a real point of promoting the use of older staff in its DIY stores as being a distinct benefit to customers. However, younger staff will need to be recruited eventually!

Activities

Unemployment in the UK fell for the 17th month in a row in March 2008. The Labour Force Survey records just 5.2 per cent of the working population as being unemployed. Labour supply in many occupations is very limited especially in south-east England and in London. This is contributing to higher annual wage settlements – up 4 per cent in 12 months to April 2008. Higher inflation is also encouraging trade union leaders to demand higher rises.

1 Explain why the annual increase in wage deals is increasing.

2 Assess the possible impact of the data above on the business strategies of a low-cost airline in (a) the HR department and (b) the marketing department.

Exchange rates

The UK is a major international trading nation. UK consumers of imported goods and UK exporters of products abroad are significantly affected by changes in the £ (sterling) **exchange rate**. If the value of £1 on the foreign exchange market rises from $2 to $2.50, then this is called an **appreciation**. A decline in value, for example from £1:$2 to £1:$1.50, is called a **depreciation**.

The impact of exchange rate changes on businesses depends on many factors:

■ Is the business an importer or exporter – or both? A depreciation of £ will raise import prices but will allow exporters to lower prices.

■ If an importer, what proportion of costs is accounted for by imported goods? If the £ depreciates, then higher import prices could be very serious for a UK-based firm dependent on imported materials.

Key terms

Structural unemployment: jobs are lost as industries decline due to structural change in the economy, e.g. the decline of UK shipbuilding and clothing manufacturing industries. This unemployment tends to be very regionally concentrated.

Frictional unemployment: occurs when people take some time to find another job after losing or leaving their previous one.

Cyclical unemployment: general unemployment that occurs across many industries due to an economic downturn or recession. It is linked with periods of negative GDP growth in the business cycle.

Exchange rate: the price of one currency in terms of another, e.g. £1 = €1.5.

Exchange rate appreciation: an increase in the value of a country's currency in terms of other currencies. This lowers prices of imported goods but may force exporters to raise prices.

Exchange rate depreciation: a fall in the value of a country's currency in terms of other currencies. This raises prices of imports but may allow an exporter to reduce prices.

Link

For information on offshoring, see Chapter 14 — Operational strategies: location, page 103.

Fig. 21.4 Will an increase in unemployment help to reduce a firm's wage costs or will it reduce demand for its products – or both?

■ Is the appreciation/depreciation substantial and does it appear to be long term?

■ How price elastic is the demand for a UK exporter's products?

■ Is the exchange rate constantly fluctuating – this can be very risky and unsettling to businesses?

Business in action

Sterling's value falls to 11 year low

The £ exchange rate against the Euro has fallen to a record low. One Euro is now worth 80p – up by 8 per cent in just four months. This means that supermarkets importing French and Italian wines are having to pay more in £ terms. Combined with the 2008 budget increase in wine duty, retailers are predicting a slowdown in the long-term growth in UK consumption of wines from these EU countries.

Table 21.6 *Evaluation of business strategies in response to £ exchange rate depreciation (opposite strategies could be considered with an exchange rate appreciation)*

Strategy	Evaluation
Reduce import content of products made in UK as imports are now more expensive	■ UK suppliers may not be available ■ Quality may be inferior
Divert marketing resources to export markets – export prices will now be lower	■ Entering overseas markets is a very big strategic decision – and often very costly. It cannot be rushed into ■ Products may not suit foreign culture/consumer tastes
Consider sale of overseas assets as these will now be worth more in £ terms	■ Will these assets be needed in the future? ■ If they are sold now, and £ falls further, then potential profit has been lost
Expand operations in the UK rather than overseas operations as buying foreign assets will now be more expensive	■ Long-term overseas expansion plans should not be derailed by small changes in the exchange rate ■ Despite the depreciation, it might still be more expensive to produce In UK than overseas.

Business in action

Thomas Cook

As the value of £ fell to its lowest level ever against the Euro in April 2008, Thomas Cook starting cancelling some of its short haul European based holidays and increased the number of its package deals across the Atlantic – the $ has depreciated against the £ in recent months.

Activities

1
a In Year 1, £1 = $2. Firm A exports goods valued at £10,000 to USA. What will be the $ price?

b Firm B imports goods valued at $15,000 from the USA. How much will it pay in £s?

2
a In Year 2, £1 = $1.5. The same transactions as above take place. What will now be the $ prices of Firm A's exports?

b How much will Firm B now pay for its imports in £?

Table 21.7 *Recent trends in £ exchange rate value*

	Euro/£	U.S.$/£
Jan 2007	1.49	1.95
Jan 2008	1.37	2.02
March 2009 (forecast)	1.20	1.96

Bank of England

Bank of England

Fig. 21.5 *Recent trends in £ exchange rate value*

Activities

Refer to Table 21.7 and Fig. 21.5.

1. What happened to the value of £ against (a) the US $, and (b) the Euro between 2007 and 2008?

2. Explain the problems of these trends in the £'s exchange rate to a business buying materials from the eurozone and exporting to the USA.

3. Why might uncertainty about the exchange rate cause problems for UK importers and exporters?

Globalisation of markets

Globalisation is not a new process but it has accelerated in recent years with the rapid growth of multinational companies and with the expansion of **free trade** with fewer **tariffs** and **quotas** on imports. The key features of globalisation that have an impact on business strategy are:

- increased international trade
- growth of multinational businesses in all countries
- freer movement of workers between countries.

As with many major economic developments, globalisation creates both potential opportunities and limitations to businesses.

Evaluation of business strategies to take advantage of globalisation

- Location abroad, outsourcing and offshoring. These strategies were evaluated in Chapter 20:
- Exporting. Although offering access to huge markets abroad, exporting carries risks and costs, including:

AQA Examiner's tip

The impact of exchange rate movements can also be evaluated by considering *how much* the exchange rate has changed by – and whether the change is likely to be short or long term. If forecast to be short term, is there any justification for significant changes in business strategy?

We have assumed that all of these changes in economic conditions will occur separately. In practice, life is not that straightforward. It is quite possible for both inflation and unemployment to increase at the same time – or for depreciation of the £ to occur at the same time as an economic downturn. Managers must then weigh up which strategies are most likely to fit in with the combination of economic factors that is taking place.

Key terms

Globalisation: The growing trend towards worldwide markets in products, capital and labour, unrestricted by barriers.

Free trade: international trade that is allowed to take place without restrictions such as protectionist tariffs and quotas.

Tariffs: a tax imposed on an imported product.

Quotas: a physical limit placed on the quantity of imports of certain products.

- setting up sales teams and support networks

- transport and translation costs

- adapting products to meet local health and safety laws

- researching local market trends and consumer tastes and adapting products, or designing new ones, to satisfy these.

Table 21.8 *The pros and cons of globalisation*

Potential benefits/opportunities	Potential limitations/threats
▨ Greater opportunity for selling goods in other countries. Opening up new markets, which may not have reached saturation as the domestic market may have done, gives the chance of higher sales, economies of scale and improved profitability.	▨ Businesses from other countries now have freer access to the UK market so there will be increased competition. Wider consumer choices will drive firms that are not internationally competitive out of business.
▨ Increased competition gives firms the incentives to become more internationally competitive. 'Hiding behind' trade barriers breeds inefficiency and this will no longer be possible.	▨ The drive for international competitiveness will also be forcing other firms to become more efficient.
▨ Pan-European or pan-global marketing strategies can be used to create a global brand identity. This saves on the costs of 'different markets – different products'.	▨ Pan-European/global strategies can fail to consider the cultural and taste differences between consumers of different nations. Firms may need to 'think global but act local' – often called global localisation.
▨ Wider choice of locations – the opportunity to set up operations in other countries and become a multinational. These locations offer, usually, lower costs and direct access to local markets. Working within each country should lead to better market information.	▨ International locations can lead to significant transport and communication problems. The risk of unethical practices by managers with delegated authority thousands of miles from head office can lead to problems.
▨ Greater freedom to arrange mergers and takeovers with firms from other nations.	▨ UK businesses are now increasingly subject to foreign takeovers, e.g. Land Rover and Jaguar by Tata (India), BAA by Ferrovial (Spain).
	▨ Increasing activity from anti-globalisation pressure groups may result in bad publicity for multinationals in particular and for those firms found guilty of environmental damage in foreign countries. There is growing concern about the environmental impact of globalisation – especially in emerging economies. Coca-Cola is under pressure to limit production in some Indian states due to shortage of water supplies.
	▨ Governments will have much less influence on business decisions, e.g. preventing closure of factories to relocate in low-cost countries.

■ **Link**

For information on location abroad, outsourcing and offshoring, see Chapter 14 — Operational strategies: location, page 102.

■ Pan-European or pan-global marketing strategies: The political and cultural backlash experienced by the multinational giants of McDonald's, Coca-Cola and Starbucks in some countries indicates the danger of trying to use a 'one strategy suits all' policy. Slowly, these and other multinationals are realising the importance of developing slightly different strategies and products to suit diverse communities around the world. This is sometimes referred to as 'global localisation'.

■ International mergers and takeovers: These have potential for great success – the BMW purchase of the Mini brand and factory in Oxford being a good example. They can also be potential disasters if the companies do not realise the huge problems caused by cultural, ethical and market differences experienced when operating companies in different countries.

■ Developments in emerging markets

This definition of **emerging markets** here is fairly loose – but it is the one used by the World Bank. The main problem with it is that it 'lumps together' countries that make up about 80 per cent of the world's population but they are actually very diverse nations.

■ **Key term**

Emerging markets (economies): economies characterised by low to middle income GDP per head.

Fig. 21.6 *Will using the same marketing strategy in all countries McDonald's expands in to be a good idea?*

AQA **Examiner's tip**

Globalisation is not just about trade and multinational companies. Increased migration to and from most countries of the world is occurring. Many economists argue that increased migration of young workers from Eastern Europe is a benefit to the UK economy.

This group of countries includes the two future economic 'powerhouses' of India and China and also countries such as Ghana, Tunisia and Chile – much smaller economies with a great deal fewer resources. The key common factor is that these economies have embarked on economic development and reform programmes and have started to 'emerge' onto the global scene with, in many cases, fast-growing economies.

In the 1980s, the fastest growing economies in the world were based in south-east Asia, including Taiwan, South Korea and Malaysia. In recent years, the giant economies of Brazil, Russia, India and China have gained prominence. These are referred to as the 'BRIC' economies.

Table 21.9 *Contrasting economic growth rates in emerging economies*

Emerging economy	Average real GDP growth rate 2000–2007 (%)
Kazakhstan	10.1
China	9.6
Mozambique	8.6
Ukraine	8.0
India	7.2

Table 21.10 *Contrasting economic growth rates in four 'developed' economies over the same period*

Developed economy	Average real GDP growth rate 2000–2007 (%)
USA	2.6
UK	2.5
Sweden	2.3
France	1.6

The message is clear from Tables 21.9 and 21.10. If a business wants to take advantage of fast-growing economies, fast-growing markets and rapidly rising consumer incomes – emerging markets are the places to be.

Evaluation of strategy for expansion into emerging market economies

■ Political uncertainty and instability: Could the trouble in Tibet spill over into general civil unrest in China and risk the profitability of investment projects there? Threats of terrorist action could dissuade investors too.

■ Cyclical variations in the economy: The phases of the business cycle are more extreme in economies where governments have not yet developed the policies needed to manage GDP growth consistently.

■ Environmental and ethical issues: Lower environmental standards and legal controls in many emerging economies offer 'low cost options' for business. But could publicity of environmental damage or unethical behaviour damage a firm's global reputation? The clothing firms GAP and Primark are still struggling to rebuild their images damaged by the admission that slave and child labour has been used to make some of their products in low-income, emerging countries.

■ Legal protection for business patents, copyrights and trade names may be less effective than in developed economies.

Case study

Starbucks – an international success story or the unacceptable face of globalisation?

The phenomenal growth of Starbucks over the last 20 years has created a brand that divides people's opinions all over the globe. Consumers often embrace its ethos completely. But anti-globalisation campaigners see it as a symbol of the worst excesses of American cultural colonisation.

Eleven thousand Starbucks cafés have opened in the last 10 years. The company plans to accelerate its expansion to 40,000 outlets worldwide. Half of these will be in emerging markets such as China, India, Russia, Brazil and Egypt. Aggressive expansion in these rapidly growing economies should allow profits growth of 20–25 per cent each year over the next five years.

Apart from growth in emerging economies, two further global strategies have recently been announced. Firstly, 22 new products have been introduced in beverages alone over the last year and the company has signed a 'hot vending' joint venture with Pepsico. Starbucks intends to expand its hot food offerings in an increasing number of outlets to appeal to a wider range of customers and to keep customers in store for longer.

Secondly, in the face of increased competition in its home US market and with falling consumer incomes and confidence, it has launched the $1 (50p) cup of coffee. This is not made freshly for each customer, but is pre-brewed and kept in hot jugs. This will be offered in other countries too if it is successful.

Expansion into emerging markets has met some opposition and other problems. In Saudi Arabia, the stores have to be segregated into 'men only' and 'family' sections and the logo of a bare-chested mermaid initially had to be covered up! In China – a nation central to Starbucks' expansion plans – the café in the capital's historic Forbidden City was forced to close as it offended thousands of traditionalists who believed that this was no location for a Western business. Starbucks also had to fight for several years to prevent Chinese firms copying its logo and using a similar name. Property rights protection is not strong in China.

Despite recent setbacks in the US market, Starbucks will continue its expansion plans but doubts have been raised by protestors about the ethics of exporting US culture and selling coffee in Jakarta, for example, for the price equivalent to the average daily earnings of an Indonesian factory worker.

www.timesonline.co.uk and www.bbc.co.uk

Questions

1 Explain, using evidence from the case study:

   a globalisation

   b emerging market economies.

2 Outline two benefits to Starbucks of continuing its ambitious expansion programme in emerging market economies.

3 Analyse two problems that Starbucks may experience from continued expansion in China.

4 Evaluate the likely chances of success of the two global strategies Starbucks has introduced, referred to in the case study.

5 Using either the example of China or India, examine using internet sources the advantages and risks of a UK-owned industry setting up an operating base in one of these countries.

✔️ *In this chapter you will have learned to:*

- identify the main economic forces that affect business strategy
- define and explain gross domestic product, business cycle, interest rates, exchange rates, inflation and unemployment
- assess the impact of the main recent UK trends in these factors on business strategy
- evaluate the importance of globalisation on business strategy
- assess the importance of emerging market economies for business strategy.

Summary questions

1 Explain how the following businesses might be affected by an economic recession:

a a discount supermarket chain such as Aldi or Lidl

b an expensive restaurant. (8 marks)

2 'In 2008, annual inflation (CPI) in the UK rose to 4 per cent. This was caused by cost push factors driving prices higher.' Explain what this statement means. (6 marks)

3 Tesco's expansion in the USA is based on opening small convenience stores which are supplied both by UK producers and by US-based producers. Any profits made by these new Fresh 'n' Easy stores is remitted back to the UK. Explain how Tesco's profits from this new expansion are likely to be affected by a depreciation of the $ against the £ sterling. (6 marks)

4 Jaguar and Land Rover were sold by Ford to Tata, an Indian company, in 2008. This is a good example of increased globalisation. Will these UK manufacturers be likely to benefit from this takeover by an emerging economy company? Explain your answer. (8 marks)

5 Find out the unemployment rate in your region. How does this compare with the national UK rate? Explain whether the difference between the two rates is a benefit or a disadvantage for local businesses. (6 marks)

6 List four foreign firms with operating bases in the UK. Does the UK economy benefit from these businesses operating here? Explain your answer. (8 marks)

7 Explain how globalisation might damage the environment. (6 marks)

8 How will the growth of emerging economies be likely to affect the demand for financial services from the City of London? (6 marks)

Essay questions

9 'Globalisation creates more opportunities for UK business than threats.' To what extent do you agree with this statement? (40 marks)

10 Discuss the impact of recent changes in the UK economic environment on UK retailers and manufacturers. (40 marks)

The relationship between business and the political and legal environment

Setting the scene

In this chapter you will learn to:

- assess the effects of government intervention in the economy

- assess the effects of government economic policies on business strategy

- evaluate the impact of political decisions affecting trade and access to markets

- discuss the impact of legislation relating to business

- evaluate responses of businesses to a changing political and legal environment.

Barratt chief calls for further cuts in interest rates

The head of Barratt Developments, the UK's second largest house builder, gave a warning that the decline in the housing market would continue unless the Bank of England cut interest rates again. He revealed that sales of his own company's new homes had fallen by 14 per cent in just a few months.

The company recently had its shares pushed out of the FTSE 100 index of leading companies after its share price fell by around 60 per cent in six months. Although Barratt's pre-tax profit rose in the 12 months to December 2007 and it was able to retain more of these profits due to the cut in corporation tax, investors are worried about the prospects for the business over the next year or so. Barratts are resisting pressure to lower the prices of their new-build houses. The company, instead, is offering to pay the stamp duty tax for first-time buyers and its Dreamstart scheme allows first-time buyers to buy 100 per cent of a property for 75 per cent of the price with an interest-free loan covering the remainder.

The increase in interest rates last year combined with the credit crunch amongst the banks has stopped the housing market dead in its tracks. The ending of the housing boom, which was partly stoked up by a period of historically low interest rates, is having a wider impact on consumer spending. As house owners now feel less wealthy than during the boom, spending on clothing, footwear and other items fell slightly last month.

Nearly all of the UK's business leaders are hoping that the Monetary Policy Committee of the Bank of England will announce further reductions in the cost of borrowing.

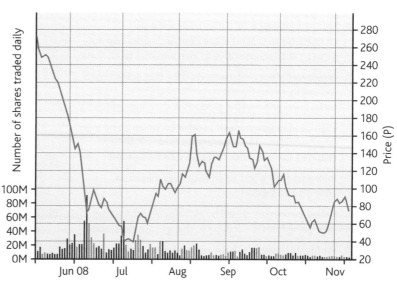

Fig. 22.1 *Barratt Developments share price chart*

Adapted from www.timesonline.co.uk

Business and

> **Discussion points**
>
> **1** Why do you think that a house builder such as Barratt Developments is greatly affected by the level of interest rates?
>
> **2** How will companies benefit from a cut in corporation tax?
>
> **3** Evaluate the likely success of the two strategies that Barratts is adopting to attract house buyers.

■ Government intervention in the economy

The UK has what is known as a 'mixed economy'. This means that the government plays a very significant role in the economy in terms of:

■ spending around 40 per cent of total GDP on important programmes such as education, health, defence, law and order and social security benefits, including pensions

■ raising a similar proportion of GDP by taxing income earners, consumers and company profits

■ owning and controlling resources such as the NHS, state schools, public corporations such as the BBC and London Transport (sometimes known as nationalised industries)

■ passing laws controlling many aspects of business activity.

Government decisions concerning these four areas is a form of **government intervention** in the economy that impacts on business strategy in major ways. Some economists argue against government

> **Key term**
>
> **Government intervention:** aims to achieve the government's objectives by controlling and supporting business, passing legislation and taking action to control the economy.

Table 22.1 *Laissez-faire versus interventionist government fiscal policies*

Laissez-faire – arguments against government financial support	Government intervention – arguments for financially supporting some industries
■ Government intervention for some industries is expensive – taxes will probably rise and this will lower consumers' living standards. Taxes on firms not receiving subsidies could rise	■ Supporting new businesses or subsidising those in trouble can increase job opportunities and reduce costs of unemployment especially in depressed regions
■ No 'level playing field' – it is unfair and anti-competitive to support some firms/industries and not others – and too expensive to give subsidies to all firms	■ Subsidies and support do not have to be long term – just enough to help a business over its most risky periods
■ Breeds inefficiency – if managers think that governments will bail them out there is no profit incentive to reduce costs, develop innovative products and increase efficiency	■ Firms can use the financial support to invest in new technology that makes them more efficient and competitive
■ Might lead to governments in other countries giving even larger subsidies – free international trade will become distorted towards those countries subsidising most	■ If subsidies are given by other governments, it might make imported goods cheaper in the UK which will benefit consumers – the EU and WTO will prevent extreme cases of government financial support
■ Businesses work best when they have minimum controls and support	■ Globalisation will lead to some business failures due to increased foreign competition – all the more reason to support other firms which could be successful in the future
■ Failing businesses caused by globalisation cannot be kept going forever – economic changes are inevitable	■ Business activity needs to be controlled but certain industries, e.g. high risk eco-energy projects or long-term investments like Airbus, will not get going unless governments provide financial support and guarantees – private investors may be discouraged from investing without this support
■ Profitable projects will always attract private investors prepared to finance it anyway	
■ Government support is like a sticking plaster – it does not solve long-term problems of poor competitiveness	

intervention on such a large scale. These **laissez-faire** economists suggest that the economy and businesses within it would be more successful without the government controlling so many resources and passing laws to govern many aspects of business life.

Laissez-faire or intervention – the debate over government support for industry

A full debate between these two economic views is beyond the scope of this book, but you should be aware of the issues. These can be examined by considering whether governments should provide financial support or subsidies to some businesses. Table 22.1 assesses the main laissez-faire and interventionist arguments on this point.

Business in action

Airbus

UK government ministers have agreed in principle a controversial state-aid package for Airbus that will allow the company to launch a new mid-sized aircraft, the A350. Britain's green light to Airbus will safeguard 10,000 high-tech jobs in the UK. Airbus has asked for £379m from Britain to launch the A350, a 250-seater aircraft which will rival the Boeing 787.

But the financial support comes at a time of government cutbacks in other areas due to the high budget deficit. Also, the US government is pursuing a case against Europe at the World Trade Organisation over alleged unfair subsidies to Airbus. Europe has responded with claims of anti-competitive support for Boeing.

Fig. 22.2 *Airbus production line*

Government economic policies

The UK government has four main economic objectives:

- continuous, stable economic growth in order to raise the population's living standards
- low inflation (CPI annual rate of 2 per cent) to maintain the value of money and reduce economic uncertainty
- low unemployment to reduce the human and economic cost of people out of work
- **balance of payments** equilibrium – over the long term, the value of imports should equal the value of exports.

Some economists add to this list:

- income and wealth redistribution
- environmental protection whilst pursuing economic growth.

The government has three main types of policies that it can use to try to achieve these objectives:

- **fiscal policy**
- **monetary policy**
- **supply side policy**.

Fiscal policy

Changes in government spending and tax levels are mainly announced in the March budget speech by the Chancellor of the Exchequer. One of

Key terms

Supply side policy: measures taken by the government to improve the efficiency of the economy (e.g. the labour market) to allow for an increase in the total supply of goods and services.

Expansionary fiscal policy: increases in government spending greater than increases in taxes, e.g. budget deficit. This increases total demand in the economy.

Links

For CPI (Consumer Price Index), see Chapter 21 — The relationship between business and the economic environment, page 164.

AQA Examiner's tip

The EU has a very complex set of rules covering what government assistance can be given to industry. Such aid usually has to be supported by an argument that without it jobs would be lost in a relatively poor region of the country. You will not be examined on these rules, but you will be expected to be able to argue for and against government financial support for some companies and some industrial projects.

the uses made of fiscal policy is to expand total demand in the economy during a downturn and contract total demand during a boom. This is called a 'counter cyclical' use of fiscal policy – trying to prevent a serious recession or an inflationary boom.

For example, during 2007 and 2008 some of the changes made included the following.

Lower basic rate of income tax

The basic rate of income tax was lowered from 22 per cent to 20 per cent. Income tax is a direct tax taken from wages, salaries and other incomes. This is an **expansionary fiscal policy** which increases total demand in the economy. This should boost economic output.

Table 22.2 *Impact on business of lowering the basic rate of income tax*

Impact on business	Evaluation
Increased consumer disposable incomes which could lead to increased demand for many goods and services.	The impact on business will depend on what is happening to interest rates and wage increases too.
Increased worker motivation as take-home pay has risen – this may encourage some workers to work overtime or to seek promotion as 'extra effort' is now rewarded with a lower tax rate.	Are workers motivated by just a 2 per cent reduction? Also, the higher rate of tax (40 per cent) was not cut and an increasing number of income earners now pay tax at this rate.

Lower corporation tax

The rate of corporation tax rate was lowered from 30 per cent to 28 per cent. (Corporation tax is on company profits.) This is an expansionary fiscal policy which should boost economic output.

Table 22.3 *Impact on business of lowering corporation tax*

Impact on business	Evaluation
Increases profits after tax: these profits could be used for paying higher dividends, increasing investment in the company from retained profits – or a bit of both!	As company profits fell in 2008 due to the impact of the credit crisis, lower corporation tax will have a limited impact in the short run.
Lower corporation tax will encourage more businesses to set up in the UK.	The corporation tax rate is still much lower in other countries such as Ireland and Poland.

Business in action

Drug maker to quit UK tax regime

Shire, one of Britain's biggest drug makers, has announced plans to move its tax base offshore. The firm's spokesman said it has applied to create a new holding company in Ireland for tax purposes. The move is set to spark a debate over Britain's level of corporation tax. The company will be paying 12.5 per cent of tax on profits instead of 28 per cent.

Higher fuel duty

Duty on fuel (petrol/diesel) was raised. These are examples of indirect taxes that are put on spending. This is a **contractionary fiscal policy** as it takes spending power out of the economy in the form of higher taxes.

Table 22.4 *Impact on business of raising fuel duty*

Impact on business	Evaluation
Higher transport costs – cost push inflation	Some firms are much more affected by road haulage costs than others
Higher inflation resulting from these tax increases may lead to demand for higher wage rises – cost push inflation	These tax increases had a small impact on inflation compared with higher costs caused by world oil and food prices and a £ depreciation that raised import prices

Higher alcohol duty

Increasing duties on beer, wine and spirits is another contractionary fiscal policy.

Table 22.5 *Impact on business of increasing alcohol duty*

Impact on business	Evaluation
Reduced spending in pubs – consumers may prefer cheaper home drinks	Demand may be price inelastic

Increased spending

Government spending on schools and universities was increased. This is an expansionary fiscal policy.

Table 22.6 *Impact on business of increasing spending on schools and universities*

Impact on business	Evaluation
Increased demand for construction company services	This occurred at the same time as the downturn in commercial property demand so some construction companies had fewer orders in 2008 than in previous years
Improvements in the quality and educational standards of the labour force should help to improve productivity for many sectors of industry	The expansion of higher education will take several years before benefits are received and there is an immediate shortage of science and engineering graduates

Increased government budget deficit

An increased government budget deficit means the government borrows more. This is an expansionary fiscal policy.

■ Business in action

Jump in public sector borrowing

The size of the government's fiscal deficit – the difference between its spending and its tax revenue – increased sharply in August 2008. Business economists accept that this deficit will help to expand the economy by pumping money into increased spending but they are

■ Key terms

Contractionary fiscal policy: increases in taxes greater than increases in government spending, e.g. budget surplus. This reduces total demand in the economy.

worried about the future. Will this mean that taxes will have to rise in the next budget to close the gap?

Table 22.7 *Impact on business of increasing government budget deficit*

Impact on business	Evaluation
This means the government is spending more in the economy than it is taking from taxes and this should increase economic growth	More government borrowing may mean interest rates have to stay higher than they would otherwise have been so that the Bank of England can finance the deficit. Also, an increased deficit will boost demand and output in the economy by raising government spending above tax revenues

Monetary policy

The Bank of England's Monetary Policy Committee (MPC) has had sole responsibility for setting interest rates since 1997. It meets monthly to fix the Bank of England's base rate. It raises interest rates when it believes there is a real risk of the UK's CPI rate of inflation rising much above 2 per cent – as the government insists that it is the MPC's job to keep annual rises in CPI between 1 per cent and 3 per cent. Clearly, if the committee feels that economic conditions mean that CPI might fall much below 2 per cent, it will lower interest rates. The data they consider includes current inflation level; unemployment rate; the £ exchange rate; levels of consumer and business confidence.

■ **Business in action**

Interest rates

The Stock Exchange index (FTSE) was boosted by the cut in interest rates by the Bank of England in April 2008. Investors in company shares are encouraged by the cut in the cost of borrowing which should help to improve consumer confidence and help to increase sales and profits of most listed companies. Some economists argue that further cuts in interest rates will be necessary before the threat of the 'credit crunch' is overcome completely.

Technically, the Bank of England does not set all interest rates. It determines only the Bank of England base rate, but most other interest rates in the economy tend to follow this key interest rate.

Impact on business of interest rate changes

An evaluation of the impact of interest rate changes could include:

■ Is the business newly formed? If so, any increase in interest rates could be very serious and reduce its chances of survival.

■ Is the business selling income elastic products? Rising interest rates reduce consumers' discretionary incomes and demand for less necessary products is likely to fall.

■ Is the business highly geared and in the middle of an expansion programme? The higher costs of loans could transform a profitable project into a potential loss maker.

■ Does the business trade abroad – either import or export? The exchange rate may be affected by interest rate changes and this could

■ Links

The impact of interest rates on business is discussed in Chapter 21 — The relationship between business and the economic environment, page 164.

change import and export prices. Higher UK interest rates will attract savings funds from abroad and this will increase the demand for the £ possibly resulting in a £ appreciation.

Supply side policies

The aim of this type of economic policy is to improve economic efficiency and increase potential for economic growth. Some of these policy actions can also be part of fiscal or monetary policy. Table 22.8 summarises supply side policies and their impact on business.

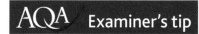

AQA Examiner's tip

It is important to evaluate the impact of interest rate changes on different businesses in different situations – it would be weak evaluation to state that all businesses will be affected equally.

Table 22.8 *Supply side policies and their possible business impacts*

Supply side policy	Possible business impact	Evaluation
Encourage new business startups to create new enterprises For example, the government financed Business Link website provides much useful advice and details of support for new business startups. New entrepreneurs formerly on state benefits receive a grant of £2,000	■ This will create more competition for existing firms ■ Successful new businesses may demand products from existing firms, increasing output and jobs	■ Any policy to assist new business start-ups will only be really successful if the whole economy is expanding and not in downturn/recession
Expand university courses to increase the proportion of the working population with specialist and flexible skills For example, UK spending on universities reached £14.2b in 2008 – and this is planned to rise by 2 per cent in real terms for several years	■ UK businesses should benefit from better qualified staff – who should be more productive ■ UK firms should be able to compete effectively in the knowledge-based global markets	■ Such policies take several years to have much impact ■ The policy of replacing student grants with loans has discouraged some from going to university ■ Other countries, e.g. China, are expanding HE provision even faster than the UK
Allow increased immigration into the UK For example, in 2007 net migration (difference between immigration and emigration) into the UK reached 240,000	■ This will increase the total labour supply available to UK firms ■ Increased labour supply helps to keep wage rises down ■ Skill shortages, e.g. building trades and IT workers, have been much reduced through immigration	■ Increased congestion caused by increased population, e.g. population rising but expenditure on transport infrastructure not keeping pace ■ Increased demand for housing can make property unaffordable for many workers in busy town and city areas
Encourage multinational investment in the UK For example, Honda's Swindon plant has been expanded with government support	■ Creates more competition for UK-based companies – may make them more efficient ■ More jobs increases incomes and this will lead to increased demand and output in the economy	■ UK-based firms might be forced out of business by competition ■ Foreign companies may use foreign managers and key workers so impact on UK job market could be limited
Reduce direct tax rates such as income tax and corporation tax See recent tax changes on pages 182–3.	■ Should encourage increased incentives for firms to invest for the future and for employees to work	■ Other countries have much lower direct tax rates than the UK so UK's relative competitiveness may not increase greatly ■ Other taxes may have to be increased to finance this policy, e.g. VAT

■ Political decisions affecting trade and access to markets

There have been two main political developments in recent decades that have transformed the UK's trading relationship with much of the rest of the world:

■ the growth of the European Union

■ the movement towards greater freedom of trade.

European Union (EU)

The UK joined this organisation in 1973. The key features of the EU that are necessary to understand its political and business significance are:

■ It is a political and economic community of 27 states (2008).

■ It traces its roots back to 1951 but the first significant union of European states was formed in 1957 with the signing of the Treaty of Rome which created the European Economic Community of just six countries.

■ The Treaty of Maastricht in 1993 established the main political ties between the states that currently exist.

■ It now has 27 member countries with a total population of 500m and accounts for 30 per cent of all world GDP. It is the largest single economic unit in the world and the largest exporter of goods and services. Despite this, the average GDP per head in the EU is around 35 per cent less than in the USA and 15 per cent less than in Japan. This difference in average living standards widened after the recent membership of countries such as Romania and Bulgaria.

Fig. 22.4 *Many economists argue that the UK economy should adopt the Euro currency*

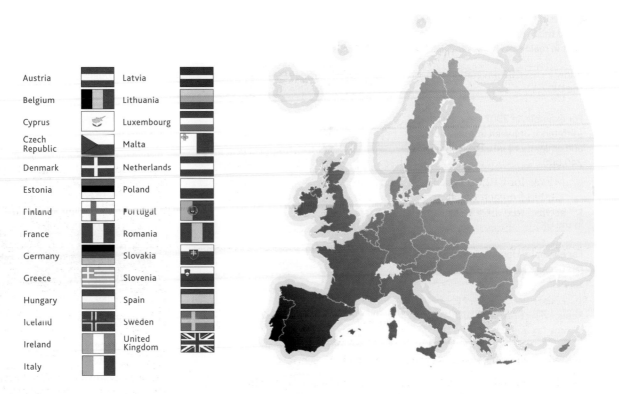

Fig. 22.5 *The EU member countries in 2009*

- There are standardised laws that apply to all member states, such as trade policy, competition policy, regional development policy, agriculture and fisheries policy. For example, EU competition policy provides for approving mergers within the EU, breaking up cartels or anti-competitive practices, ensuring free trade takes place and preventing state aid to industry.

- The EU has created a Single Market between all member states. There should be no barriers or obstacles in the movement of goods, capital, people or services. There is a Common Customs Tariff for all goods and services entering the EU.

- Fifteen EU members use the Euro which was created in 1999 as the EU's common currency – the UK decided not to join this European Monetary Union (EMU).

- Other non-member countries are keen to apply for membership of the EU, such as Turkey and Ukraine, and this would further increase the size and complexity of the administration required to run the EU.

- There are several important EU institutions that govern and control its workings. The two main ones are the European Commission, the executive and law initiating body, and the European Parliament which has elected representatives from all member states who vote on new laws.

Impact on UK business of two possible future developments

UK adopting the Euro

By adopting the Euro, the UK would join the eurozone by becoming a member of the European Monetary Union.

Business in action

Nissan head threatens to pull out of UK

The head of Nissan in the UK has joined the debate over the UK membership of the Euro. He is worried that further investment at the firm's huge Sunderland plant could be at risk unless the UK joins the Euro.

Nissan believes the Euro would cut out risks of £ exchange rates changing when it is importing components from the eurozone and when exporting cars there. For example, if the company sold 100 Micras for €12,000 each to a French importer, it would receive £8,000 for each car at an exchange rate of £1:€1.50. But if the £ appreciated after the contract was signed, but before the cars were paid for, Nissan would receive fewer £s for each car.

Fig. 22.6 *Nissan Micra cars are manufactured in the UK for export around the world – a depreciation of the £ would make imported parts more expensive but Nissan would be able to reduce export prices*

Activities

Read Business in action: Nissan head threatens to pull out of UK.

1. If the exchange rate for the £ depreciated to £1:€1.2, how much would Nissan receive for each car sold to the French importer?

2. What would happen to Nissan's profits from this contract?

3. Give a numerical example of how Nissan could lose out from the purchase of components from the eurozone if the £ sterling depreciated during the contract period.

Table 22.9 *Potential impacts of the UK adopting the Euro*

Possible benefits to UK business	Possible limitations to UK business
■ A reduction in transaction costs when buying or selling in the eurozone – it is expensive to change currencies when trading abroad	■ Initial one-off conversion costs – accounting systems, tills, catalogues, display material and price lists will all need to be converted into Euros. This has been estimated at between £12bn and £15bn
■ Reduced uncertainty caused by exchange rate movements when buying or selling within the eurozone – see Business in action: Nissan head threatens to pull out of UK	■ Transparent prices throughout the eurozone – as UK firms will now have to price products in Euros, they must be competitive with the best firms in the area. They cannot 'hide behind' a pricing system that is influenced by the £ exchange rate and claim that this is causing them to be uncompetitive
■ Transparent prices from eurozone suppliers – as all goods and services traded within the eurozone will be priced in just one currency, it will be easy to see which is providing the best value	■ The key factor may be the £:€ exchange rate at which the UK joins the eurozone. In 2007, this averaged £1:€1.48 which most economists believed was too high and made UK products uncompetitive. In contrast, by 2008, it had fallen to £1:€1.20
■ Increased trade and capital movements. Using a common currency and the increased ease of money transfers will encourage trade in products and investments between the UK and the eurozone	■ Eurozone interest rates are set by the European Central Bank. This bank would consider UK economic conditions if the UK adopted the Euro – but also the economic conditions in other EU countries. Losing Bank of England independence means interest rates may now be set too high or too low for UK business conditions
■ Multinationals who are discouraged from investing in the UK while the £ still exists may be willing to set up operations after UK membership	

Table 22.10 *Potential impact on the UK of further EU expansion*

Potential benefits to UK business	Potential limitations to UK business
■ Huge new markets accessible to UK firms without any barriers to trade – these economies have great potential for growth with many consumer markets not at maturity, unlike in the UK. The potential for economies of scale through increased sales will exist	■ Low cost imports from new member countries may drive UK suppliers out of business
■ Potential for easier mergers and takeovers of businesses in these economies	■ Eastern European countries may experience more political and economic instability than in the more developed countries of the existing EU
■ Easier and cheaper to outsource business operations to countries with relatively low wage, but well qualified, workforces. Using cheaper EU suppliers will help to keep UK businesses competitive	■ Many of the potential new member states have relatively low GDP per head so they will contribute little to EU funds but will be eligible for large payouts. This will increase the EU funding costs and taxes may have to rise in existing member countries to pay for this. Grants to existing member states are likely to be cut
■ Immigration of workers from new member countries will boost the UK labour force, increase supply of labour for some skills and help to keep down wage rates and wage costs in the UK	■ EU decision-making and law-making will be slowed by the increase in numbers of countries to consult and views to consider

Expansion of the EU by allowing other countries to join

Table 22.10 summarises the possible impact on UK business if existing non-member countries, such as Turkey, are successful in their applications to join the EU.

World Trade Organisation and the pressure for free international trade

This international body was set up in 1995 with the aim of promoting free trade between member nations and reducing **protectionism**. The importance of the WTO is based on the increase in world trade that results from its agreements between member states. This increase in trade – a feature of globalisation – raises world prosperity, but not necessarily evenly around the globe. Without WTO agreements to remove protectionist barriers, the world would probably divide into competing trading blocks with huge trade barriers between them. This would reduce trade, output and employment and possibly result in worldwide recession.

The work of the WTO is, in many ways, a 'double-edged sword' for UK businesses. On the one hand, it means that UK firms can increasingly compete in export markets on equal terms with locally based firms. On the other hand, UK markets are more open to imports from highly competitive world producers than ever before and UK firms must become competitive with them or be forced out of business.

■ Business in action

Chinese trade surplus hits new records

Bad news for European firms struggling to compete in industries dominated by Chinese companies such as clothing, footwear and electronics. The Chinese value of exports rose by 33 per cent in the year to January 2008 and the trade surplus reached a record level of $15.9 billion in that month alone.

Fig. 22.7 *Chinese exports heading for Europe – these have caused many traditional European industries such as clothing and footwear to cut output and jobs*

■ The impact of legislation relating to businesses

Business activity in the UK is constrained by many laws, but, by being seen to implement these laws fully and perhaps by exceeding the statutory requirements, a business can create opportunities too. The main categories of laws that affect business are employment (including health and safety), consumer protection, planning, environmental protection and competition.

Employment (including health and safety)

Examples of legislation include:

■ Disability Discrimination Act 1994: Employers may not treat a disabled person less favourably than other people without due reason, for example in the requirements of the job.

■ Minimum Wage Act 1998: No worker in the UK may be paid less than a fixed wage rate per hour (£5.80 in April 2008, with lower rates for workers aged less than 21).

■ Employment Relations Act 2000: A trade union with membership over 50 per cent of a firm's employees can demand union recognition and collective bargaining.

■ Health and Safety at Work Act 1974: This has many provisions including providing and maintaining safety equipment and safe systems of work.

Activities

Read the 'Ryanair risks big fine over adverts' Business in action.

1 Why does the government believe that consumers need protection from this kind of practice?

2 Assess the likely short term impact on Ryanair's sales of this form of advertising.

3 Evaluate the long term impact on firms of being found guilty of breaking consumer protection laws.

Link

Competition policy is discussed in Chapter 25 — The relationship between business and the competitive environment, page 209.

AQA Examiner's tip

No questions will be set by AQA that require a detailed knowledge of specific laws. Instead, a broad understanding of the scope of the main laws and their business impact is all that is required.

Consumer protection

Examples include:

- Sale of Goods Act 1979: Three main conditions: goods must be of 'merchantable quality' (i.e. with no obvious flaws or problems), be fit for the purpose they are sold for and must be as described by the seller.
- Consumer Protection Act 1987: Brought UK law into line with that of the EU. In order to satisfy the conditions of the Single Market, the whole of consumer protection is increasingly run by EU law not UK law.

Business in action

Ryanair risks big fine over adverts

Ryanair is facing prosecution and a substantial fine for repeatedly misleading passengers about the availability of its cheapest fares. Ryanair had, it was claimed, advertised prices that did not include taxes and charges and had failed to make clear 'significant restrictions that would exclude customers from taking advantage of the lowest prices'.

■ Planning

The Town and Country Planning Acts 1947 and 1990, for example, place restrictions on industrial and residential developments in all rural and urban areas. A lengthy planning permission procedure has to be followed.

Environmental protection

For example, the Environmental Protection Act 1990 sets out strict rules on emissions into the air, sea and rivers, with a system of inspection and heavy fines on businesses that exceed certain emission limits.

Competition

One example of legislation related to competition is the Enterprise Act 2002.

We could devote many pages to all of the important UK and EU laws that govern and limit business activity. This, you will be pleased to hear, is not the point of Business Studies A Level. Managers employ lawyers to give them clear guidance of all the latest legal changes from either Westminster or Brussels. This book adopts the view that detailed legal knowledge is *not required*. The focus is on *why* government has passed these laws and *what* the impact on business strategy might be as a result of them.

■ Why are there laws that constrain business?

There are a number of reasons:

- to prevent exploitation of employees by powerful businesses: The traditional view is that managers will always pay the lowest possible wages and offer the worst conditions that workers can be found to work in. Even if this is not really true for many businesses today, the government lays down strict minimum standards of working conditions and pay levels so that workers in vulnerable jobs, for example unskilled, and with little bargaining power or those doing dangerous work, can avoid being taken advantage of by profit-maximising businesses

- to improve industrial relations in the UK by making trade unions take key steps before calling strike action (for example, a secret ballot of all members): This area of employment law was thought necessary after the UK recorded some of the worst records of strike action in Europe in the 1970s and 1980s

- to prevent exploitation of consumers: Goods and services are becoming increasingly complex and consumers cannot be expected to understand everything that they buy. Consumers are also buying so much more than before due to higher incomes that the need for protection is greater. Also, society is much less willing to tolerate the 'buyer beware' principle – today's attitude is much more that, if something goes wrong with the product or service, it must be the supplier's/producer's fault

- to protect the natural environment from pressures of urban sprawl, industrial development and industrial processes that can do great damage to air and water quality: Increasing concern about global warming is putting pressure on both the UK and EU lawmakers to introduce stricter regulations on air pollution from industry located in EU member states.

Negative impact on business of legal controls

- Cost: All of the laws referred to will lead to increased costs for business. These costs arise from two main sources:
  - administration or 'red tape' costs in ensuring standards are recorded and monitored
  - compliance costs from meeting the provisions of the Acts, for example higher wage costs, higher safety maintenance costs, higher product replacement costs under consumer protection laws, higher emission control equipment costs.

- Unfair advantage: Many countries outside of the EU do not have the same level or complexity of legislation covering business activities. This could give businesses operating in these countries an unfair cost advantage.

- Restrictions: These make it more difficult to do business, for example planning laws and red tape.

- Product designs may have to be adapted to meet new rules and regulations, for example on consumer safety requirements for new toys.

> ## AQA Examiner's tip
>
> When asked about the impact of legal controls on business, a good form of evaluation is to assess the cost of meeting the legal requirements against the benefits to the business of fully meeting its legal obligations.

Business in action

Chinese applications take less time

James Dyson, head of Dyson consumer products business, commented that in 16 weeks, the Chinese firm that bought out Rover cars, had managed to obtain planning permission, build a factory and start production of cars. His own planning application for a factory in the west of England took 16 weeks to be considered by the local council.

Positive impact on business of legal controls

- Legislation ensures that workers are paid at least a minimum wage and this could increase work incentives for low-paid workers.
- Improved health and safety at work reduces accidents and days lost

through injury and increases the chances of workers being able to satisfy their 'security' needs.

■ Reduced UK strike record and improved industrial relations have helped to reduce disruption and increase productivity in UK businesses.

■ Planning and environmental controls have prevented large-scale destructions of the countryside and the environment which makes the UK a more attractive destination for tourists and multinational businesses wishing to invest in the economy.

■ Consumer confidence about products and services and their quality has increased and this encourages consumers to spend – especially on complex and technical goods.

■ Accepting EU laws has put UK business on a 'level playing field' with the rest of the EU. All EU countries should observe the same laws on consumer protection, workforce safety and environmental controls so no business should, within the EU, be able to gain an unfair competitive advantage by operating more cheaply with less strict legal controls.

Legal controls: final evaluation

Businesses could adopt several strategies in response to tighter legal controls. Here are two:

■ Introduce them in advance of the legal changes or even make sure that the business exceeds the minimum standards laid down. For example, offer extended guarantee periods, increase workers' wages by more than the annual percentage for the minimum wage, offer health and safety measures above the legal requirements, reduce pollution below levels set by the law. Potential gains include:

  – easier to recruit the best qualified staff, low labour turnover

  – good publicity

  – marketing advantages – consumers more assured to buy from this business

  – much less chance of breaching the law and incurring fines.

■ Locate abroad, for example, in developing countries where legal restrictions are less and, as a result, costs of production are lower. Potential drawbacks include:

  – may be viewed as being unethical – taking advantage of poor countries and poor workers to drive down business costs

  – consumer resistance to purchasing products sourced in this way – but how sensitive are consumers to this issue?

  – there may be consumer health issues if food products are processed or electrical products made in countries with low legal requirements.

Case study

UK economic policy achieves 15 years of economic growth

The recent performance of the UK economy has been remarkable – and only the downturn caused by the banking problems in 2008 seem likely to spoil the record of success. Inflation, controlled by monetary policy, has only once exceeded 3 per cent (CPI) since 1997. This has been achieved, though, with quite regular variations in the level of interest rates. Economic growth, measured by real GDP, has averaged 2.5 per cent over this period – faster than the other big economies of the EU. Unemployment, as a proportion of the working population, is amongst the lowest in the developed world. The top rate of income tax is only 40 per cent – lower than many other EU economies although the corporation tax rate is still not very competitive.

The government still aims to double the provision of university places in coming years to achieve its goal of 50 per cent of the school leaving population having access to higher qualifications. Trade union reforms, brought about by collective employment laws, have led to low strike rates and much better and more cooperative relations between unions and bosses.

Problems are now appearing, however. The government's ambitious fiscal policy spending plans and the recent cut in VAT have created a huge budget deficit. The squeeze on inflation has left UK interest rates higher than in the USA and unemployment has started to increase rapidly due to the recession. The 25 per cent depreciation of the £ against the Euro that occurred during 2008 causes much uncertainty in large parts of UK industry. Above all, the true long term risks of the credit crunch and the shortage of bank lending to consumers are still to be revealed.

Questions

1 Explain the difference between fiscal policy and monetary policy.

2 Outline the impact a lower rate of corporation tax could have on UK businesses.

3 Analyse the likely impact of frequent changes in the level of UK interest rates on either the car retailing industry or the consumer electronics industry.

4 Discuss whether UK industry would benefit from the UK adopting the Euro currency this year.

5 Find out all of the 'discrimination laws' that exist to protect employees in the UK. Assess the potential costs and benefits of a firm meeting all of these legal obligations.

☑ *In this chapter you will have learned to:*

- assess the reasons for governments intervening in the economy
- outline the government's main economic objectives
- discuss the potential impact on businesses and business strategy of changes in fiscal, monetary and supply side policies
- assess the reasons for government legal intervention in business activities
- evaluate the impact of laws on businesses and consider both the opportunities and constraints that they represent.

Summary questions

1 How might businesses benefit from the government achieving:

 a higher economic growth

 b lower inflation? (8 marks)

2 Select one UK business that is likely to be greatly affected by an increase in UK interest rates and explain one strategy it could adopt to reduce this impact. (6 marks)

3 Outline how a large employer of labour in the UK such as the Post Office, might be affected by:

 a an increase in the minimum wage rate

 b a reduction in income tax rates. (6 marks)

4 Outline how a government might use fiscal policy to increase the level of demand and output in the UK. (8 marks)

5 What would be the potential costs and benefits to a restaurant of encouraging the local press to view the health, safety and cleanliness of its kitchen which exceed minimum legal standards? (8 marks)

6 Are all UK businesses likely to benefit from supply side policies? Explain your answer. (8 marks)

7 Would all UK businesses be at a competitive disadvantage if the UK government introduced the toughest anti-pollution laws in the world? Explain your answer. (6 marks)

8 How might a UK petrol company respond to higher taxes on fuel imposed by the government? (6 marks)

9 Do you think the government should pass more laws to control business activity? If so, why and which laws would you suggest? (10 marks)

10 Would a UK business such as Rolls-Royce aero engines benefit or lose from fewer restrictions on international trade? (8 marks)

Essays

11 'Recent government intervention in the economy has created more opportunities than constraints for UK businesses.'
To what extent do you agree with this statement? (40 marks)

12 Discuss the likely impact on the success of UK businesses of UK membership of the eurozone (adopting the Euro currency). (40 marks)

The relationship between business and the social environment

  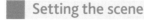

In this chapter you will learn to:

- understand the changing nature of the social environment

- understand the changing nature of the ethical environment

- assess the effects of changes in the social environment on businesses

- assess the effects of changes in the ethical environment on businesses

- evaluate the responses of businesses to changes in their social and ethical environment.

Fig. 23.1 *It's not easy being green!*

Key term

Social environment: the environmental factors that influence business behaviour including the characteristics of the population and natural environment in which it exists.

Setting the scene

Claiming to be green might be easy – being green is not

Since Kermit the frog sang about the hardship of being green in the 1970s, the term has become universal. Some of the most polluting industries are amongst the loudest to vaunt their 'green' credentials. Energy firm Edf, for example, is running a nostalgia-laden advertisement that starts with the song, 'It's not easy being green' originally trilled by Kermit. Retailers, from Carphone Warehouse, with its 'green' mobile phone charger, to political parties such as the Conservative Party, with its motto 'Vote Blue to go Green', all claim to be green. High-street firms, especially supermarkets, have jumped on the bandwagon.

Mike Childs, head of campaigns at Friends of the Earth, says being green is hard for any company, 'because mass retailing is based on consumption'. But he underlines an inherent challenge, 'We haven't a hope in hell in tackling climate change unless business is part of solution.' Outside the UK, there are signs of a shift, which recognises the inherent challenge facing firms. Norway, for example, has forbidden terms including 'green', 'environmentally-friendly', 'clean', and 'natural' in car adverts on the grounds that no vehicle is actively beneficial for the environment. Ogilvy's Mr Sutherland argues that we are quick to blame firms but they rely on consumers spending. 'Consumers will buy Ecover washing-up liquid or recycled loo roll, then fly to Latin America for a holiday – clearly the former doesn't begin to justify the latter as far as the environment is concerned.'

news.bbc.co.uk

Discussion points

1. To what extent do you believe it is possible for businesses behave in a 'green' manner? Justify your answer.

2. In what ways have supermarkets 'jumped on the bandwagon'?

3. Do you think it is the responsibility of large firms to behave in an environmentally-friendly manner?

4. Should the government intervene to enforce firms to meet strict environmental targets?

5. Is there a conflict between environmental friendliness and consumerism? Explain your answer.

The social and ethical environment

Businesses need not only react to forces from within the organisation, but also a host of external factors including the **social environment** in which they operate. The social environment is influenced by the make-up of society, i.e. the demographics of the population and the behaviour

■ **Activity**

1 How do you think society has changed in the last 10, 20 or 30 years?

2 How has the make-up of society changed?

3 How have attitudes within society changed?

4 How have businesses tried to respond to these changes?

and attitudes of society. When looking at the behaviour and attitudes of society, we are going to consider it from the angles of environmental concerns and a broader perspective of ethical behaviour.

Impact of changes in the social environment

In order to respond effectively to the social environment, it is necessary to understand and respond to changes in both the human and non-human aspects of it. How we behave, our relationships, our gender, religion and ethnic group, our education and work, the conditions and communities we live in, and our attitude towards ourselves and others are all part of our social environment.

Demographic factors

Demographics refer to the characteristics of the population and key factors influencing these characteristics. Demographic factors which define the communities in which we live and, therefore, in which businesses operate are determined by factors such as births, deaths, migration and relationships. The government, through the census, collates and publishes statistics about the population. Some of the key features of the UK population as of mid-2006 were:

■ The resident population was 60,587,000.

■ Eighty-three per cent lived in England, compared to 4.9 per cent in Wales, 8.4 per cent in Scotland and 2.9 per cent in Northern Ireland.

■ The average age was 39.0 years, an increase from 34.1 years in 1971.

■ One in 5 people were under 16.

■ One in 6 people were over 65.

■ Every year since 1901 (except 1976), there have been more births than deaths (natural change).

■ The growing population was as a result of natural change and net international migration (see Fig. 23.2).

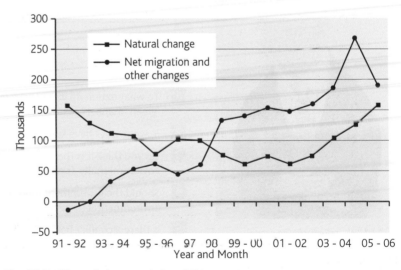

Fig. 23.2 *UK population growth since 1991*
www.statistics.gov.uk

■ **Activity**

How would the characteristics and trends given for the UK in mid-2006 affect decision-making within the following businesses/organisations?

■ A large house builder, such as Barratts or Persimmon

■ Supermarkets

■ NHS

■ Schools

■ A national newspaper

Environmental issues

Businesses have an impact on the environment in which they operate and increasingly are becoming aware of their responsibility towards trying to reduce any negative impact they have on society. Equally, businesses are seeing an expanding market for environmentally friendly products as society as a whole becomes more aware. Environmental issues are wide reaching and across the globe cover concerns such as:

- slumping urban air quality and increasingly intensive droughts
- food miles and carbon footprint
- use of non-sustainable resources
- global warming.

As society as a whole becomes increasingly aware of, and concerned about, these issues, there is increasing pressure for business leaders, governments and environmentalists to work together.

Many large organisations carry out an environmental (or green) audit in order to assess their own performance and identify areas for improvement. This allows businesses to set targets and measure their performance against them. This is reported in a business's **Corporate Social Responsibility (CSR)** Report.

Fig. 23.3 *Green issues are a major responsibility for businesses*

Key term

Corporate Social Responsibility (CSR): a firm's decision to accept responsibility for its social, environmental and ethical actions, often reported through a CSR report.

Business in action

Marks & Spencer: How We Do Business – The Five Pillars

Marks & Spencer, like many other high street retailers, has set itself some challenging environmental and ethical targets to meet by 2012. Below is the introduction to their Corporate Social Responsibility Report, How We Do Business:

> The five pillars represent the five key areas where we believe we can make our business both more sustainable and kinder to the environment. These five areas are: Climate Change, Waste, Sustainable Raw Materials, Health and being a Fair Partner.
>
> Each pillar has its own goal. By 2012 we aim to:
> - become carbon neutral
> - send no waste to landfill
> - extend sustainable sourcing
> - help improve the lives of people in our supply chain
> - help customers and employees live a healthier lifestyle.

plana.marksandspencer.com

Although many larger businesses accept their responsibilities towards environmental issues, there are other occasions where either the government or pressure groups are the driving force behind changing business behaviour. In March 2006, the UK government warned that it would force retailers to charge for plastic carrier bags unless the number of free bags they issued was drastically reduced. *The Grocer* magazine carried out a poll to gauge retailers' reactions to this government warning.

1 What are the advantages to the government of businesses accepting responsibility for environmental issues?

2 What are the advantages to society of businesses accepting responsibility for environmental issues?

3 What are the advantages to businesses of businesses accepting responsibility for environmental issues?

4 Do you think the government is correct to intervene in environmental issues? Justify your answer.

■ **Activity**

Analyse how businesses may alter aspects of their marketing in order to respond to different shopper types. Refer to Table 23.2.

■ **Key terms**

Ethical environment: the moral beliefs and attitudes from both inside and outside a business that influence its behaviour.

Public relations (PR): actions taken by business to help achieve a positive relationship with its stakeholders.

AQA Examiner's tip

Take care in the examination not to confuse ethical actions with legal requirements.

The results are shown in Table 23.1.

Table 23.1 *Retailers' reactions to government warning on charging for plastic carrier bags*

Question	Yes	No
Do you agree with the government's plans to introduce a charge for plastic carrier bags in 2009?	62%	38%
Have you made any efforts to reduce carrier bag usage in your stores?	91%	9%
Do you intend to introduce initiatives to reduce carrier bag usage this year?	86%	14%
Do you think independent retailers have a part to play in reducing carrier bag usage?	91%	9%

The Grocer, *29 March 2008; phone and email poll*

Impact of changes in the ethical environment

Ethics refers to a general code of what is deemed to be morally right or wrong. Businesses have to decide on how big a role ethics will play in their decision-making. Ethical behaviour is thought to be the correct course of action, but it is not legally binding, hence the scope for choice. Businesses may often be faced with an ethical dilemma when the morally correct action may not be the most cost-effective action. The **ethical environment** defines the ethical issues and considerations a business faces as well as the views, attitudes and behaviours of its target market. Ethical issues include:

■ animal welfare, for example testing on animals, battery farms

■ importing of products or manufacturing abroad, for example labour conditions, impact on UK economy

■ nature of the product, for example tobacco and alcohol

■ advertising, for example pester power, high-fat products.

Many large businesses include an ethical audit as part of their Corporate Social Responsibility (CSR) report. More cynical consumers and critics accuse large organisations of using their environmental and ethical stances as a marketing tool, or as a **public relations** exercise to gain the approval of stakeholders and a means to higher profit margins, rather than adopting such policies because of a genuine belief in or desire to do good.

■ **Business in action**

Ethical attitudes among consumers

It is of benefit to business to understand the ethical stance of their consumer. According to research into shoppers' behaviour, they can be split into five distinct groups as shown in Table 23.2.

Table 23.2 *Ethical attitudes among consumers*

Shopper type	Characteristics
Conscience Casuals	They show little or no interest in ethical shopping.
Blinkered Believers	Their concern is focused on a single ethical issue.

Shopper type	Characteristics
Aspiring Activists	They express an interest in many ethical areas but will not go out of their way to shop ethically.
Focused Followers	They do shop ethically but pick and choose their areas of interest.
Ethical Evangelists	The most dedicated – will buy ethically whatever the cost and across a broad range of products.

The Grocer, *March 2008*

Case study

Lush – an ethical brand?

Lush are against animal testing, use very little packaging and 70 per cent of their ingredients are vegan. Some may see these as glowing credentials, but founder Mark Constantine refuses for it to be labelled as a purely ethical brand. In an interview with *The Grocer* magazine, he says:

'I can tell you about the organic ingredients or not. I can tell you about the unpackaged bits or not. I don't think anyone should buy a cosmetic because its unpackaged, I think they should buy it because it's effective and good value for money.'

He explains that although, yes, they are an ethical brand, if people were no longer interested in hearing about ethics Lush would stop telling you about it, but would not stop being an ethical brand.

The Grocer, *March 2008*

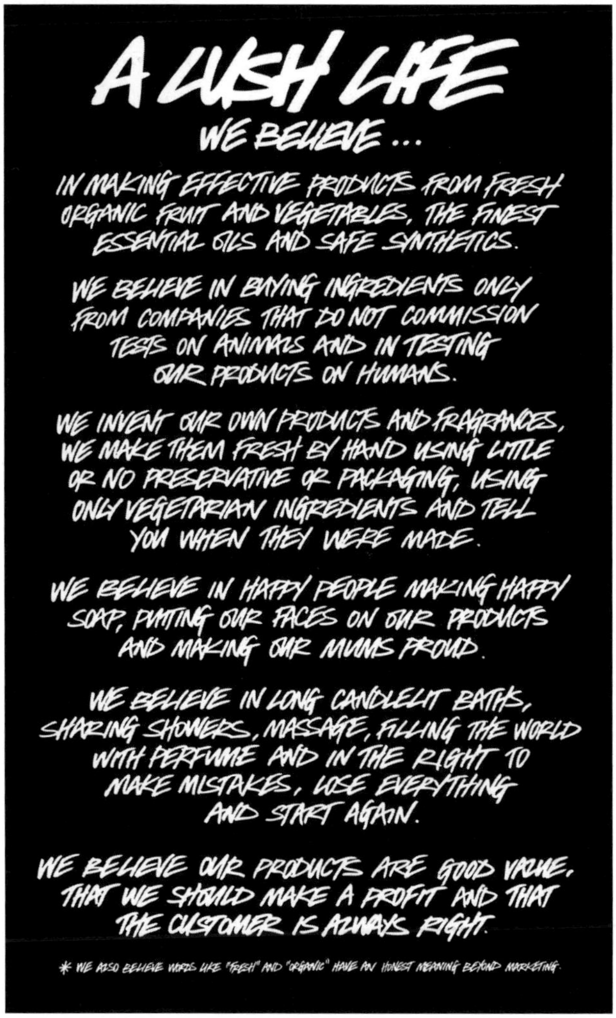

Questions

1. In the context of Lush, what do you understand by the term 'ethical brand'?

2. Analyse the impact of the social and ethical environment on firms such as Lush and other manufacturers and retailers in the cosmetic industry.

3. To what extent do you think Lush's ethics are key to their success?

Fig. 23.4 *The Lush mission statement*

✅ *In this chapter you will have learned to:*

- understand the changing nature of the social environment
- understand the changing nature of the ethical environment
- assess the effects of changes in the social environment on businesses
- assess the effects of changes in the ethical environment on businesses
- evaluate the responses of businesses to changes in their social and ethical environment.

Summary questions

1 What is meant by the term 'social responsibility'? (3 marks)

2 Explain one social responsibility a fast-food outlet such as McDonalds or Burger King has towards each of the following:

a employees

b customers

c the local community

d suppliers. (12 marks)

3 Explain two advantages to a firm of accepting its social responsibility. (8 marks)

4 What is meant by the term 'business ethics'? (3 marks)

5 Identify one business you believe to behave ethically and explain its ethical behaviour. (6 marks)

6 Identify one business you believe not to behave ethically and explain its unethical behaviour. (6 marks)

7 How might firms use their ethical or environmental credentials as a PR exercise? (10 marks)

24 | The relationship between business and the technological environment

In this chapter you will learn to:

- analyse the nature and scope of technological change on business

- assess the effects of technological change on business

- evaluate the strategies that business might adopt in response to technological change.

PhotoBox – the opportunities and threats of technological change

Some companies only exist as a result of technological change. PhotoBox is one. Without the digital revolution in cameras, the business would simply just not exist. Although they had always been interested in photography, PhotoBox founders were driven by what could be achieved by the rapid developments in technology. They saw a gap in the UK market for developing customers' digital images and were surprised that no other business was offering the same service. While the core business of printing pictures is fairly standard, PhotoBox has used technology to offer advanced customer services:

- computer software keeps track of orders and monitors quality

- customers' pictures can be stored on the PhotoBox website so friends can see what you are up to

- pictures can be printed and despatched quickly or put on calendars, key rings and so on

- cameras and accessories can be purchased online.

Technology can create its own problems too:

- Cheaper computers, photoprinters and websites allow easy access to new rivals entering the market and improvements in home inkjet printers allow more people to develop their own pictures.

- In addition, just having a website and some products to sell does not guarantee success. Why did Tesco recently close its internet e-commerce clothing business?

- Just using the new technology may not effectively compete with the likes of ASOS who, as well as using the latest technology, developed a marketing proposition of products, prices and delivery reliability that has the customers flocking to them.

news.bbc.co.uk

Discussion points

1. Is the future success of PhotoBox guaranteed now that it uses the latest technology?

2. Kodak came late to the digital revolution in cameras and processing. What drawbacks may it have experienced as a result of this?

3. How could a business try to assess whether adopting a new technology will be profitable or not?

4. What impact is new technology having on operations management and HR management in businesses such as restaurants and car manufacturers?

Fig. 24.1 *PhotoBox is just one of many companies that exist as a consequence of recent technological changes*

Technological changes in business

Technological changes have been dramatic and far reaching over the past decade – and promise to continue to be so over the next ten years. There are few businesses that have been untouched by it, but some have turned it more to their advantage than others. Table 24.1 outlines some of the more obvious business applications of **Information Technology**.

Table 24.1 *Common business applications of technology and evaluating business strategies towards them*

Information technology system	Common business applications	Advantages	Potential limitations of adopting this application
Wordprocessing	Use in all departments for secretarial tasks. Typing, printing, storing, amending all forms of written letters and messages for internal and external communication	▪ Speed ▪ Accuracy ▪ Ease of amending documents ▪ Fewer secretarial staff needed – managers can operate the system with some training ▪ Links with use of e-mail for quick internal/external communications	▪ Now so widespread that not adopting this technology would be unusual ▪ Staff training will be needed if non-secretarial staff are required to undertake their own secretarial functions
Pagemaker and publishing programs	Specialist publishing programs can create magazine and newspaper pages for high quality printing direct from the computer. The marketing department can produce its own promotional material. Internal business 'newspapers' can be produced to aid internal communications	▪ May reduce need for use of professional publishing firms – reducing costs ▪ Documents can be amended quickly, e.g. promotional leaflets changed for different countries ▪ Professional appearance given to company publications	▪ Cost of the software and systems plus staff training – these are not easy programs to use to a very high standard

Databases	■ Used in all departments where the storing, filing and retrieving of large quantities of data is necessary ■ Human Resources department for keeping of personnel records ■ Marketing department for storing details of all customers, addresses, numbers of products purchased, most frequently purchased products ■ Operations department for stock handling, electronic ordering of new supplies, application of JIT stock control process ■ Finance department for recording all transactions including debtor payments and for producing up to date accounting data to management	■ Replaces vast quantities of paper records ■ Rapid retrieval of information saves time ■ Linking two sets of data, e.g. customers and preferred products, allows focused promotional campaigns ■ Stock control in retail stores much more effective with electronic tills that relay information directly to central stockholding computer and then to supplier for automatic re-ordering ■ Credit control more effective with up to date debtor records ■ Widespread use in both stockholding situations and customer data handling	■ Possible issues include: –Meeting all of the requirements of the Data Protection Act (data must be used only for specific purposes, must not be shared without the consent of the individual, etc.) –IT problems can quickly jeopardise the operation of a JIT system –RFID (radio frequency identification) of retail goods has raised doubts about individual freedoms if goods are still being tracked after purchase!
Spreadsheet programs	■ Financial and management accounting records can be updated and amended ■ Cash-flow forecasts and budgets can be updated in the light of new information. Changes in expected performance can be inputted to the spreadsheet and changes in total figures are made automatically ■ Income statements and balance sheets can be drawn up frequently	■ Flexibility and speed – changes to accounting records can be made quickly and the impact of these on total figures can be demonstrated instantly ■ 'What if' scenarios in budgeting and sales forecasting can be demonstrated, e.g. what would happen to forecasted profits if sales rose by 10% following a 5% cut in price?	■ Allows more frequent centralised control of cost and profit centre accounts – risk of excessive and overbearing centralised control and monitoring?
Computer Aided Design (CAD)	■ Nearly all design and architectural firms now use these programs for making and displaying designs, e.g. cars, house plans, furniture, garden designs ■ Designs can be shown in 3D and turned around to show effect from all angles ■ Speeds up the development of new products	■ Saves on expensive designer salaries as work is now much quicker ■ More flexibility of design as each customer's special requirements can be easily added ■ Can be linked to other programs to obtain product costings and to prepare for ordering of required supplies	■ Staff who fail to learn this technique are unlikely to be employed for long

Computer Aided Manufacturing (CAM)	■ These programs are used to operate robotic equipment that replaces many labour intensive production systems ■ Used in operations management in manufacturing businesses	■ Labour costs are reduced as machines replace many workers ■ Productivity is increased and variable cost per unit lower than in non-computerised processes ■ Accuracy is improved – less scope for human error ■ Flexibility of production is increased – modern computer controlled machinery can usually be adapted to make a number of different variations of a standard product and this helps to meet consumers' needs for some individual features ■ All of these benefits can add to a firm's competitive advantage	■ The main issues here are cost of the equipment, the need for frequent and expensive updates and the redundancy of semi-skilled workers whose jobs have been replaced by machines ■ Teething problems with new systems can lead to delays in achieving the claimed efficiency and quality benefits ■ R&D into new and more efficient processes can be hugely expensive
Internet/intranet	■ The internet is the worldwide web of communication links between computers ■ Marketing department – for promoting to a large market and taking orders online ■ Operations management – business to business (B2B) communication via the internet is used to search the market for the cheapest suppliers ■ Human Resources uses these programs for communicating within the organisation ■ Intranets allow all staff to be internally connected via computers ■ Intranet allows links between computers within the same company to allow e-mailing and access to a wide range of online services	■ Cost savings from cheap internal and external communications ■ Access to a much larger potential market than could be gained through non-IT methods ■ Web pages project a worldwide image of the business ■ Online ordering cheaper than paper-based systems ■ B2B communications can obtain supplies at lower costs ■ Internal communication is quicker than traditional methods ■ Improved communication technology is allowing much greater 'teleworking' – staff working at home but still linked to the office	■ Too many e-mails. This is causing huge logjams in company employees' electronic intrays – leading to some firms introducing e-mail free days ■ E-retailing has to be carried out very effectively to reassure customers, e.g. about credit card security and return of unwanted goods

■ Business in action

Social networks – opportunities for retailers?

Retailers need to wake up to the potential of social networks in order to tap into the huge numbers of consumers using the sites.

Analyst house Gartner says social networking sites are starting to attract a broader spectrum of consumers with the rise of career-based networks such as LinkedIn and shopping-based sites.

Hung LeHong, research vice president at Gartner, said retailers have previously seen social networks as relevant only to younger consumers so have not given them the attention they deserve.

Lehong added retailers could create social communities for product feedback and use social networks as an effective marketing tool.

Gartner's tips for retailers wanting to get in on the social network action include looking beyond the big names of Facebook and MySpace due to the huge amount of activity in the area.

Retailers should also look into the potential of viral marketing campaigns on social networks, as well as building third-party applications.

Amazon, for example, recently unveiled its social shopping application for Facebook.

But Gartner warns social networks aren't yet ready for commerce so retailers shouldn't jump in before they have understood implications.

www.silicon.com/retailandleisure

Assessing the business impact of technological change

The main potential benefits of technological change for business are:

■ new products: R&D departments will be busy exploiting new technologies to create innovative products
■ cost savings, especially in operations management: These may be difficult to assess accurately if they are gained over several years in the future
■ improved efficiency and better customer service – a key operations management objective
■ new marketing opportunities – creating new openings for the marketing department to exploit. The internet will continue to have a huge impact on the way goods and services are marketed.

These benefits will all assist a business towards higher levels of efficiency and competitiveness.

There will always be potential limitations and drawbacks and the scale of these will depend greatly on how technological change is managed by senior staff.

The potential limitations of technological change include:

■ rapid obsolescence of existing technology: the current processes and systems in the business may have to be radically changed, for example stock management systems
■ HR management issues, for example training and possible redundancies, and the need to manage people effectively to encourage them to accept changes

■ **Key term**

VoIP: voice over internet protocol – making telephone calls via the internet.

■ **Activities**

Read the 'VoIP a perfect fit for Gieves & Hawkes' Business in action.

1 Explain the benefits to this company of the new IT upgrade.

2 How did the existing processes and systems within the business change as a result of this IT upgrade?

3 Discuss likely disadvantages to the company from 'getting rid of one receptionist' and 'hot-desking and tele-working'.

■ Link

The main issues involved in change management are covered in Chapters 26–31, pages 217–265.

- capital cost, training cost, maintenance cost: These costs will need to be included in any investment appraisal assessment of a new technology investment

- management culture may not be prepared to accept it: there are still some managers who may resent the influence of IT experts and resist too much technological change, especially if they do not fully understand it.

When assessing whether a particular technological application or development is worthwhile for a business, investment appraisal can be used. Clearly, as with all projects that involve estimating future returns or costs, the forecasted cash flows used in investment appraisal – perhaps especially when assessing technological projects – are subject to considerable guesswork and potential inaccuracies.

Making strategic choices about technology must also involve qualitative factors such as the:

- attitude and culture of management to technological change that they may not understand themselves

- attitude and culture of workers to technological change and the impact this will have on their working lives – or indeed, on the survival of their jobs

- potential gains to customer service which may be real and long lasting – but difficult to quantify

- unknown risk of obsolescence and the increased expense that replacing equipment that may have been only recently purchased entails

- the existing processes and systems used within the business – such as production methods, stock management systems and current marketing methods. To what extent will these have to be amended in response to rapid technological change?

■ Link

Chapter 29 — Key influences on change process: culture, page 244, looks in detail at management culture and how this might either support or restrict change.

Fig. 24.2 *Technological change offers efficiency gains – but will these machines soon be outdated?*

■ Link

For the calculation of payback, see Chapter 6 — Making investment decisions, page 38.

■ Business in action

Glasgow NHS to use RFID to keep tabs on equipment

NHS Greater Glasgow and Clyde has implemented a wireless networking project in the Royal Alexandra Hospital (RAH) that involves tracking medical equipment with RFID tags.

The initial driver of this part of the project is to reduce the amount of time maintenance staff waste in locating portable medical equipment, such as defibrillators, infusion pumps and blood monitors.

However, there is expected to be a knock-on effect of medical practitioners also being able to lay their hands on equipment when needed, thereby improving the level of patient care.

According to RAH clinical scientist Jason Britton, the hospital loses between £20,000 to £40,000 per year in wasted staff time.

He told silicon.com: "Devices can get lost in the system for years before they are discovered."

The wireless network was installed in May 2007 by Carillion IT Services and tagging started roll out in September last year and is ongoing. So far, seven wards have been provided with active-tagged equipment and readers, with a further 15 to receive the same, plus out-patient facilities.

Only 40 tags have so far been delivered to the hospital but Britton estimates around 1,500 tags will eventually be deployed.

The initial phase of the project to install a wi-fi network and RFID tags cost up to £70,000.

www.silicon.com/publicsector

Case study

E-tailing comes of age

Online retailing increased by 32 per cent in 2008 compared to high street sales growth of 1.2 per cent according to industry analyst Verdict Research. E-tailing now accounts for almost 7 per cent of total retail spending. Verdict forecasts that by 2012 this share will double to 14 per cent. Seventy-four per cent of consumers surveyed by Verdict said the internet was better for cheaper goods and 67 per cent agreed that it is better for comparing prices.

Typical of the move to e-tailing was the decision by Dixons to:

- close many of its high street stores
- rebrand those remaining into 'Currys.digital'
- move the Dixons brand completely online.

The strategy cost £7m but was expected to increase sales as well as deliver administration cost savings of £3m annually.

'I am very excited about the prospects for the Dixons brand as a pure play e-tailer,' said the Chief Executive of Dixons. 'Consumer buying behaviours are developing with the growth in broadband usage and we constantly innovate to support how our customers shop.'

E-tailing is now an indispensable part of the fashion industry too. Yoox.com is a virtual boutique that saw over 3 million visitors per month in 2008. When another site, Net-a-Porter, partnered fashion label Halston one dress style sold out in 45 minutes after the launch of the site. There is also potential for young new designers, keen to enter the industry, to show off their styles to a huge online audience.

However, when consumer spending started to fall towards the end of 2008, online traders reported lower 'conversion rates' (online shoppers actually buying) and there were signs of the market reaching maturity. Tesco withdrew its clothing ranges from Tesco Direct after its initial claim of 'selling online will enable us to reach a greater number of customers eager to buy items from our collections' seemed not to be supported by sales figures.

In addition, there are still familiar customer complaints about 'difficult to use sites', 'delays in postal deliveries' and 'it was not as it seemed on screen', so perhaps high street shops are not doomed after all. 'The high street will not die,' said Neil Saunders, director of Verdict Research. 'Internet retailing is certainly set to become more significant, but shopping is a tactile process and for many people it is a leisure activity – e-tailing does not really deliver on those two things.'

Adapted from www.talkingretail.com and www.silicon.com/webwatch

Activities

Read the 'RFID' Business in action on page 206 and answer activities 1 and 2.

1 Using the mid-point of the average forecast cost savings, calculate the payback period for this investment.

2 Do you think that the other potential advantages of this scheme could be valued in financial terms? Explain your answer.

3 Assess the likely accuracy of investment appraisal in this case.

4 On what other grounds, apart from financial ones, could this project be assessed?

Questions

1 Outline three reasons for the recent growth in online retailing.

2 Analyse the potential benefits to an electrical and computer retailer such as Dixon's from going exclusively online.

3 How might Dixon's have assessed the advanatges and disadvantages of the decision to go completely online?

4 Would you recommend other retailers to close their stores and sell exclusively via the internet? Justify your answer, using appropriate examples.

5 Use the internet to look up one of the sites of a major UK online retailer (or use one of the sites referred to above). Assess the impact it has on consumers and discuss how it could be improved to encourage more browsers to purchase from it.

☑ *In this chapter you will have learned to:*

- understand the scope and pace of technological change
- assess the response of businesses to technological change
- evaluate how a business might assess whether a particular technological change should be introduced.

Summary questions

1 Give three examples of products that, because of the technological advances, exist today yet did not exist three years ago. (3 marks)

2 Assess the factors a retailer should consider before launching an internet e-tailing site. (9 marks)

3 Explain two applications of technology that are particularly relevant for manufacturing businesses. (6 marks)

4 Explain two applications of technology that are particularly relevant to service sector businesses. (6 marks)

5 What are the limitations of investment appraisal techniques when assessing new technology applications in business? (6 marks)

6 Using examples to illustrate your answer, why is obsolescence such a problem for businesses given the current pace of technological change? (6 marks)

Essays

7 'The key to successful manufacturing business today is a positive management attitude to technological change.' To what extent do you agree with this view? (40 marks)

8 Discuss the strategies that a UK retailing business could adopt to the increasing acceptance of e-tailing or internet selling. (40 marks)

25 The relationship between business and the competitive environment

In this chapter you will learn to:

- analyse the meaning and significance of an industry's competitive structure
- assess the ways in which an industry's competitive structure can change
- evaluate strategies businesses could adopt in response to changes in the competitive environment.

Setting the scene

The package holiday industry – where to now?

The recent changes in the package holiday industry have transformed its competitive structure. Ten years ago there were many companies offering family-oriented package holidays – flights, accommodation, transfers and so on all included in the basic price. Today, after the recent merger of Thomsons (TUI) and First Choice, there are just two main players in the market.

What has caused this radical change in the industry? Two main factors – the internet and changing consumer preferences. The spread of internet use has allowed virtually every hotel chain and airline operator to set up in competition with the package holiday companies. Hotels offer to arrange flights, transfers and 'all in packages'; airlines offer car hire and hotel deals. Even websites such as toptable.co.uk, a restaurant booking service, is distributing hotel rooms through its site and plans to offer further travel products. So, there are fewer traditional package holiday companies – but the two that remain face more competition from non-traditional rivals than ever.

Consumer preferences have also changed as well as their internet buying power. Higher incomes have meant that the typical family holiday in a beach resort is no longer good enough – more activities, more exclusive destinations, fly–drive–cruise packages: anything but the traditional two weeks in Benidorm.

How have TUI and Thomas Cook responded to these changes in their industry? Firstly, by integrating to gain economies of scale and reduce direct competition in travel agents – the First Choice and TUI merger was just the most recent in a series of mergers and takeovers. Secondly, by diversifying into more luxury and activity-based breaks with less competition such as Exodus and Sunsail Flotillas.

business.timesonline.co.uk

Discussion points

1 Do you think the number and size of competitors matters to any business?

2 How did competition increase for the traditional travel company despite the number of companies declining?

3 Assess the likely chances of success of the two strategies used by travel companies.

Competitive structure of industry – what does this mean?

Apart from the obvious point that one provides a service and the other a product, what would you say were the key differences between the hairdressing industry and the petrol retailing industry? Table 25.1 gives a list of differences – you could probably add to it.

Table 25.1 *Contrasts in competitive structure between hairdressing and petrol retailing*

Differences	Hairdressing	Petrol retailing
Number of firms in the industry	There are 7,000 members of the National Hairdresser Federation – and many hairdressers do not belong to this organisation	Apart from a few independent operators, there are 13 major petrol retailing businesses – but the industry is dominated by the main supermarket chains and the Big Three: Esso, Shell and BP
Product differentiation	Very different quality and range of services offered at most hairdressers	Virtually none – although the Big Three are trying to promote premium fuels such as Shell Optimax as offering more power and better economy
Price differences	Huge differences – dependent upon location, quality of service, reputation	Very slight differences – apart from remote local monopolies that can charge a few pence per litre more
Ease of entry into the market	Easy – no qualifications needed to set up a business, no licence required, can be done from home	Difficult – health and safety/fire service licence required, access to wholesale supplies of fuel, large location, expensive equipment needed

Economists enjoy giving names to different forms of **competitive structure**. Hairdressing is classified as being **monopolistically competitive**. This is because it is highly competitive with many firms, yet they each try to establish a differentiated service that gives them a degree of control over prices. Petrol retailing is an example of what economists call an **oligopoly**.

Another competitive structure is **monopoly** – a single supplier. For example, London Transport is a monopoly provider of underground trains in London – but it does face competition from other transport providers.

Why is competitive structure important?

The number of competing firms in an industry, their strength and the ease of entry for new firms have an impact on:

- the amount of choice for consumers
- the level of competition in terms of price, promotion, new product developments
- the profitability of businesses in the industry
- the likelihood of illegal collusive agreements – arrangements between firms to limit open competition between them.

Changes in the competitive structure

New competitors

The entry of new firms into the industry increases competition.

The airline industry is notable for increased competition in recent years. Until the 1980s, the global airline industry outside of the US was dominated by national 'flag carriers' that were often state owned. Governments imposed significant restrictions on the entry of new firms into the industry and on the routes that non-flag carriers could operate. The industry was heavily regulated and the entry of new firms was rare. Over the last 20 years, the EU market has followed the US down the road of deregulation. Nationalised flag carriers have been privatised to be run as profit-seeking businesses. The EU has made subsidies to national airlines illegal and enforced an 'open skies' policy on all member states to allow any operator from any EU country to fly within and between

Key terms

Competitive structure: the number and strength of competing firms in an industry and the ease of entry for new competitors.

Monopolistic competition: a competitive industry with many firms, easy to enter and good knowledge amongst consumers about prices and products but with each firm producing differentiated products.

Oligopoly: industry with competition amongst a relatively few businesses.

Monopoly: in theory, an industry with just one supplier but the UK and EU definition is of a firm with at least 25% market share or a legal monopoly.

all member states. Entry barriers fell and many new low cost airlines – spearheaded by Ryanair and Easyjet – have been established and expanded rapidly.

Examples of strategies adopted by the traditional airlines in response to increased competition:

- integration, for example, Air France with KLM and Lufthansa with Swissair
- new routes and new services, for example flat beds, showers and massage facilities in first class
- cost cutting, for example BA has outsourced its ticketing administration to India
- better branding – focusing on the service differences with the low cost carriers.

Dominant businesses

The existence of a main and dominant business can have a huge impact on the nature or level of competition in a market. The lack of big competitors often means that:

- there is less choice for consumers
- the dominant firm may charge higher prices than would exist in a more competitive market
- it will take any action it can to maintain its dominant position.

Microsoft is a classic example of a dominant firm. It has over 90 per cent market share of computer operating systems. It has been accused of using this monopoly power to exploit consumers by putting pressure on computer manufacturers to install only its internet browser on new machines.

Changes in the buying power of customers

If customers – or final consumers – become more or less powerful then this will change the competitive nature of a market.

Tesco and other large supermarkets are huge customers for their suppliers. They have been accused of using excessive bargaining power over suppliers. This has become an issue since the industry has become increasingly oligopolistic. The market share of the big four grocery retailers has reached 75 per cent (April 2008), up from 51 per cent in 2002 – this gives each firm more buying power over suppliers.

Fig. 25.1 *The level of competition in this industry has increased in recent years as more airlines have been set up*

Business in action

Tesco flexes its muscles with the big suppliers

The age of the 'super supermarket' seems to have put the likes of Unilever – suppliers of branded cleaning and food products to all major grocery retailers – firmly in their place.

As Tesco's commercial and trading director stood up to address a conference of Tesco's suppliers, a picture of a derelict house was beamed on the wall. Pricing was the fundamental factor in Tesco's success, he said, and if suppliers did not get their pricing right, then their businesses, like the house in the picture, would collapse!

He went on to claim that some suppliers – amongst them international manufacturers – had not been giving Tesco the lowest

Link

This topic links with the issue of ethical business behaviour. See Chapter 23 — The relationship between business and the social environment, page 195.

Activities

Read the 'A lesson in loss for Suppliers' Business in action and answer activities 1 & 2.

1. Why do retail customers such as Sainsbury have so much power over firms such as Uniq?

2. Suggest three possible strategies Uniq could adopt to attempt to increase profitability from its sandwich and desserts products.

3. Evaluate the likely chances of success of any one of these strategies.

prices possible. 'Give us better prices or watch this space,' he warned his stunned audience.

As annual profits are being announced, the shifting balance of power between the supermarket giants and the supplying manufacturing companies has again been thrown into focus. Last week Tesco announced phenomenal profit results – but Unilever and Colgate-Palmolive have issued profit warnings and Cadbury Schweppes admitted it was finding the going tough.

http://business.timesonline.co.uk/article 486615

Business in action

A lesson in loss for suppliers

Does winning a contract with one of the major supermarkets lead to untold wealth and success? Should a supplying business go 'all-out' to gain such a contract? Possibly – if the alternative is to retrench the business, close factories and lose jobs. But, all is not a bed of roses when a contract with one of the big food retailers is signed. It can lead to huge pressure to continually cut costs and improve quality – with, sometimes, little prospect of long term profit. Uniq, formerly Unigate, does not have any problem devising, manufacturing and selling sandwiches and desserts to the likes of Tesco and Marks & Spencer. Revenues last year reached £736m. Its problem is making any profit whatsoever from the process. Resistance in negotiations can be fatal – as when it lost the Sainsbury's desserts contract last year.

Buying power of consumers

These are the final purchasers and user of a product. Consumer power is changing too – just as the power of the supermarkets has increased, so the buying power of consumers has changed the nature of competition in some markets. Again, the internet has been a driving force in improving consumers' power and allowing groups of consumers to influence business product strategy and pricing decisions.

Business in action

2007 hailed as the 'year of consumer power'

Consumer campaigning on an unprecedented scale through websites and social networks has led to a series of corporate climbdowns, backflips, reversals and U-turns over everything from Mars bars to excessive bank charges and carrier bags. Consumers are increasingly taking advantage of new information sources, price comparison websites, online pressure groups and websites such as Uswitch to flex their buying power and change energy and telephone service providers. British Gas has admitted to losing 1.1m customers in just 12 months – and reduced its prices as a result.

Mars UK did a backflip and changed back to only vegetarian ingredients in most of its chocolate bars after 6,000 e-mails to its customer service centre. The Vegetarian Society had posted the necessary address on its own website. Fiona Dawson, MD of Mars UK said, 'The consumer is our boss – we had lots of feedback from customers who were not going to buy our products because of the change towards some animal-based ingredients such as rennet.'

Over 6,000 students used Facebook to protest about plans by HSBC to scrap interest free student overdrafts. Faced with the potential loss of so many student accounts, the bank backed down.

Adapted from http://lifeandhealth.guardian.co.uk

Changes in the selling power of suppliers

The number and power of suppliers can change over time and this will affect the nature of competition in an industry. The more concentrated and controlled the supply of raw materials, components and important businesses services are, the more power suppliers will have. This power is likely to be used to restrict supply and drive up prices. A significant reduction in the number of suppliers is likely to focus power in the hands of fewer firms and give them more bargaining power over customers.

Business in action

Weak and strong suppliers

Industries using diamonds, such as jewellery and electronics, face the huge supplying power of DeBeers which has a dominant market share. Food-processing companies, in contrast, can buy agricultural produce from many small and weak farmers. Retail stores can fill their shelves with many competing products from different producers.

Having only two producers in a market concentrates supplier bargaining power in few hands – but it does not always lead to strong suppliers. Although both Airbus and Boeing are big and powerful, the threat of substitution is enough to limit their power over airlines.

Competition policy

Markets with few suppliers have a tendency for anti-competitive **collusion**. Agreements between suppliers – called cartels – limit competition and greatly increase supplier power. This form of action is illegal in most countries and is investigated and controlled by **competition policy**.

The competitive environment in UK and EU industries is governed and controlled by competition policy. If there was no competition policy, dominant firms and businesses that act together would reduce competition, reduce choice and increase prices.

The main objectives of competition policy in the UK are now greatly influenced by the EU, which aims to achieve consistency in all member countries. These aims are to:

- protect consumers' interests by encouraging free competition
- outlaw practices and agreements between businesses that restrict competition such as price fixing agreements

Activities

Read the '2007 hailed as the "year of consumer power"' Business in action and answer the following activities.

1 How has the internet increased consumer buying power over some businesses?

2 Should a business always change its strategies if large numbers of consumers complain and threaten to withdraw their custom? Explain your answer.

Key terms

Collusion: firms working together – called a cartel – to fix prices or agree on output levels to reduce competition.

Competition policy: aims to prevent the abuse of monopoly power so that competition in markets is not restricted.

- investigate the behaviour of dominant, monopoly firms in an industry
- investigate proposed large-scale mergers or takeovers that would create a dominant firm position.

These policy aims are carried out by the Office of Fair Trading (OFT) and the Competition Commission. These government bodies can:

- impose fines on firms that are restricting competition in unfair ways such as fixing prices – up to 10 per cent of a firm's annual revenue
- refuse permission to proposed mergers and takeovers that are likely to be against the public interest
- release reports to the media about collusion and this creates much bad publicity against the companies involved.

Business in action

European Competition Commission imposes €899m fine on Microsoft

The EU fine of €899m on Microsoft was imposed because the monopoly provider of computer operating systems did not comply with an earlier ruling. This stated that it should give out details of its operating system, for a reasonable fee, to competitors to allow them to offer customers 'interoperable' alternatives to Microsoft's software.

http://europa.eu

Fig. 25.2 The construction industry is the latest large-scale investigation by the Office for Fair Trading into anti-competitive practices

Business in action

OFT names building firms in 'bid-rigging' scandal

The OFT has formally accused many of the UK's largest construction firms with participating in illegal bid rigging in order to increase profits. Multi-million pound fines are expected as a result of the OFT investigation. It is claming that building firms, when bidding for large contracts such as new schools or hospitals, agree on the level of their bids before submitting their prices to the customer. In one case, the winning bid for a college contract was 25 per cent higher than it would otherwise have been because the bidding companies had agreed on artificially high bids.

http://timesonline.co.uk

Evaluation of business strategies in response to changes in the competitive environment

According to a famous management writer, Michael Porter, there are three broad competitive strategies that firms can adopt in response to changes in their competitive environment: cost leadership, differentiation from rivals and focus, a combination of the first two but focused on niche markets. Table 25.2 summarises and evaluates these strategies.

Table 25.2 *Porter's three competitive strategies*

Competitive strategy	Steps to be taken	Evaluation of strategy
Cost leadership, e.g. low-cost airlines	Tight cost control achieved by: ■ pressure on suppliers ■ supervision of labour ■ products designed for ease of manufacture ■ low-cost distribution ■ incentives based on meeting strict cost-based targets ■ investment in new capital	■ May not prevent even lower-cost new entrants, benefiting from imitation, coming into industry with new technology ■ Market resistance to low-cost image and frequent reductions in service offered to cut costs ■ Inflation in costs, e.g. jet fuel, that narrow the relative cost and price advantage over competitors – the cost advantage may no longer outweigh the brand advantages of other suppliers
Differentiation from rivals, e.g. BMW differentiates itself from most other car manufacturers with quality and sporting imagery – this allows value added products to be sold successfully	■ Focus on product engineering and technical advances ■ Corporate reputation for quality and technological leadership ■ Creative marketing flair ■ Stress traditional virtues ■ Investment in R&D ■ Ensure attractiveness for skilled labour, managers, designers	■ The cost and price differences between new entrants, e.g. Korean and Chinese car manufacturers, may become too great for brand loyalty to be maintained ■ Subject to variations in business cycle – likely to be an income elastic product. In recessions, consumers' willingness to pay for differentiated products may fall ■ Imitation may reduce brand identity
Focus – a combination of the cost leadership and differentiation strategies but focused on niche markets, e.g. First Choice offering specialist/activity holidays	■ A combination of the decisions above but directed at a niche market, e.g. First Choice developing own holiday resorts to offer focused holidays to niche groups of holidaymakers	■ Existing niche suppliers may have developed specific products, have brand loyalty or undertaken effective market research that allow them to be even better focused. The 'Explore' business has a huge following amongst 'activity tourists' ■ Additional costs of operating in a niche market (fewer economies of scale) remove the benefit of operating a focused strategy

■ Case study

Taxi firm hails bright future

Manganese Bronze, the Coventry based maker of black cabs, plans to fight the increasing competition for its iconic products. Although the firm is the dominant supplier of cabs to London taxi drivers, the famous black cab faces increasing competition in other markets as other manufacturers such as Peugeot adapt existing vehicles into suitable taxi models. These manufacturers have huge cost advantages over Manganese Bronze as they produce hundreds of thousands of the basic vehicle model that they are converting into taxis. In contrast, the UK firm makes a few thousand TX4 black cabs each year. They are not cheap – the current model costs between £30,000 and £43,000, depending on specification.

Management at Manganese Bronze are making important strategic decisions. Firstly, they have signed a joint venture agreement with Shanghai LTI to start production of its taxis in China which will

Fig. 25.3 *Can new competitive strategies increase the profits for the makers of the famous black cab?*

hopefully be sold in large numbers in Asia. Secondly, the company has developed a new model with green credentials – a battery powered taxi! Based on the existing model, it strips out the diesel engine and replaces it with an electric motor and batteries. The electric cab will have a range of 100 miles before it needs recharging and will cost just 4p a mile to run – about half the cost of the diesel version. The plug-in taxi will be available in 2010 – but it will cost even more to buy than the current model.

www.independent.co.uk

Questions

1 Analyse how Manganese Bronze has been affected by:

a increased power of oil suppliers

b entry of new firms into the taxi manufacturing industry.

2 Analyse the strategies that Manganese Bronze has adopted in terms of Porter's competitive strategies.

3 Evaluate the likely chances of sales and profits success of the two strategies Manganese Bronze has adopted.

4 McDonald's restaurant chain has experienced higher ingredient costs, increased competition and consumer buyer resistance due to some of its policies. Research the strategies that the business is adopting to deal with these cost and competitive pressures.

In this chapter you will have learned to:

■ assess the ways in which the structure of an industry can affect the level of competition within it

■ analyse factors that can occur within an industry to change its competitive environment

■ evaluate the strategies that a business could adopt in response to changes in the competitive environment.

Summary questions

1 Distinguish between monopoly and oligopoly, and give an industrial example of each. (4 marks)

2 Give an example of a market that has experienced new entrants that have changed the level of competition in the market. (2 marks)

3 Give an example of an industry (other than computers) that is dominated by a single well-known business. (2 marks)

4 Explain four factors that might lead to an increase in the market power of suppliers. (8 marks)

5 How might EU Competition Policy have an effect on the level of competition within a market? (6 marks)

6 Distinguish between, using relevant examples, the strategies of cost leadership and differentiation. (8 marks)

Essays

7 To what extent do you consider that UK businesses will be adversely affected by greater competition in the future? (40 marks)

8 'The announcement by Tesco plc in 2008 of record profits of £2.75bn proves that supermarket power over suppliers is increasing and this trend should be stopped.' To what extent do you agree with this view? (40 marks)

Introduction

Change in business is inevitable. However, it is not always bad. Change can create both opportunities and threats for business. Changes can result either from internal factors within the business – such as a change of owner or chief executive – or externally, such as slower economic growth or technological developments. Many changes in business are relatively minor and incremental, but some change is rapid and structural and needs effective management if it is to be used to increase a firm's competitiveness.

Examples of significant causes of change are:

- technological developments that make existing products obsolete but create new product opportunities
- takeovers that result in new management styles and operating strategies
- environmental accidents that require an immediate business response.

These and other significant business changes need to be planned for and managed effectively if the business, and the people who work for it, are not to be swept along by events rather than being in control of them.

Change should not be viewed negatively and with anxiety. In fact, businesses can gain competitive advantage if they use change to further their own objectives. If management make necessary changes within an organisation before these are forced upon them, then consumers and other stakeholders are likely to react favourably to the business. As we will see in this section, creating a culture of innovation can transform a business and its future prospects. Opportunities are there to be grasped and a negative approach to change will only exaggerate the threats and not the positives that can result.

This final part of Unit 4 of the AQA Business Studies specification focuses on analysing the impact that change can have on business and on evaluating the different ways that businesses might react to it. There are some common themes running through the chapters that follow. One of these is that change management entails thoughtful planning and sensitive implementation and, above all, consultation with and involvement of the people most affected by the changes. Change can be unsettling and demotivating, so it needs to be understood and managed in a way that the staff of an organisation can cope with. As you work through these chapters, you will do well to remember the four key stages of managing change in any organisation. These will all be explained in detail. They are:

- identifying the key causes and areas of change
- preparing and planning for change
- implementing change
- creating a culture of change.

Chapter 26: Internal causes of change

This chapter focuses on some of the major causes of change from internal sources – changes in the size of the business. The key distinction between internal and external growth is explained as well as the reasons why a business might actually cut back its operations (retrench). Changes in ownership and leadership are common reasons for changes affecting people within an organisation. The consequences of poor business performance and the changes that result from this are also analysed in this chapter.

Chapter 27: Planning for change

Without planning, effective change management becomes very difficult. Corporate plans are frequently used to lay out the overall aims and strategies of a business and include an analysis of the internal and external factors on them. Planning for the unexpected (contingency planning) is of growing importance to businesses given the increase in social awareness of the impact of business accidents on the wider world and the legal costs that can follow a workplace disaster.

Chapter 28: Key influences in the change process: leadership

Change will not be managed effectively without appropriate leadership. Different leadership styles can be adopted and there are both internal and external factors that influence the styles generally used in any organisation. This chapter also assesses the importance of leadership in the change process.

Chapter 29: Key influences on the change process: culture

Whether a business is prepared for change and is able to cope with it depends on a great deal on the culture of the organisation. A business that is bureaucratic and bound by rules will be less likely to be able to benefit from change than one that allows employees to adopt an entrepreneurial, risk-taking approach to major issues. This chapter considers the major types of organisational culture and how they affect ability to deal with change.

Chapter 30: Making strategic decisions

Major sources of change, whether they are internal or external, often lead to significant changes in the strategy of a business. This chapter analyses the value of different approaches to decision-making and the main influences on corporate decision-making.

Chapter 31: Implementing and managing change

Major changes in the direction or structure of a business have to implemented and managed effectively if they are to make the business more and not less effective and competitive. This chapter analyses the techniques that can be used to implement and manage change successfully and also considers those organisational factors that can restrict and promote change.

As well as dealing with industrial disasters, BP management has to implement and manage change brought about by environmental legislation and consumers increased demand for biofuels

26 Internal causes of change

In this chapter you will learn to:

- identify the different causes of internal change

- analyse the different methods by which a business can grow including mergers and take-overs

- examine other reasons for changes in ownership

- recognise the need for some businesses to become smaller or retrench

- analyse the impact that poor business performance might have on the need for a business to change.

Setting the scene

First Choice to merge with TUI

Travel firm First Choice is to merge with the tourism division of Germany's TUI to form Europe's top tour operator. The new firm, TUI Travel, will have 27 million customers and £12bn in sales. It will be based in Luton in the UK, at the current TUI Thomson headquarters, and its shares will be listed on the London Stock Exchange. First Choice said there would be 'job duplication' and some jobs would be lost as it would close its current Gatwick Head Office. The merger has been approved by the European Competition Commission which investigated claims by consumer groups that the combined business would have too much market power.

The merger deal follows one month after the UK travel firm MyTravel agreed a merger with Thomas Cook. The holiday industry is changing and all travel companies are aiming to cut costs when many travellers are booking their own holidays and hunting the best deal online.

First Choice said in a statement that, 'There is a good strategic fit between these two businesses because the UK company focused on activity and speciality holidays, while TUI had built up its reputation based on low-cost holidays. It provides the opportunity to cut costs and achieve sustainable revenue growth from offering a complete range of holidays to customers.'

Both TUI and First Choice recorded losses last year and TUI recently announced a cost-cutting retrenchment programme with up to 3,600 jobs being cut across its European operations.

newsvote.bbc.co.uk

Discussion points

1. What seem to be the major potential benefits to these two companies from the merger?

2. Should holidaymakers and staff employed in these companies be pleased or concerned about this merger?

3. What internal changes will be necessary within these two businesses for the merger to be successful?

4. Is cost-cutting inevitable in the holiday industry, do you think?

Change in organisational size

The owners of some businesses want the firm to remain small for reasons of remaining in control, avoiding taking too many risks and preventing workloads from becoming too heavy. Why do other business owners and directors of companies seek growth for their business? There are a number of possible reasons:

- increase profit: if the main aim of the owners and directors is profit, then expanding the business and achieving higher sales is one way of becoming more profitable
- increase market share: this will give a business a higher market profile and greater bargaining power with both suppliers (for example, lower prices) and retailers (for example, best positions in the shop)
- increase economies of scale: see Chapter 12
- increase the power and status of the owners and directors: for example, the opportunities to influence community projects and government policy will increase if the business controlled by the owners or directors is large and well known
- reduce the risk of being a takeover target: a larger business may become too large a target for a potential 'predator' company.

Internal growth

Business growth can be achieved in a number of ways and these forms of growth can lead to differing effects on stakeholder groups, such as customers, workers and competitors. The forms of growth can be categorised as either **internal growth** or external growth.

An example of internal growth would be a retailing business opening more shops in towns and cities where it previously had none. This growth can be quite slow with, perhaps, only a few branches or shops opening each year. However, it can avoid problems of excessively fast growth, which tends to lead to inadequate capital (overtrading), and management problems associated with bringing two businesses together that often have different attitudes and cultures.

■ **Business in action**

Starbucks confirms rapid growth strategy

Howard Schultz, the chairman of Starbucks, confirmed growth plans for the world's largest chain of coffee shops. The business will open at least 10,000 new cafes over the next four years by using internal growth. Schultz said at the company's annual meeting that he planned to double the size of the business in five years. At the end of 2007 there were over 15,000 stores worldwide.

China will be the main focus of this growth strategy. The US giant opened its first Chinese branch in 1999 and now has over 200 Chinese branches. 'No market potentially has the opportunities for us that China hopefully will,' said Schultz. Like many Western retailers, Starbucks sees China as its key growth area due to its fast growing economy, lack of strong local competitors and sheer size of population. The business is also expanding its network of branches in Russia and Brazil.

There are plans to increase sales of non-coffee products to reduce its reliance on just hot drinks. It has expanded its sale of audio books and music and Sir Paul McCartney, the former Beatle, will be the first artist to release an album on Starbucks 'Hear Music' label. This rapid internal expansion has not been without problems. Consumer Reports magazine recently ranked McDonald's coffee ahead of Starbucks saying it tasted better and cost less. This could be due to the time-saving equipment that has been added to new Starbucks branches that use automatic espresso machines instead of

---

Link

Economies of scale are discussed in Chapter 12 — Operational strategies: scale and resource mix, page 90.

Key term

Internal growth: expansion of a business by means of opening new branches, shops or factories (also known as organic growth).

Fig. 26.1 *Starbucks has expanded rapidly through internal growth*

Activities

1. Why would you describe Starbucks' growth strategy as being an example of internal growth?

2. Suggest two reasons why Starbucks has adopted a rapid expansion strategy.

3. Analyse the possible advantages of focusing growth in China.

4. Explain why Starbucks is planning to reduce its reliance on just selling coffee.

5. Do you think Starbucks is right to plan to expand so rapidly? Explain your answer.

extracting espresso shots in the traditional way. The chairman has also criticised the time-saving policy of designing stores uniformly rather than with some local decoration.

www.iht.com; www.bbc.co.uk

External growth

External growth is often referred to as 'integration' as it involves bringing together two or more firms in a **merger** or **takeover**. This form of growth can lead to rapid expansion, which might be vital in a competitive and expanding market. However, it often leads to management problems. These are caused by the need for different management systems to deal with a bigger organisation. There can also be conflict between the two teams of managers (who will get the top jobs?) and conflicts of culture and business ethics. External forms of growth are summarised in Fig. 26.2 and their impacts, advantages and disadvantages in Table 26.1.

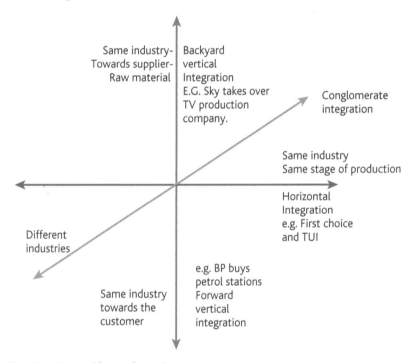

Fig. 26.2 *External forms of growth*

Synergy and integration

When two firms are integrated, the argument is that the bigger firm created in this way will be more effective, efficient and profitable than the two separate companies. Why might this be the case?

- It is argued that the two businesses might be able to share research facilities and pool ideas that will benefit both of the businesses. This is only likely to be the case if the two firms deal with the same kind of technologies.

- Economies of operating a larger scale of business, such as buying supplies in large quantities, should cut average costs.

- The new business can save on marketing and distribution costs by using the same sales outlets and sales teams.

Key terms

External growth: business expansion achieved by means of merging with or taking over another business, from either the same or a different industry.

Merger: an agreement by shareholders and managers of two businesses to bring both firms together under a common board of directors with shareholders in both businesses owning shares in the newly merged business.

Takeover: when a company buys over 50 per cent of the shares of another company and becomes the controlling owner of it. It is often referred to as 'acquisition'.

AQA Examiner's tip

If a case study makes reference to a merger or takeover and a question is based on this, the first sentence of your answer should classify the type of integration it is and define it.

Table 26.1 *Different types of integration, their common advantages and disadvantages, and the impact they often have on stakeholder groups*

Type of integration	Advantages to business	Disadvantages to business	Impact on stakeholders
Horizontal integration – same industry, same stage of production	■ Eliminates one competitor and gives more market share and power ■ Potential for further economies of scale ■ Increased power over suppliers to achieve lower costs ■ Scope for rationalising production, e.g. by concentrating all output on one site as opposed to two with potential cost savings	■ Rationalisation may involve redundancies and bad publicity ■ May lead to Competition Commission investigation if market share now exceeds 25% – this will make it a 'legal monopoly' ■ Potential management style and culture conflicts	■ Consumers now have less choice and prices could either rise (less competition) or fall (passing on the benefits of economies of scale) ■ Workers may lose job security as a result of rationalisation ■ Remaining competitors may be under greater pressure to reduce costs ■ Suppliers may fear greater pressure being put on them, by the larger integrated business, to cut prices
Vertical backward integration – same industry but a supplier of the business	■ Gives control over quality, price and delivery times ■ Allows joint research and development into improved quality and design of components and materials ■ Business may now control supplies of materials to competitors ■ Absorbing the supplier's profit margin may reduce cost of essential supplies	■ May lack experience of managing a supplying company – a successful retailing business might not necessarily manage a manufacturing business effectively ■ Supplying business may become complacent due to having a guaranteed customer	■ Competing businesses that depended on supplies from the former independent business may have to find alternative sources of supplies ■ Consumers may obtain improved quality and more innovative products ■ Control over supplies of an important resource or component may limit competition and choice for consumers
Vertical forward integration – same industry but with a customer of the business	■ Business is now able to control the promotion and pricing of its own products ■ Obtains a secure outlet for its own products ■ Business now has direct contact with customers and this could provide useful market data ■ Retailers' profit margin absorbed so prices could be reduced	■ Lack of experience in managing the 'forward' stage of production, e.g. a manufacturing company may not have the skills needed to operate a retailing concern efficiently ■ Dominance of this firm's products in the retail outlets may be rejected by consumers looking for choice and variety	■ Consumer choice may be limited in these retail outlets ■ Prices may be higher (lack of competing products) or lower (profit margin absorbed so prices may be marked down) ■ Staff in the retail business may have less delegated authority if the business dictates how its products are to be displayed and marketed

| Conglomerate integration – different industry | • Diversifies the business away from its original industry and markets, and spreads risks

• Other industry may be faster growing than the one the business was originally in

• May be benefits of synergy if the processes and techniques of one industry can be effectively adopted in another | • Lack of management experience of the industry being entered

• There could be a lack of clear focus and direction now that the business is spreading its interests across more than one industry | • Greater opportunities for workers to gain experience in other markets

• More job security as business risks are spread across more than one industry |

In practice, many mergers and takeovers fail to gain true **synergy**, and shareholders are often left wondering what the purpose of the integration really was. Many examples of business integration have not increased shareholder 'value' for the following reasons:

- The integrated firm is actually too big to manage and control effectively – a diseconomy of scale.
- There may be little mutual benefit from shared research facilities or marketing and distribution systems if the firms have products in different markets.
- The business and management culture, for example the companies' approaches to environmental issues, may be so different that the two sets of managers and workers may find it very difficult to work effectively and cooperatively together.

Retrenchment

In some circumstances it may be necessary for a business to contract its operations in order to reduce costs. It often involves job losses and other cutbacks. The process of making a business smaller is called downsizing or **retrenchment**.

Retrenching the operations of a business is a difficult decision to take and may have serious long-term implications. Staff will have reduced job security and motivation may be adversely affected. Customers may be lost as products or services are withdrawn. Other stakeholders may lose confidence in the business as a result of negative publicity resulting from the difficult decisions being made. However, not taking drastic action to cut costs at times of market change, increased competition or economic recession can lead to total failure of a business.

Business in action

Big cutbacks at estate agents

One of the country's largest estate agents has announced the loss of hundreds of jobs and the closure of 12 branches. A spokesman for LSL Property Services, the owner of Your Move offices, said that, 'Our larger competitors are doing similar things. They have no choice as the number of property transactions could fall by 20 per cent this year.' The President of the National Association of Estate Agents said that 'larger agents are always the first to act when there is a slowdown as their costs are higher.'

Adapted from www.timesonline.co.uk, 5 January 2008

Key terms

Horizontal integration: merging with or taking over another business in the same industry at the same stage of production.

Vertical integration: merging with or taking over another business in the same industry but at a different stage of production.

Backward vertical integration: merger with a supplier business.

Forward vertical integration: merger with a customer business.

Conglomerate integration: merging with or taking over another business in a different industry.

Synergy: literally means that 'the whole is greater than the sum of parts', so in integration it is often assumed that the new, larger business will be more successful than the two, formerly separate, businesses were.

Retrenchment: the reduction of business costs in order to become more financially stable, increase profits and to move out of loss-making areas of operation.

Fig. 26.3 *Estate agents are some of the first businesses to close branches and retrench their operations during an economic downturn*

Link

Economic downturn is discussed in Chapter 21 — The relationship between business and the economic environment, page 164.

AQA   Examiner's tip

If an examination question refers to a merger or takeover, do not forget that they often cause businesses as many problems as they solve.

Link

The issue of leadership style is covered fully in Chapter 28 — Key influences on change process: leadership, page 236.

Key term

Management buy-out (MB-O): a form of ownership change where a company's existing managers acquire a significant part or all of the business.

Steps to take in the retrenchment process

The implications of this difficult decision can be eased and some credibility retained if the following steps are taken:

- consult with staff representatives on numbers of jobs to be lost
- give clear reasons for retrenchment
- state clearly when retrenchment will take place
- explain the assistance the employer intends to give retrenched workers
- reassure staff to be retained about their job security, pension rights and salary levels.

Changes in owners/leaders

Integration with another business is only one way in which the ownership of a business might change. According to a recent survey by Grant Thornton Accountants, 48 per cent of the owners of UK small and medium-sized businesses anticipated a change in business ownership for their firm and 30 per cent expected this change to occur within five years. The same survey reported that apart from selling the business to another firm – a takeover – the most common forms of ownership change were passing the business on to the next generation, management buy-out, flotation on the Stock Exchange and sale to employees.

Passing the business on to the next generation

This is very common with family businesses. The transition to the next generation could be quite smooth and seamless, but much depends on the leadership style of the younger generation. If it is very different to that of the retiring generation, then the impact on staff, the forms and extent of delegation and decision-making styles could be substantial.

Management buy-out (MB-O)

Management buy-out (MB-O) is now frequently used by existing business owners to dispose of all or part of the assets of the firm. Recent UK examples include New Look, Virgin Interactive and Virgin Megastores which are now known by the name of Zavvi.

Claimed advantages of management buy-outs

- The senior managers become the owners too, so they have the added incentive to work hard and take effective decisions as growth of the business will increase the value of their investment substantially. There is clearly now no divorce between management and control.
- By buying out a single business unit from a large corporation, the style of leadership may become less bureaucratic and decision-making should become quicker.
- The sale of the division to internal managers will raise capital for the parent company and will allow it to concentrate on other areas of its operations.

Potential limitations of management buy-outs

- Many MB-Os are financed with high debt levels and high gearing. This makes them very vulnerable to economic changes such as higher interest rates. If the business fails because of this, management will lose their jobs as well as their investment. This can add considerably to the stress on senior management.

- The business unit, if bought from a large parent company, will now lose the financial and technical support of this larger corporation.

Flotation on the Stock Exchange

Flotation on the Stock Exchange involves conversion to a public limited company. This is only likely to be a feasible option when the business has clear growth plans and can justify the raising of further capital by the sale of shares on the open market. Two main options exist for owners. The Alternative Investment Market (AIM) supports smaller companies that want their shares to be traded publicly. Larger businesses with a longer trading record may opt for a listing on the main London Stock Exchange.

The benefits of a flotation

- Flotation rewards the success of the entrepreneurs/business owners.
- It allows the business access to capital for expansion.
- It gives the business a higher market value as there will be a greater number of potential buyers of shares than when it was a private limited company. This increases the personal wealth of the original owners.
- The status of the business is improved.

Potential limitations of a flotation

- The cost of arranging the flotation may be too high, for example publication of a detailed prospectus.
- There is the potential for conflict between ownership and control – the main shareholders may not now be the managers and there could be conflict of objectives.
- Greater disclosure of accounting and other data is required.
- There is a risk of takeover if over 50 per cent of shares are sold by original owners.

Business in action

Moneysupermarket.com to float on London Stock Exchange

Simon Nixon, the co-founder of the price comparison website Moneysupermarket.com, is expected to pocket £200m from a flotation of the company on the Stock Exchange. All employees will be offered £3,000 in shares to help retain and motivate them. Capital raised from the flotation will be used to develop the services of the business.

www.PersonnelToday.com

Sale to employees

This is a variation on a management buy-out as under this scheme all existing employees may be given the right to buy a stake in the business. The firm is likely to retain the existing business and management structures. The employees are likely to be much more motivated as they have an opportunity for capital gain if the business is successful. This should help to ensure the future survival of the firm.

Poor business performance

Substantial or persistent losses or declining profits are another cause of business change. Owners of a business will expect to receive an adequate return on their investment and, if this is not achieved, then either changes in management or changes in business strategy can be expected to be the inevitable result. The previous section gave examples of plcs that changed ownership and senior management as a consequence of poor performance. The example of HMV is a good one to base our analysis on.

Business in action

HMV

HMV profits plunge as CD market evaporates

Profits at HMV, the music retailer, plunged by 73 per cent in 2007. Sales in the UK and Ireland fell by 3.4 per cent over the same period. The main reasons for this poor performance were given as 'difficult conditions for consumers' and the 'changing nature of the CD market with more music being downloaded than ever before'. Last year the Chief Executive was replaced by Simon Fox who pledged to make substantial changes.

HMV goes digital to halt decline

The HMV share price fell by 13 per cent after the high street retailer gave warning that profits would be lower than expected as it revealed details of a three-year 'turnaround strategy'. This strategy includes:

- management changes, including the departure of the Products Director
- sale of the Japanese division
- closure of loss-making stores
- increased product range, including MP3 and MP4 players, as well as speakers and other accessories
- new-style stores based on the pilot Dudley branch with a juice bar, mini Apple store, digital kiosks to allow music downloads and an Xbox Live zone
- partnerships with Universal and 20th Century Fox to sell their film content on HMV's website.

http://business.timesonline.co.uk

In the case of HMV (see above), poor business performance was largely caused by technological changes altering consumer buying habits and a slow response by the original HMV management to the changing market conditions. The changes that were brought about are typical of those that occur in persistently poorly performing companies:

- management changes
- strategy changes.

These will always have an impact on the staff who work in the organisation and the products and services it sells. In HMV's case, these changes seem to have met with some success as the latest data suggests increasing sales are being recorded by its stores.

Key term

Private equity ownership: when wealthy investors buy out a business which is usually underperforming and take it over with the intention of transforming its management and performance.

Private equity ownership

One of the major developments in recent years leading to a change of ownership for some businesses, including well-known public listed companies, has been the growth of **private equity ownership**.

Madame Tussauds, Boots and EMI are some of the best examples of companies that are now privately owned and not publicly listed on the Stock Exchange. Private equity ownership of well-known companies has received a great deal of criticism in recent years. The main arguments against this trend are that:

- substantial tax benefits are given to private equity investors and there is less public scrutiny as the accounts no longer have to be published
- unions argue that these investors are only interested in short-term profits and 'asset stripping' of undervalued assets. Jobs are often lost in the 'dash for short-term profits'.

Private equity investors respond by claiming that:

- the companies taken over were often underperforming and the injection of new management talent will lead to growth of these businesses
- there is now no divorce or division between ownership and control as the private equity investors both own and operate the business. There can be no conflict of objectives between owners and managers.

Case study

Jet Airways takes over Air Sahara

India's largest private airline, Jet Airways, says it has agreed to buy out its smaller rival, Air Sahara, for $140m. The take-over gives the airline a combined market share of about 32 per cent. Jet Airways acquires the aircraft, equipment and landing and take off rights at the airports Air Sahara had. 'This deal is definitely going to be good news for Jet Airways shareholders,' Jet Airways founder and chairman, Naresh Goyal, said at a press conference in Mumbai. Some analysts are predicting substantial synergy from this take-over. Better deals from aircraft manufacturers are expected. Streamlining the two head offices into one unit should reduce fixed costs. The interlinking of the different air routes should allow more passengers to be offered connecting flights with the new enlarged airline.

Before the take-over could go ahead, it had to be approved by the Indian Ministry of Company Affairs. There was some concern that the take-over could lead to a monopolistic position as Jet Airways will now enjoy a dominant position on many domestic air routes.

www.bbc.co.uk, 12 April 2007

Case study

Daimler sells Chrysler after failed merger

After nine years of trying to make the merger of two large car makers work successfully, Mercedes Benz has at last admitted defeat and sold its 80 per cent stake in the US-based operator, Chrysler. The merger never increased returns to shareholders and it failed in its original aim of creating a global motor company to compete effectively with General Motors, Ford and Toyota.

Management problems in controlling the merged businesses were huge. Distance between Germany (Mercedes Benz) and the USA (Chrysler) made communication difficult. The car ranges of the two companies had very little in common so there were few shared components so economies of scale were less than expected. Culture clashes between the two management approaches led to top-level director disputes over the direction the merged business should take.

www.timesonline.co.uk, 15 May 2007

Questions

1 How would you classify the type of integration used in both of these case studies? Explain your answer.

2 If Jet Airways were now to merge with an aircraft manufacturer:
   a How would this merger be classified? Explain your answer.
   b Explain two potential benefits to Jet Airways of this potential merger.

3 Analyse the likely impact of the Jet Airways takeover of Air Sahara on any two stakeholder groups.

4 Using the Daimler–Chrysler case study and any other researched examples, discuss why many mergers and takeovers fail to give shareholders the benefits originally predicted.

5 Identify a recent, well-publicised merger or takeover. For a six monthly period, research all newspaper articles or website articles on the performance of the newly enlarged business. Does the integration seem to have achieved lower costs and higher profits? Comment on your findings.

✔ *In this chapter you will have learned to:*

■ recognise that change can result from growth of a business

■ differentiate between internal and external growth

■ evaluate the impact on stakeholder groups of the different forms of external growth or integration

■ differentiate between other forms of ownership change

■ analyse why poor business performance often leads to internal business changes and changes of ownership.

Summary questions

1 Differentiate between internal and external business growth. Give some actual business examples. (6 marks)

2 Ford has recently sold Land Rover and Jaguar. Explain possible reasons why Ford's takeover of these two businesses was not as successful as originally predicted. (8 marks)

3 Examine the potential advantages and disadvantages to Sony of a decision to buy-out a chain of electrical retailers. (8 marks)

4 General Electric is a large engineering-based company but it also owns NBC Universal, a major US television channel. Analyse the potential advantages and disadvantages of this form of conglomerate growth. (8 marks)

5 Hornby Hobbies was a failing toy business before it was bought out by its own managers. Explain why this management buy-out might have contributed to the firm's later success. (8 marks)

6 Six years after the MBO, Hornby Hobbies was floated on the London Stock Exchange. Examine the likely reasons for this decision. (6 marks)

7 If Sainsbury and Tesco planned to merge:

a Explain what form of integration this would be. (2 marks)

b How might the government respond to this proposal? (6 marks)

8 BP owns oil fields, petrol refineries and petrol stations. What benefits do you think it has from integrating in this way? (6 marks)

Essays

9 Discuss the likely impact on stakeholder groups if Asda integrated, by takeover, with Morrison's supermarket. (40 marks)

10 'The ability of management to adapt to internal change is the key to a firm's long-term success.'
To what extent do you agree with this view? (40 marks)

Planning for change

In this chapter you will learn to:

■ explain the main features of a corporate plan

■ analyse the main purposes of corporate plans

■ assess the main internal and external influences on corporate plans

■ assess the value of corporate plans

■ discuss how contingency planning is carried out and the value of it.

Planning for the worst pays off

When arsonists destroyed the head office of Kent-based marketing agency FDS Group, chairwoman Allison Williams ensured her 75 employees were relocated and the business fully operational within three working days. 'Having a disaster recovery plan as part of our corporate plan helped to re-house the entire business in days and sent out a strong positive signal to our customers,' said Allison. 'Our contingency planning routines meant that our data was backed up off-site. We made use of our contacts in the local business community and had two temporary offices to view within 24 hours. The company secretary made sure the insurance company's loss adjustor was on-site by noon of the day after the fire. I've never been so proud of my staff and suppliers fell over themselves to help us too. There was no time to dwell on the situation – most of our customers are blue-chip businesses and they wanted the reassurance that we could be operational again as soon as possible.'

Managers from FDS held several informal meetings with customers within days of the fire to reassure them that it was 'business as usual'. This was also part of the firm's contingency plan. This demonstration of the firm's commitment to its customers paid off as it showed that customers' needs were valued above everything else.

Adapted from www.businesslink.gov.uk

Discussion points

1. Explain whether you think the time spent by this business in planning for disasters was worthwhile or not.

2. What problems might this business have experienced if it had not 'prepared for the worst'?

3. Do you think that even very small businesses should engage in some form of contingency planning? Explain your answer.

Corporate plans

What do corporate plans contain?

A typical **corporate plan** will include:

■ the overall objectives of the organisation within a given time frame. These could be:
  - profit target
  - sales growth
  - market share target

Key term

Corporate plan: a methodical plan containing details of the organisation's central objectives and how it intends to achieve them.

the strategy or strategies to be used to attempt to meet these objectives. For example, to achieve sales growth the business could:

- increase sales of existing products – market penetration

- develop new markets for existing products – market development

- research and develop new products for existing markets – product development

- diversify – new products for new markets

the main objectives for the key departments of the business derived from the overall objective.

Link

Corporate aims and objectives are discussed in Chapter 20 — Understanding mission, aims and objectives, page 155.

Fig. 27.1 *A corporate plan – linking objectives and strategies*

Links

The functional objectives of key departments are discussed as follows:

- Chapter 2 — Understanding financial objectives, page 9

- Chapter 7 — Understanding marketing objectives, page 48

- Chapter 11 — Understanding operational objectives, page 84

- Chapter 16 — Understanding HR objectives and strategies, page 121.

What are corporate plans for?

Potential benefits

The value of corporate planning for several years ahead is that senior managers have a clear focus and sense of purpose for what they are trying to achieve and the means they should use to reach these aims. Hopefully, they will communicate this sense of purpose and focus to all managers and staff below them in the organisation – and this is an important requirement for corporate plans to be effective. An important benefit of any corporate plan is the control and review process. The original objectives can be compared with actual outcomes to see how well the business's performance matched its aims.

The whole planning process is a very useful exercise as well. When effectively done, actually preparing for and producing the corporate plan can have the benefits of forcing senior managers to consider the organisation's strengths and weaknesses in relation to its environment and to think about how all of the different functional departments of the firm interrelate.

Potential limitations

Plans are great if nothing else changes. The best-laid plans of any business can be made obsolete by rapid and unexpected internal or external changes. This does not mean that planning is useless – far from it, as part of the planning process may well be looking ahead to consider how to respond to unforeseen events – see contingency planning below. What change does mean, however, is that if a business puts, say, a five-year plan into effect and then refuses to make any variations or adaptations to it, no matter how much external environmental factors might change, then this inflexibility will be punished. The planning process and the plans that result from it should be as adaptable and flexible as possible to allow them to continue to be relevant and useful during periods of change.

The value of corporate plans

The fact that there are very few businesses without a formal planning process for the future suggests that corporate planning is very important. The plan is not just for senior management consumption. It will be essential to share the contents of such a document with:

- potential investors when a share sale is considered
- major lenders to the organisation
- other stakeholder groups, for example the government if requesting development grants for expanding into an area of high unemployment
- all staff – in the form of a specific and tangible objectives for all departments, sections and individuals that will be based on the original objectives and strategies contained in the corporate plan.

The main influences on a corporate plan

Internal influences

Internal influences on a corporate plan include:

- financial resources
- operating capacity
- managerial skills and experience
- staff numbers and skills
- culture of the organisation.

External influences

External influences on a corporate plan include:

- macro-economic conditions
- Bank of England and government economic policy changes
- likely technological changes
- competitors' actions.

■ Contingency planning

Contingency planning is also known as 'business continuity planning' or 'disaster-recovery planning' which perhaps give a better idea of what it is for. Unplanned events can have a devastating effect on businesses of any size. Crises such as fire, floods, damage to stock, illness of key staff, IT system failure or accidents on the business's premises or involving its vehicles could all make it difficult or impossible to carry out normal everyday activities. At worst, important customers could be lost or the firm could go out of business altogether.

Effective contingency planning allows a business to take steps to minimise the potential impact of a disaster and, ideally, prevent it from happening in the first place. The key steps in contingency planning are:

1 Identify the potential disasters that could affect the business: Some of these are common to all businesses but others will be specific to certain industries. For example, the oil industry must plan for oil tankers sinking, explosions at refineries and leakages in oil and gas pipelines.

■ **Link**

Organisational culture is discussed in detail in Chapter 29 — Key influences on change process: culture, page 244.

AQA Examiner's tip

The relative importance of these factors will vary from business to business. A company producing income elastic luxury products may find its corporate plan is most influenced by macro-economic forecasts. The directors of a small company may consider that the plan for their business is most constrained by internal financial limits.

■ **Key term**

Contingency planning: preparing an organisation's resources for unlikely events

2 Assess the likelihood of these occurring: Some incidents are more likely to occur than others and the degree of impact on business operations varies too. It seems obvious to plan for the most common disasters, but the most unlikely occurrences can have the greatest total risk to a business's future. These issues need to be balanced carefully by managers when choosing which disaster events to prepare for most thoroughly.

3 Minimise the potential impact of crises: Effective planning can sometimes cut out a potential risk altogether. When this is not possible, the key is to minimise the damage a disaster can do. This does not just mean protecting fixed assets and people, but also the company's reputation and public goodwill, as far as possible. This is often best done by the publicity department telling the truth, indicating the causes when known and giving full details of how to contact the business and the actions being taken to minimise the impact on the public. Staff training and practice drills with mock incidents are often the most effective ways of preparing to minimise negative impact.

4 Plan for continued operations of the business: As in the Setting the scene case study, prior planning can help with alternative accommodation and IT data – the sooner the business can begin trading again, the less the impact is likely to be on customer relationships.

Business in action

Cadbury's had a plan ready

The risk of salmonella contaminating millions of chocolate bars put Cadbury's corporate plan in doubt (see the Case study below). The problem was caused by a leaking pipe in Cadbury's UK factory, but the company's contingency plan swung into action. Over a million chocolate bars were recalled by the company, they were disposed of in a completely safe way and the Food Standards Agency was informed. Retailers were fully compensated for stock that was destroyed. Cadbury's apologised to all customers. Business consultants doubted whether the incident would cause any long-term damage to the company's image or brand names because of the detailed contingency plan that was put into operation.

Activities

Read the 'Cadbury's had a plan ready' Business in action and answer the following questions.

1 Outline two other incidents or 'disasters' that could have a major impact on Cadbury's sales and reputation.

2 Evaluate the importance of contingency planning in this case.

Fig. 27.2 *The Buncefield oil depot disaster would have been even more destructive without detailed contingency planning*

Table 27.1 *The benefits and limitations of contingency planning*

Benefits	Limitations
■ Reassures staff, customers, local residents that concerns for safety are a priority	■ Costly and time consuming – not just the planning process but the need to train staff and have practice dry runs of what to do in the event of fire, IT failure, terrorist attack, accident involving company vehicles, and so on.
■ Minimises negative impact on customers and suppliers in the event of a major disaster	■ Needs to be constantly updated as the number and range of potential disasters can change over time
■ Public Relations response is much more likely to be speedy and appropriate with senior managers being used to promote what the company intends to do, by when and how	■ Staff training needs increase if labour turnover is high
	■ Avoiding disasters is still better than planning for what to do if they occur

Case study

New goals for Cadbury Schweppes

Cadbury Schweppes is a major multinational confectionery and drinks business. In 2003, the directors published some details of their new corporate plan which set specific goals for the company to be achieved over the next three years. In 2007, it reported that these had been achieved.

For example, one objective was to 'profitably and significantly increase global confectionery market share'. The success was measured by 'a 60 base point increase in global market share' and an '11 per cent increase in emerging markets revenue growth per year'.

A second objective was to 'profitably increase regional beverage sales'. The 2007 Company Report noted that, 'we have increased revenue from US sales of beverages by 4.7 per cent per year over this period.'

Buoyed by these successes, the directors set out new company goals and strategies for 2007/2008. These included:

■ Goal: 'Deliver superior shareholder returns'. Strategy: 'Relentless focus on cost reduction and efficiency improvement'.

■ Goal: 'Be the best regional beverages business'. Strategies: 'Further innovation of products and expand consolidation of bottling plants'.

Adapted from www.investis.com

Questions

1. What is meant by the term 'corporate plan'?

2. Explain how Cadbury Schweppes might measure its success in achieving the two goals outlined in the case study.

3. Analyse two factors that might make it difficult for Cadbury Schweppes to achieve the two goals contained in the case study.

4. Evaluate the usefulness of corporate planning to a multinational business such as Cadbury Schweppes.

☑ *In this chapter you will have learned to:*

- explain the meaning of corporate plan and what a corporate plan contains
- evaluate the factors that influence a firm's corporate plan and the reasons that might prevent it from being achieved
- assess the value of corporate plans
- understand the key stages in the process of contingency planning
- evaluate the usefulness of contingency planning.

Summary questions

1   Outline three benefits to a company of establishing a corporate plan. (6 marks)

2   What are likely to be the most significant factors that influence the corporate plan of a family-owned company producing exclusive leather furniture? (8 marks)

3   Why is it important to update a corporate plan? (4 marks)

4   Examine the benefits to an oil company such as BP of undertaking extensive contingency planning. (10 marks)

5   Why is staff training an essential part of an effective contingency plan? (4 marks)

6   Assess the major actions you would expect an airline business to take in the event of a crash involving one of its aircraft. (8 marks)

Essays

7   'Contingency planning is a waste of resources as major accidents are often unavoidable but, in any case, they rarely occur.'
To what extent do you agree with this view? (40 marks)

8   'The value of a corporate plan to a firm's long-term success cannot be overestimated – it is the key to future profitability.'
Discuss this view. (40 marks)

Key influences on the change process: leadership

Setting the scene

In this chapter you will learn to:

- analyse the meaning of leadership and compare different leadership styles
- assess internal and external factors influencing leadership style
- understand the role of leadership in managing change
- evaluate the importance of leadership.

Jack Welch – the greatest business leader of all?

As CEO of General Electric, Jack Welch took over when the business had a value of $12bn. Twenty years later, on his retirement, this had grown to $500bn. His huge success and reputation was built on using a very human process to drive change through GE's vast organisation. He had respect for the individual as the main force in organisational change. Under Welch's leadership, managers had wide authority to build their GE divisions into entrepreneurial units. Two of his famous quotes were:

- 'The individual is the source of all creativity and innovation and our people must accept the truth that the best way to manage people is just to get out of their way.'
- 'Getting in great talent, giving them all the support in the world and letting them run is the leadership philosophy of GE.'

www.leadershipprofiles.com

Discussion points

1. What do you understand by the term 'a good leader'?
2. What kind of business leader did Jack Welch seem to be?
3. How important do you think leadership is to the success of a business?
4. Jack Welch once said, 'The role of a leader is to express a vision, encourage people to accept it and then implement it.' Can you think of a good business example of this?

Key term

Leadership: influencing and directing the performance of group members towards achieving the goals of the organisation.

Leadership

There are many diverse definitions of **leadership**. Many of them include the following features:

- exerting influence on others
- motivating and inspiring people
- helping team/organisation members to realise their potential
- setting a good example
- encouraging the team/organisation members to achieve the organisation's goals.

Peter Drucker, a famous writer on business issues, suggested that 'the only definition of a leader is someone who has followers'. This must be true – but it does not tell us much about what the practice of leadership actually involves. This short definition of leadership is very much to the point: leadership is about influencing and directing the performance of group members towards achieving the goals of the organisation.

It is important to differentiate between leadership and **management**. Management has been defined as the process of setting objectives and taking decisions to make the most efficient use of an organisation's resources. Table 28.1 summarises the key differences between leadership and management.

> **Key term**
>
> **Management:** the process of setting objectives and taking decisions to make the most efficient use of an organisation's resources.

Table 28.1 *Key differences between leadership and management*

Leadership	Management
Motivating and inspiring others	Directing and monitoring others
Innovators who encourage others to accept change	Problem solvers
Stems from personal qualities or traits	Official position of responsibility in the organisation
Natural abilities and instincts	Skilled and qualified to perform role
Believes in doing the right thing	Believes in doing things right
Respected and trusted by followers – they want to follow because of leader's personality	Listened to by others because of status – not necessarily because of personality
Creates and develops a culture of change	Accepts and conforms to the 'norms' of the organisation

Effective leadership

Effective leadership is based on key personal skills and qualities. The four most important are:

- ability to communicate: To lead others effectively it is essential to be able to communicate with them. By communicating with clarity and authority, leaders should be able to inspire their 'followers' (or workers) to want to work hard to achieve the aims of the organisation

- willingness to listen: The best communication is two-way, which means that the leader must be able to send messages clearly and with authority and must also be able to listen to others. Failure to accept the need to receive and act upon messages as well as to send them will lead to ineffective leadership

- capable of critical thinking: Critical thinking means thinking logically and not being influenced by personal wants or desires. Leaders should solve problems by gathering data and weighing up alternatives before making a decision. This will inspire confidence of their 'followers' that there is a clear sense of direction and a logical path to follow

- great self-motivation and determination to succeed – and an ability to enthuse others to be self-driven too.

> **AQA Examiner's tip**
>
> Do not take these five leadership styles as being absolutes. For example, it is possible for a range of democratic styles to exist or for some managers to be extremely authoritarian and for others to be mildly authoritarian.

Leadership styles

Leadership style refers to the way in which managers take decisions, change and deal with their staff. There are five distinct management styles:

- **Autocratic** (or authoritarian) **leadership:** These leaders make decisions without consulting others. They set objectives for the business themselves, issue instructions to managers and staff and then check to ensure that they are carried out. Such leaders have set views on how the business should be managed and run. They believe it is both more efficient and quicker to take all decisions centrally.

> **Key term**
>
> **Autocratic leadership:** leaders take decisions on their own with no discussion.

Democratic leadership: leaders discuss with workers before making decisions.

Paternalistic leadership: leaders will listen, explain issues and consult with the workforce but will not allow them to take the final decision.

Bureaucratic leadership: leaders use rigid and complex rules and procedures to direct and lead the organisation.

Laissez-faire leadership: leaders leave their colleagues to get on with their work so there is no supervision or control.

■ **Democratic** (or participative) **leadership:** These leaders engage in discussion with workers before taking decisions. There is, therefore, considerable scope for involvement and participation. This can have benefits to both the organisation with better informed decisions and to the individual with higher levels of motivation.

■ **Paternalistic leadership:** Paternalistic literally means 'father-like'. The paternalistic leader will decide what is best for the business but will have sought the opinions of staff first and will finally explain the decision to them. The paternal leader treats the workforce as a family unit and emphasises the meeting of the social and leisure needs of the staff.

■ **Bureaucratic leadership:** These leaders use rigid and complex rules and procedures to direct and lead the organisation. Truly bureaucratic organisations have a hierarchical structure, clearly defined job roles, lack of flexibility in applying organisational rules and recruitment by competence not flair.

■ **Laissez-faire leadership:** These leaders leave their colleagues to get on with their work without supervision or control. It can be effective if the leader monitors what is being achieved and communicates this back to the team regularly.

Table 28.2 compares these five leadership styles.

Table 28.2 *Five leadership styles compared*

Style	Main features	Limitations	Possible applications
Autocratic/ authoritarian	■ Leader takes all decisions ■ Gives little information to workers ■ Supervises workers closely ■ Only one-way communication	■ Demotivates workers who want to contribute and accept responsibility ■ Decisions do not benefit from workers' knowledge and experience	■ Defence forces and police/ fire services where quick decisions are needed and the scope for discussion is limited ■ In times of rapid change or crises when decisive action might be needed to limit damage to the business
Democratic/ participative	■ Worker involvement is encouraged – this could lead to better decisions ■ Two-way communication is used which allows feedback from workers ■ Job enrichment is more likely to be achieved	■ Consultation with staff can be time-consuming ■ On occasions, quick decision-making will be required ■ Should staff be involved in all aspects of a business? Some issues might be too sensitive, e.g. job losses, or too secret, e.g. development of new products	■ An experienced and flexible workforce is more likely to benefit from and contribute to this style of leadership ■ In changing situations that demand a new way of thinking or a fresh solution, staff input can be valuable
Paternalistic	■ Managers do what they think is best for the business and the workers ■ Consultation and explanation take place but final decision rests with managers. No true participation at work ■ Managers want workers to be happy in their jobs	■ Some workers may be frustrated and demotivated with the apparent attempts to consult while not having any real influence or power ■ It might be difficult for management to take tough decisions if some staff lose out as a result	■ Used by managers who have a genuine concern for workers' interests but who feel that managers know best in the end ■ When workers are young or inexperienced and participative style might be inappropriate

Bureaucratic	Clearly defined rules	Slow to respond to new situations	In large organisations where consistency and rational decision-making are important, e.g. government departments
	Impersonal	Excessive use of paperwork and forms	
	Centralised decision-making – especially to deal with new or unusual situations	Enterprise not encouraged	
	Tightly defined job descriptions	Power concentrated at the top	
Laissez-faire	Little if any management supervision	Ineffective if it is used as a result of weak managers not exerting control when it might be needed	When teams contain very experienced and self-motivated staff
	Feedback on progress towards agreed targets		When creativity is crucial to success, e.g. scientific research or advertising agencies

■ McGregor's Theory X and Y

This famous distinction between two extreme types of leader was based on research undertaken by Douglas McGregor to establish leaders' assumptions about the workers they were responsible for. These assumptions influence how managers lead and direct their staff. McGregor coined the terms 'Theory X leaders' and 'Theory Y leaders'. The key points of difference between these two extreme leadership assumptions are summarised in Table 28.3.

Table 28.3 *Theory X and Theory Y*

Theory X leaders believe most workers:	Theory Y leaders believe most workers:
do not like work and will avoid it if possible	find work as natural as rest or play
need to be controlled and monitored to make sure they put in effort at work	do not naturally dislike work
are motivated by money not the chance of accepting responsibility	will seek and willingly accept responsibility under most circumstances
seek security not job enrichment at work	are motivated by means other than control and threats
	are capable of showing initiative and imagination in helping their business to succeed

Clearly, a manager with assumptions of workers based on Theory X will tend to use an autocratic style of leadership. Managers with assumptions about workers based on Theory Y will tend to adopt a more democratic and participative approach to allow workers to show their initiative and accept responsibility.

In practical terms, most managers' views and assumptions about workers will lie somewhere between these two extreme positions and may well be influenced by the experience and skills of the groups of workers they deal with. There is clear evidence, though, that since the 1950s when McGregor was developing his ideas, management attitudes generally have moved a long way from the Theory X extreme view that assumes workers are all mediocre and lack talent and commitment.

Procter & Gamble

McGregor was employed by Procter & Gamble to help design a new factory in Augusta, USA. It was designed along Theory Y principles with self-managing work teams of 12 workers, common objectives agreed with management and regular meetings to improve communication. Productivity was 30 per cent higher than other factories in the company.

■ Factors that influence leadership style

The most important point to remember about leadership styles is that no single approach to leadership is appropriate at all times and in all circumstances. There is no single right way to manage an organisation or to lead people that suits all situations. The factors that determine the most appropriate leadership style at any one time are internal and external to the business.

Internal factors

Internal factors that influence leadership style are:

- the skill levels and experience of the team: The greater these are, the higher the chance of a democratic style proving to be effective
- the work involved: Is it routine or creative? Would an error put the entire business at risk?
- the preferred or natural style of the leader: Some leaders are more inclined towards being autocratic or democratic than others
- the time limit: Must a quick decision be taken? In such a case, perhaps there is no time for participation.

Business in action

The manager of a food manufacturing business trains new machine operatives using a bureaucratic style to ensure that the workers know the precise procedures that achieve the right standards of product quality and workplace safety. The same manager adopts a participative style of leadership when seeking product improvements from a quality circle team of workers.

External factors

External factors that influence leadership style are:

- the economic environment: Rapid decisions taken at a senior level may be needed to secure the survival of a business during a recession
- the nature and speed of change in the industry: Ideas for technological change often come from teams of committed workers who have been given considerable scope for participation and problem-solving
- legal changes: If changes are necessary due to new laws, such as those governing health and safety at work, then a directive approach may be needed to ensure that they are effectively applied in the workplace.

A good leader will find him or herself switching instinctively between styles according to the people and work they are dealing with and the external environment of the organisation. This is often referred to as 'situational leadership'.

Leadership and managing change

The essential differences between leadership and management are made clear when discussing organisational change. **Managing change** means:

- setting new objectives that recognise the need for change
- ensuring that adequate resources – financial and staffing – are made available for the changes to be put into effect
- appropriate planning needs to be in place to ensure that the proposed change is put into effect.

Contrast this with **leading change**:

- establishing a vision for the business and attracting staff towards it
- motivating staff at all levels so that the change is looked upon positively. This will lead to significant improvements in the behaviour of workers and reduce their resistance to change
- putting change at the centre of the culture of the organisation – not just tacked on as an afterthought.

As Jack Welch (see Setting the scene) said, 'Change before you have to' and this means pro-active leaders who will make change a force for good rather than managers who just put the resources for change in place.

Assessing the importance of leadership

The significance of clear and effective leadership to the success of a business cannot be overemphasised. This is never more true than during a period of rapid and structural change in the organisation. This applies to painful and traumatic changes such as downsizing and redundancies but it also applies to positive changes that affect the working lives of those in the business.

AQA Examiner's tip

If the question refers to an 'appropriate leadership style', a very effective form of evaluation is to indicate that there are several factors that will determine this and that what is appropriate in one case may be unsuitable in another.

Activities

Identify what might be the most appropriate leadership style to adopt in each of the following situations. Be prepared to explain and justify your answer in each case:

1. Training of staff in applying the company's Ethical Code of Conduct.

2. Trying to find a solution to a long-standing quality problem on a bread production line.

3. An oil company responding to an environmental disaster resulting from a crash involving one of its tankers.

4. Teams of IT software designers working on major new IT developments.

Business in action

Reckitt Beckinser

Bart Becht's leadership at Reckitt Beckinser has made all the difference to this cleaning products and detergent business. Sales are up 44 per cent in four years and profits up nearly 300 per cent since 1999. A clear vision – focus on growth markets only, such as dishwasher powder – and a team-based approach to looking at ways to cut costs have transformed this company. He travels up to 300,000 miles a year to visit company departments abroad, attracts and employs highly talented staff and quickly cuts out underperforming products.

Fig. 28.1 *Bart Becht has shown sterling leadership skills at Reckitt Beckinser*

In an organisation where there is faith in the senior managers, employees will look towards their leaders for a number of things:

- clear vision and sense of direction
- support and commitment to their welfare
- confident and effective decision-making
- effective planning

■ timely and full communication.

These leadership virtues are then most likely to result in successful acceptance of change.

In organisations with poor leaders, employees expect nothing positive. In a climate of mistrust, employees learn that leaders will act in irrational ways with little understanding of the impact their decisions can have on the staff working around them. In these cases, not only must the organisation deal with the practical issues of unpleasant changes but also the deadweight of employees who have given up, have no faith in the system or in the ability of leaders to turn the organisation around.

■ Case study

New leader – new style

Henly Soaps plc is a major producer of cosmetics and beauty products. It used to be the market leader in the UK market, but sales fell by 20 per cent over a recent five-year period. A new Chief Executive, Sheila Banks, was appointed two years ago and given the responsibility of turning the business around. Under the old management team, a paternalistic style of management had persisted from the days when the business was a family-run firm. Harsh decisions had been avoided but labour turnover had been very low as workers enjoyed substantial social benefits.

Sheila had a vision for the business to become number 1 in the UK with a new range of 'eco-friendly' make-up and soaps. She also planned to enter the European market, but realised that this would need a new team of managers with authority to take decisions relevant to this new market. She spent most of her first month in the job visiting all five production plants, the research laboratory and administration offices. She met all staff in small group meetings and encouraged them to express their thoughts on the future of the business. She explained the need for change and the risk to the whole business if changes were not introduced quickly. After brief negotiations with unions, two of the lowest productivity factories were closed. Plans were announced to launch the new soap and cosmetic ranges made in a brand new factory. Staff who had lost their jobs were offered employment first, but they had to agree to give up social benefits and re-train so that they could make an effective contribution to the company's new quality control system. During this period of upheaval, productivity increased and absenteeism fell. Union leaders accepted the new strategies and even offered funds to help re-train the workers. After six months, market share had risen by 15 per cent and favourable reports appeared regularly in the financial press about Sheila's 'effective leadership'.

Questions

1 Explain what is meant by the term 'effective leadership'.

2 Outline two potential implications of paternalistic leadership for this business and its employees.

3 Analyse the leadership styles Sheila seemed to adopt at Henly's.

4   To what extent will it be important to the success of Henly's that Sheila and her senior directors vary their leadership style to deal with different circumstances?

5   Use the Times Power 100 as a starting point to investigate the degree of success and styles of leadership of any two of the UK's most powerful business leaders.

✓ *In this chapter you will have learned to:*

■ explain the nature of leadership and its importance to the success of a business

■ assess the suitability of different leadership styles to different business situations

■ understand the difference between leadership and management, especially in cases of organisational change

■ assess the importance of leadership in managing people.

Summary questions

1   What makes a good leader, in your opinion? (6 marks)

2   Explain the key differences between the paternalistic and democratic styles of leadership. (6 marks)

3   Give examples of business situations when an authoritarian style of leadership might be appropriate. (5 marks)

4   Do you think a business manager should just have one style of leadership and 'stick with it'? Explain your answer. (8 marks)

5   Explain the difference between managing and leading change in a manufacturing business that needs to increase productivity to maintain competitiveness. (8 marks)

6   Do you think a business could still be successful even though leadership is poor within the firm? Explain your answer. (8 marks)

7   Explain, with examples from within your school or college, the difference between leadership and management. (6 marks)

Essays

8   'During periods of rapid external change the role of the leader – more, even than a good manager – becomes crucial to success.'
Discuss this view. (40 marks)

9   'Good business leaders are born not trained.'
To what extent do you agree with this view? (40 marks)

Key influences on the change process: culture

Setting the scene

Culture change to meet increased competition

DLM is a European airline that underwent a spectacular turnaround. Under a new Chief Executive, the company switched from a product and technology focused business to a market and customer service oriented one. Under the old organisational culture, the pilots, technicians and autocratic managers were the company's heroes. Planning and sales were based on maximising flight hours with the most modern aircraft possible. Worsening profits forced a change of approach. The new CEO understood the changing and increasingly competitive air travel market and the need to cater for the needs of current and potential customers.

Those needs were best known by the employees with face-to-face contact with the customers – cabin crew and ground staff. These people had never been asked for their opinions. They had just been a disciplined group of uniformed 'soldiers' trained to follow clear rules and procedures. The CEO changed all this. These staff are now considered to be 'on the firing line' and the organisation was completely restructured to support them, not to order them around. Superiors are now advisers, simulation training is given in customer relations and the staff are given considerable independence in dealing with customers' problems on the spot. They only check with their senior managers after the event – which involves much confidence in employees' judgement with all the risks this entails.

Customer numbers and profits have been on a steady upward flight path since these changes in culture were introduced.

Discussion points

1. What do you understand by the term 'organisational culture' from this case study?

2. Explain why the new CEO thought that he had to make changes to this culture.

3. Why did the changes made by the CEO seem to have been introduced so successfully?

Organisational culture

What is organisational culture?

A commonly used definition of **organisational culture** is 'the way we do things around here'. This means how the people within the organisation view the world and respond to it in trying to achieve certain goals.

It is widely understood that different organisations have distinctive cultures. This is very true of businesses as well as other organisations such as schools and colleges. The culture of a steel company will be very different to that of a nursing home. Similarly, some school cultures are driven by the need for better examination results while others view that educating the 'complete person' is more important. The culture of an organisation gives it a sense of identity and is based on the values, attitudes and beliefs of the people who work in it, especially senior management.

Values, attitudes and beliefs have a very powerful influence on the way staff in a business will act, take decisions and relate to others in the organisation. They define what is 'normal' in an organisation. So it is possible for the same person to act in different ways in different organisations. What we do and how we behave – in society in general and in business in particular – is largely determined by our culture.

The main types of organisational culture

Many management writers have used different ways to identify and classify the types of organisational culture. These are the most widely used culture types:

- **power culture**: This is concentrating power among just a few people. It is associated with autocratic leadership. Power is concentrated at the centre of the organisation. Swift decisions can be made as so few people are involved in making them
- **role culture**: This is most often associated with bureaucratic organisations and is where each member of staff has a clearly defined job title and role. People in an organisation with this culture operate within the rules and show little creativity. The structure of the organisation is well defined and each individual has clear delegated authority. Power and influence come from a person's position within the organisation.
- **task culture**: This is based on cooperation and teamwork, where groups are formed to solve particular problems. There will be lines of communication similar to a matrix structure. Such teams often develop a distinctive culture because they have been empowered to take decisions. Team members are encouraged to be creative.
- **person culture**: this is where individuals are given the freedom to express their views and make decisions for themselves. There may be some conflict between individual goals and those of the whole organisation but this is the most creative type of culture.
- **entrepreneurial culture**: This encourages management and workers to take risks, to come up with new ideas and test new business ventures. Success is rewarded in an organisation with this culture but failure is not necessarily criticised as it is considered an inevitable consequence of showing enterprise and risk taking.

Activity

For each of the different types of culture, suggest one business situation in which it would be the most appropriate culture to adopt.

Changing organisational culture

Possible reasons for change

Many businesses have turned themselves around, converting potential bankruptcy into commercial success. Very often this transformation

AQA Examiner's tip

Culture is such a powerful force in any organisation that you should take every opportunity in your answers to A2 questions to make reference to it as a factor that helps explain managers' decisions and behaviour.

Key terms

Power culture: concentrating power among just a few people.

Role culture: each member of staff has a clearly defined job title and role.

Task culture: based on cooperation and teamwork.

Person culture: when individuals are given the freedom to express themselves fully and make decisions for themselves.

Entrepreneurial culture: encourages staff to take risks, to come up with new ideas and test out new business ventures.

AQA Examiner's tip

As with leadership styles there is no one right or wrong culture for a business. The appropriate culture will depend on the firm's objectives, the type of market it operates in and the values and expectations of managers and employees.

Do not expect all departments in a business to have the same culture. It can be very different. Would you expect the team working with IT all day to have the same jargon, patterns of behaviour, values and beliefs as HR staff or the marketing team?

has been achieved by changing the culture of the business. The existing culture of a business can become a real problem when it seems to stand in the way of growth, development and success. Here are some examples of situations when changing culture would seem to be essential:

■ A traditional family firm which has favoured members of the family for promotion into senior posts converts to a public limited company. New investors demand more transparency and recognition of natural talent from recruited employees.

■ A product-led business needs to respond to changing market conditions by encouraging more staff involvement. A team or task-based culture may need to be adopted.

■ A recently privatised business, formerly run on bureaucratic principles, needs to become more profit-oriented and customer-focused. An entrepreneurial culture may need to be introduced for the first time.

■ A merger or takeover may result in one of the businesses having to adapt its culture to ensure consistency within the newly created larger business unit.

■ Declining profits and market share may be the consequences of poorly motivated staff and a lack of interest in quality and customer service. A person-based culture might help to transform the prospects of this business.

Activity

Think of two further situations that might require a change of business culture.

Business in action

Porsche

Perhaps one of the reasons for the astonishing success of the Porsche motor manufacturing business is the culture embodied by the views of its boss, Wendelin Wiedeking. 'The Porsche philosophy is that first comes the client, then come the workers, then the suppliers and finally the shareholders. When the first three are happy then so are the shareholders.' Compare this with the typical view in US and UK-based businesses that often promote 'shareholder culture' as being most important. These differences in outlook and culture help to explain why high profile integrations between BMW and Rover Cars and then Chrysler and Mercedes-Benz were such disasters.

Fig. 29.1 *The collapse of the Chrysler/Mercedes-Benz merger was largely due to culture differences*

The problems of changing organisational culture

Changing the value system of a business and attitudes of all staff who work for it is never going to be an easy task. The process could take several years before all staff and processes have been fully 'converted'. It means changing the way people think and react to problem situations. It can mean directly challenging the way things have been done for years. It can also involve substantial changes of personnel, job descriptions, communication methods and working practices.

Much work has been done on analysing the best way to bring about change to an organisation's culture. The key common elements to these different approaches are:

■ Concentrate on the positive aspects of the business and how it currently operates and enlarge on these. This will be much easier and more popular with staff than focusing on, and trying to change, negative aspects.

■ Obtain the full commitment of people at the top of the business and all key personnel. If they cannot or will not change, it might be easier to replace them altogether. Unless the key personnel model the behaviour they expect to see in others, change will be very difficult to achieve.

■ Establish new objectives and a mission statement that accurately reflect the new values and attitudes that are to be adopted – and these need to be communicated to all staff.

■ Encourage bottom-up participation of workers when defining existing problems or when devising new solutions. The biggest mistake could be to try to impose a new culture on workers without explaining the need for change or without giving them the opportunity to propose alternative ways of working.

■ Train staff in new procedures and new ways of working to reflect the changed value system of the business. If people believe in the change and understand the benefits of it, then it will become more acceptable to them.

■ Change the staff reward system to avoid rewarding success in the old ways and ensure that appropriate behaviour that should be encouraged receives recognition. People need to be reassured that if they adjust to the new approach then they will gain from it.

> ■ Link
>
> See Chapter 20 — Understanding mission, aims and objectives, page 155.

> ■ Activity
>
> A housing development for disabled workers has been owned and operated by a profit-making private company for many years. A charity has just been successful in buying the development from the company. Explain the steps the new management might have to take to change the culture of the organisation.

Fig. 29.2 *The six critical success factors for changing organisational culture*

British Airways

British Airways used to be a nationalised, state-owned business. It was overstaffed and customers' satisfaction ratings were low. Privatisation brought a profit focus to all strategic decisions. Staff numbers were reduced, but productivity and profits increased. Managers were encouraged to be enterprising in taking decisions to increase customer numbers and profits. The new culture brought risks too. In 2008 BA agreed to pay compensation to thousands of passengers who, for two years, had been overcharged a fuel surcharge that BA had illegally fixed with Virgin Atlantic. Possibly additional staff training may have helped to demonstrate those circumstances where 'how we do things around here' might conflict with legal obligations.

■ Evaluating the importance of organisational culture

The significance and power of an organisation's culture to drive people's behaviour and attitudes should not be underestimated. Most of us do not want to be seen to do the wrong thing within any group of people that we work with and this feeling is particularly strong within a business environment. However, the impact of culture goes beyond the desire of most people to conform with accepted values. The following examples help to reinforce the importance of organisational culture:

■ The values of a business establish the norms of behaviour of staff – what is and what is not acceptable in certain situations. For example, is it acceptable in this organisation to offer bribes to attract large contracts 'as long as we are not found out'?

■ Culture determines the way in which company managers and workers treat each other. For example, if the Chief Executive is open and receptive to new ideas and proposals from senior managers, then this approach is likely to filter through the whole organisation – to its potential long-term benefit.

■ A distinctive organisational culture can support a business brand image and relationships with customers. For example, Body Shop almost invented the ethical trading culture. Will this approach to business now change after its takeover by L'Oreal?

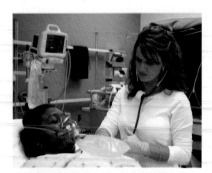

Fig. 29.3 *Should targets and budgets be allowed to influence patient care and treatment?*

■ Culture determines not just how decisions are made – with the participation of staff or by top managers alone – but also the type of strategic decisions that are taken. For example, the culture of NHS target setting and rewards for meeting short waiting times within Accident and Emergency departments is, it is claimed, encouraging hospital managers to decide to leave patients in ambulances for up to two hours. How different would it be if doctors were taking these decisions?

■ Organisational culture has been clearly linked to the economic performance and long-term success of organisations. Businesses dedicated to continuous improvement with staff involvement have been shown to be more profitable in the long term. For example, Toyota is the prime example of success based on this principle.

Regal Supermarkets – a case study in cultural change

As one of the UK's largest family-owned chain of supermarket stores, Regal Supermarkets had established a culture amongst its staff that had contributed in no small way to its many years of growth. Loyalty to the family managers was very high. In fact, staff often commented on the whole business being like a 'big family'. Staff were promoted for long service and loyalty. Relationships with suppliers had been built up over many years and long-term supply contracts were in place. Customer service was a priority and was especially important as Regal never intended to be the cheapest shop in the towns it operates in. However, profits were not high and the younger members of the owning family lacked the skills to take over.

It was clear to some industry experts that some of these values and attitudes had to change once it was sold by the family and converted into a public limited company. The new Chief Executive, Sally Harte, had experience in the US as Wal-Mart's chief food buyer. She announced on the first day of her appointment that, 'This business is like a sleeping giant. There is so much shareholder value that I can unlock to allow for higher dividends and to underpin a higher share price.' Within five weeks, 50 per cent of the directors and key managers had been replaced. Suppliers' terms were changed, on Sally's insistence, to '5 per cent below the cheapest or we drop you' and the staff salary and pension scheme was replaced for new recruits with flexible pay and conditions contracts. Staff turnover increased sharply.

Sally had not predicted the adverse media coverage of these changes. 'I am only trying to adapt the organisational culture of this business to one which allows us to be successful in a highly competitive national market place where consumers want low prices and fresh goods.'

Questions

1. Explain one possible reason why Sally thought it necessary to change the organisational culture of Regal Supermarkets.

2. Outline the type of culture that Sally seems to be introducing at Regal Supermarkets.

3. Analyse the key steps that Sally should have taken to manage cultural change more effectively.

4. To what extent will the change in culture guarantee future success for this business?

5. Compare the organisational culture of any club or society that you are a member of or know well with the culture of Wal-Mart. Use the BBC and Times websites to access articles about Wal-Mart and its US and UK operations.

☑ *In this chapter you will have learned to:*

■ explain the key features of organisational culture

■ analyse the main types of organisational culture

■ explain some of the important steps that need to be taken to change an organisation's culture successfully

■ assess why organisational culture is important.

Summary questions

1 If you were appointed to a management position in a well-known business, what evidence would you look for to allow you to identify or classify the culture of the organisation? (6 marks)

2 Explain the possible problems of changing the culture of a business with a small but loyal staff and customer base. (8 marks)

3 How might a business attempt to establish a people culture? (6 marks)

4 Explain two reasons why the culture of a fast-food restaurant might need to be changed. (8 marks)

5 Explain two reasons why workers may resist attempts to change the culture of the organisation they work for. (8 marks)

6 Examine the differences between bureaucratic and entrepreneurial culture, including examples of different circumstances in which each type of culture might be appropriate. (10 marks)

Essays

7 Discuss the factors that will determine the extent to which a new Chief Executive of an oil company, with a poor safety record and bad reputation for oil spills, will be able to change successfully the culture of the organisation. (40 marks)

8 'In markets with increasing competition resulting from globalisation, it is essential for all businesses to adopt an entrepreneurial culture if they are to succeed.' To what extent do you agree with this view? (40 marks)

Making strategic decisions

In this chapter you will learn to:

- differentiate between strategic and tactical decisions

- examine the importance of information management to strategic decision-making

- evaluate different approaches to decision-making

- assess the main influences on corporate decision-making.

Setting the scene

Caffè Nero and Asda: contrasting strategies to achieve growth

Although both companies have similar objectives – sales growth leading to profitability – Asda and Caffè Nero present an interesting contrast in business strategy. The coffee bar operator is going for market development. Gerry Ford, Caffè Nero's chairman who led the management buy-out of the business in 2007, has set a target of 100 branches to be opened in Turkey. He said that he was 'also looking around Europe and scouting out China'. He is confident of success in Turkey. He has appointed Isik Asur, a Harvard Business School graduate who used to run the Starbucks operation in the country. He knows all about the changing consumer tastes in the country as well as the political, social and economic environment there.

Asda – number 2 supermarket chain in the UK – has decided on the strategies of market penetration and product development to build sales growth. New food stores will be opened in the next few years in an attempt to gain ground on Tesco. It aims to be the lowest price supermarket to increase food sales further. In addition, it is expanding rapidly into non-food retailing. It plans to open ten new Asda Living stores selling a huge range of items for the home – but not food.

Different businesses in different markets will often decide on different strategies for the future – even though overall objectives may be similar.

Discussion points

1. Why do companies like these need long-term plans to help achieve their objectives?

2. Suggest six facts about the Turkish consumer market and economy that Caffè Nero would have found useful before taking this strategic decision.

3. Compare and contrast the different strategies being adopted by these two companies and comment on possible reasons why these were decided upon.

4. What factors might influence the long-term plans or strategies adopted by a business?

Fig. 30.1 *Strategies are designed to achieve corporate objectives*

Key term

Business strategy: a long-term plan of action to achieve the objectives of the business.

Business strategy

What is a business strategy?

A **business strategy** is the plan that directs the activities of the business over a long period of time. Deciding on new business strategies is a vitally important role of senior management. Taking the appropriate strategic decisions will make or break a business. This chapter focuses on the key features of business strategic decision-making.

■ Business in action

Business strategies

Tesco's long-term objectives of increasing global sales and profits has led to the recent strategy of opening many convenience stores in California – its first venture into the US market. In 2008, Airbus Industries set the objective of remaining profitable in difficult economic circumstances – the directors took the strategic decision to rationalise by closing some factories and making redundancies.

Strategic or tactical decisions?

There are important differences between **strategic decisions** and **tactical decisions**. Table 30.1 illustrates some of them.

Table 30.1 *The differences between strategic and tactical decisions*

Strategic decisions	Tactical decisions
■ Long-term consequences for the business	■ Usually short-term consequences
■ Usually have implications for all departments of the business	■ Often taken within one department
■ Taken at senior management level	■ Taken by middle management
■ Difficult to reverse	■ Can be reversed if unsuccessful
■ Often involve considerable investment of resources	■ Fewer resources need to be committed to putting these decisions into effect

■ Business in action

Strategic and tactical decisions

The Tesco example given earlier clearly involved a strategic decision. The move into the US market was very expensive, was very high profile resulting in huge publicity for the business and, once the decision was made, would be difficult to reverse without considerable wastage of resources and a loss of public image.

In contrast, a decision by Volkswagen to reduce the price of its Fox model in order to reach sales revenue targets could be reversed quickly if the cut in price of 5 per cent did not lead to an increase in car sales of more than 5 per cent. This was a tactical decision.

■ The significance of information management

Strategic management – taking strategic decisions – requires detailed information if it is to be successful.

Essentially, then, **information management** means getting the right information to the right person at the right time. When that information is recorded and collated using IT and used for decision-making the term **management information system (MIS)** is often used.

An effective MIS would provide senior managers with:

■ data about options that would allow a more accurate choice

■ Key terms

Strategic decisions: result in changes to long-term plans, involve many resources and are difficult to reverse.

Tactical decisions: involve meeting short-term targets, require fewer resources to implement and may be easy to reverse.

Information management: the collection and assessment of information from one or more sources and the distribution of that information to the appropriate managers.

Management information system (MIS): a computer system designed to help managers plan, take decisions and control business operations.

- simulated results of what would happen if a particular decision was taken
- up-to-date information about the performance of all profit centres and individual products.

The quality and accuracy of strategic decisions will greatly depend on the accuracy and relevance of the information used by managers when making the final choice. While computers and management information systems cannot create business strategies by themselves, they can assist managers in understanding the effect of their strategic decisions. However, even the most comprehensive information management system will not guarantee business success. Managers still need to analyse information appropriately, take effective and timely decisions and manage all resources in the business towards the desired goal. Mere information is not enough.

One model of strategic decision-making suggests that there are three main stages in the process:

1 strategic analysis
2 strategic choice
3 strategy implementation.

Strategic analysis

This involves trying to find answers to all of the questions shown in Table 30.2. This will require detailed information management and extensive analysis of data gained from many different sources.

Table 30.2 *Areas of focus for strategic analysis*

Answers needed to these questions	Potential sources of information
Where does the business stand at present and what are its main strengths and weaknesses?	▪ **SWOT analysis**
Which markets could the business compete in?	▪ Market research data ▪ Research and development results of new products
How do competitors operate in these markets and how successful are they?	▪ Market research data ▪ Competitor analysis
How can the business perform better than the competition in these markets?	▪ Competitor analysis ▪ Test market results
What are the likely costs of each of the strategic options?	▪ Past data from previous, similar decisions ▪ Cost forecasts from marketing and operations departments
What are the likely sales and revenue gains from each of the different options?	▪ Market research data ▪ Test market results
What are the likely chances of success or failure of each of the different options?	▪ Success rates from similar strategic decisions ▪ Competitor analysis – success/failure rate of similar strategies
What external, environmental factors affect the business's ability to compete?	▪ **PEST analysis** – analysing political, economic, social and technological constraints

Activity

Give two examples of strategic decisions and two examples of tactical decisions that a high-street banking business could take to increase numbers of customers holding current accounts.

Key terms

PEST analysis: the assessment of the external political, economic, social and technological factors that may present constraints on strategic decisions made by a business.

Key terms

Scientific decision-making: an attempt to make logical business decisions on the basis of data that is analysed and tested.

AQA Examiner's tip

Remember that effective information management can make all the difference between a successful business decision and one that 'almost made it'.

Link

For SWOT analysis, see Chapter 10 — Developing and implementing marketing plans, page 75.

Link

Ansoff's matrix is a useful analytical tool for assessing the risk of different business strategies. Risk – and the degree of it that managers are prepared to accept – is an important consideration when making strategic choices. See Chapter 9 — Selecting marketing strategies, page 66, for an explanation of Ansoff's matrix.

Fig. 30.2 *Computer-based management information systems are now a key part of information management*

Business in action

Strategic analysis

Sony's victory over Toshiba in the high definition DVD battle was a huge blow for the innovative Japanese company. This new technology meant that little backdata had been available to Toshiba's management when assessing the likely chances of success of its HD-DVD technology.

The opening of a new Starbucks café carries relatively little risk as this strategic decision is informed and assisted by huge amounts of data about the success of previous café openings.

Strategic choice

This stage involves evaluating and choosing between strategic options and will also require management access to much detailed information. Data will be needed to allow calculation of investment appraisal measures, break-even levels and forecasted returns on capital employed. Care should be taken when analysing most of this data as it will largely be based on forecasted figures. Computerised simulations would be an essential part of information management at this stage.

Strategy implementation

When a strategy has been decided on, then the task of management is to translate this into action by organising resources and motivating people so that the long-term plan is put into effect. Once in place, the strategy will need to be monitored and reviewed using budget data and actual results – variance analysis. This process will also require regular and frequently updated information management.

Activity

Assume that Dell Computers are considering entering the home TV market with their own branded flat-screen TVs. Outline what data about the market, competitors and the economy the management would need to analyse before taking this decision.

Different approaches to decision-making

The process outlined above – data analysis, choice and implementation – is often referred to as the **scientific decision-making** approach.

Pure or 'natural' scientists, such as chemists, will use the equipment and resources at their disposal to try to solve a problem or test an idea until a logical and rational deduction is made or an answer is arrived at. This is the typical approach used by research scientists in laboratories. How can this method be adapted to business decision-making? One of the best ways of illustrating this is to look at the decision-making model in Table 30.3. The stages should be completed in the order shown and if enough time and resources are allocated to each stage, the chances of the strategic decision eventually failing will be much reduced.

An extreme, alternative approach to decision-making is to use experience and intuition – and not refer to any data at all. Some entrepreneurs claim to have such a 'feel' for a new business opportunity that they do not need

Scientific	Hunch, i.e. based on a manager's intuition
■ Reduces risk of strategic failure by simulating the outcome of different options	■ Much cheaper than scientific approach as it is costly to collect and analyse data – can small businesses afford this?
■ Decisions that fail after test marketing will be halted – potentially saving huge sums for the business	■ Much quicker as it takes time to use the scientific method – in a fast changing market, could a firm lose 'first mover advantage' by strictly following this scientific model?
■ Analysis of market and other data should result in a better decision or it might even suggest or open up other market opportunities	■ Scientific method does not guarantee success anyway – even a successful test market does not mean that the majority of the target population respond positively to this strategic change
	■ Hunches could work well if the business has taken many similar decisions before

Table 30.3 *Scientific decision-making versus intuitive decision-making*

the cost and time devoted to the scientific approach to tell them what they already know. There are potentially high risks with this intuitive or 'hunch' approach, but it is much quicker than employing the scientific approach.

■ The main influences on corporate decision-making

The main influences on corporate decision-making are summarised in Table 30.4.

Table 30.4 *The four main factors that will influence important strategic decisions*

Influence on corporate decision-making	Impact on decisions
Corporate objectives	■ This should be clearer to you by now. The objectives are the key determining factor in business strategy. An objective of rapid sales growth might be more effectively achieved in the long run by product innovation and market development than by adopting a market penetration strategy.
Ethical position	■ Some strategies may carry more of an ethical risk than others. Should Gap continue with the strategy of using Far Eastern sources of supply despite the problems the company has experienced in ensuring they adopt the ethical code of conduct?
	■ This ethical stance may be real or perceived as such by customers. If a business that is looked upon as being basically ethical in its commercial affairs is seen to be acting against normal moral standards, it may pay a high price in lost consumer confidence and poor publicity.
	■ In 2008 Tesco was arguing for controls over price discounting of alcoholic drinks – to curb binge drinking amongst the young. This seemed to be a truly ethical position. The *Times* newspaper then reported that Tesco was in fact the biggest discounter of alcohol!
Resources available	■ This is always a major consideration. Some strategic choices may be beyond the resources of certain businesses. Product innovation can be very rewarding – but huge investments may be required for many years before returns are received.
	■ Lack of suitably skilled staff or poor facilities may also limit the strategic options open to management.
	■ If resources become very scarce, for instance during a recession, a strategy may even have to be adapted or reversed.

Relative power of stakeholder groups	■ Powerful stakeholder groups could make an impact on strategic decisions. Environmental groups have pressurised petrol companies to make biofuel products available in many stations. The 'dash to organic products' by food retailers has been influenced by media pressure and well advertised campaigns by celebrity chefs.
	■ In contrast, the declining power of UK trade unions could not prevent job losses by offshoring companies, as with Burberry's closure of its UK factory in order to source quality clothing products from China.

AQA Examiner's tip

These factors may often conflict, of course, and a good answer on business strategy would recognise that the relative importance of these influences could also vary over time. Investment in alternative energy sources was never a high priority for the major oil companies. The combination of high oil prices, environmental pressure and the objective of being perceived as socially responsible has led to dramatic changes in investment strategy by these businesses.

Case study

New objective needs new strategies

The private equity buy-out of Artco Furniture has put a new management team in charge. The declared objective of the new directors is to 'slim the business down, refocus it and prepare it for public limited company status'. Many of the smaller retail stores, offering excellent consumer service in smaller towns with no other furniture shops, are to be sold. They are popular with consumers but high labour costs make them unprofitable. The furniture and home decoration superstores will be expanded. There will be a huge push to gain market share by internet selling. In addition, Eastern Europe will be the location of new store openings. Existing furniture ranges will be sold in these shops. 'We can't redesign everything to their taste, but they have been starved of good furniture for decades so our current ranges will still sell,' suggested the Marketing Director.

New designs will be bought in from abroad as the existing design team will be closed with some job losses. This decision and the shop closures will result in 1,200 job losses. One market analyst said that the business was putting the interests of its existing and future shareholders before those of the workers and unions. A recent report in *The Independent Manager* magazine suggested that if these decisions were perceived as being unethical by the public, the cost gains of the new strategies could be cancelled out by lower sales.

Questions

1 Why did new strategies have to be devised for this business?

2 Outline the usefulness of an up-to-date management information system for the directors when deciding which stores to close.

3 Analyse the data needed by the business before deciding on the market development strategy in Eastern Europe.

4 Evaluate the factors that will influence the success of these new strategies.

5 Use the internet to research recent private equity buy-outs of firms such as HMV, EMI and Boots. Assess how the strategies of these businesses have changed since these buy-outs.

✅ *In this chapter you will have learned to:*

- recognise the key features of a strategic decision

- assess the importance of effective information management to successful strategic decisions

- discuss the relative merits of scientific decision-making and intuition

- evaluate the importance of key influences on strategic decisions.

Summary questions

1 Explain the main differences between a strategic decision and a tactical decision. (4 marks)

2 What do you understand by the term 'management information system'? (3 marks)

3 Use examples to outline why accurate information would be essential before a Boots management team took a decision about launching a new range of cosmetic products. (6 marks)

4 Have you seen 'Dragons' Den' on BBC TV? When deciding whether to invest in a new project or not, do the Dragons seem to use the scientific decision-making method or intuition? Explain your answer. (6 marks)

5 Under what circumstance could a hunch decision prove to be more effective than one taken using the scientific model? (6 marks)

6 Explain two influences that will affect a strategic decision by a US business to close a clothing factory and outsource production to Thailand. (8 marks)

Essays

7 'I have the simple but strong belief: how you gather, manage and use information will determine whether you win or lose.'

(Bill Gates, Chairman of Microsoft)

To what extent does information management determine the competitiveness of a business? (40 marks)

8 Using recent examples to support your answer, discuss the key factors that can influence major strategic business decisions. (40 marks)

Implementing and managing change

In this chapter you will learn to:

- explain the main stages to be followed when an organisation implements and manages change

- assess the role of project champions and project groups in implementing and managing change

- analyse and assess the main factors that promote change in an organisation

- analyse and assess the main factors that lead to change resistance in an organisation.

Setting the scene

IT drives business change at Volkswagen

Radical changes to the way the IT department supports departments within VW have led to significant cost reductions and quality improvements. VW produce and sell cars in the world's most competitive marketplaces. It faces the twin threats of changing consumer tastes and Asian rivals who operate with much lower labour costs. Constant change is needed to maintain competitiveness. VW have a clear vision for all major changes it introduces – to reduce costs, improve quality and reduce product development times. These will combine to increase sales. The number of IT applications has been reduced from 4,000 to just 300 and the company is also set to cut thousands of jobs across all departments over the next two years.

The complete redesign of the work of the IT department started in 2005. Traditionally the IT department provided support to other departments when and how necessary. IT now has a 'horizontal' IT team that connects different parts of the business together into processes rather than departments. So, for example, the IT team will bridge the gap between market research, designers who know how to design a new car and the production team who know best the process of building it. Chief technology officer, Stefan Ostrowski, explained that, 'we want to design quality cars that are easy to build – IT acts as the link between the different departments that are involved in this process.'

VW trained 400 IT staff in business processes and in how to mediate between different departments. IT staff are rotated to different business areas every four years to give staff new skills. 'Communication was also a key part of this change as if IT does not explain its new role in clear business language you will not change anything,' concluded Ostrowski.

www.computerworlduk.com

Discussion points

1. Why did VW realise that constant change is necessary?

2. Why do you think a clear vision or objective is important before making changes?

3. Explain why improved communication and training were key features of the successful changes to the work of the IT department within VW.

4. Do you think important business changes could ever take place without the support of staff? Explain your answer.

■ Techniques for implementing and managing change

Understand what change means

Change is the continuous adoption of business strategies and structures in response to changing internal pressures or external forces. Change happens whether we encourage and welcome it or not. To take control of it and to ensure that it is a positive, and not a negative process, businesses must have a vision, a strategy and a proven and adaptable process for managing change.

Today, change in business is not the exception but the rule – it has become an accelerating and ongoing process. Table 31.1 gives some common causes of change. 'Business as usual' will become increasingly rare as global, economic and technological upheavals necessitate a business response. **Change management** requires firms to be able to cope with dramatic one-off changes as well as more gradual evolutionary change:

- Evolutionary or incremental change occurs quite slowly over time. For example, the swing towards more fuel-efficient cars has been happening for several years. These changes can be anticipated or unexpected – the decision to increase the London congestion charge was announced months in advance, but a sudden oil price increase may not have been expected. Obviously, incremental changes that are easy to anticipate tend to be the easiest to manage.

- Dramatic or revolutionary change, especially if unanticipated, causes many more problems. Civil conflict in Kenya in 2008 forced many safari holiday companies to re-establish themselves in other countries or markets. In extreme cases, these dramatic changes might lead to totally rethinking the operation of an organisation using a 'clean slate'. This is called **business process re-engineering**.

Recognise the major causes of change

The major causes of change are given in Table 31.1.

Understand the stages of the change process

This is a checklist of essential points that managers should consider before attempting to introduce significant changes in an organisation:

- Where are we now and why is change necessary? It is important to recognise why a business needs to introduce change from the situation it currently finds itself in.

- New vision and objectives. For substantial changes, a new vision for the business may be needed – and this must be communicated to those affected by the change.

- Ensure resources are in place to enable change to happen. Starting a change and then finding that there is too little finance to complete it could be disastrous.

- Give maximum warning of the change.

- Staff in particular should not be taken by surprise by change – this will increase their resistance to it.

- Involve staff in the plan for change and its implementation. This will encourage them to accept change and lead to proposals from them to improve the change process.

■ Key terms

Change management: planning, implementing, controlling and reviewing the movement of an organisation from its current state to a new one.

Business process re-engineering: fundamentally rethinking and redesigning the processes of a business to achieve a dramatic improvement in performance.

AQA Examiner's tip

When discussing how change will affect a business and its strategies, try to analyse whether the change was incremental or dramatic, anticipated or unanticipated.

■ Activities

1 Identify some recent changes in the external business environment that have an incremental impact on business.

2 Identify other recent changes that have occurred that have had a dramatic impact on business.

Table 31.1 *The major causes of change*

Nature of change	Examples of change	Managing change
Technological advances – leading to new products and new processes	■ Products: new computer games, iPods and iPhones, hybrid powered cars ■ Processes: robots in production; CAD in design offices and computer systems for stock control	■ Need for staff retraining ■ Purchase of new equipment ■ Additions to product portfolio – other products to be dropped ■ Need for quicker product development which may need new organisational structures and teams
Macro-economic changes – fiscal policy, interest rates, fluctuations in the business cycle	■ Changes in consumers' disposable incomes – and demand patterns that result from this ■ Boom or recession conditions – need for extra capacity or rationalisation	■ Need for flexible production systems – including staff flexibility – to cope with demand changes ■ Explain need for extra capacity or the need to rationalise ■ Deal with staff cutbacks in a way that encourages staff who remain to accept change
Legal changes	■ Changes to what can be sold (raising age of buying cigarettes) or when (24-hour licences for public houses)	■ Staff training on company policy on sale of cigarettes and alcohol ■ Flexible working hours and practices
Competitors' actions	■ New products ■ Lower prices – based on higher competitiveness/lower costs ■ Higher promotion budgets	■ Encourage new ideas from staff ■ Increase efficiency by staff accepting the need to change production methods ■ Ensure resources are available to meet the challenge

■ **Link**

See Chapter 16 — Understanding HR objectives and strategies, page 121, for more about 'soft' HRM.

AQA **Examiner's tip**

Use your understanding of communication gained from Chapter 16 to assess the importance of two-way communication in motivating staff to accept change.

■ **Key term**

Force field analysis: an analytical process used to map the opposing forces within an environment (such as a business) where change is taking place.

■ Communicate. The vital importance of communication with the workforce runs through all of these other stages.

■ Introduce initial changes that bring quick results. This will help all involved in the change to see the point of it.

■ Focus on training. This will allow staff to feel that they are able to make a real contribution to the changed organisation.

■ Sell the benefits. Staff and other stakeholders may benefit directly from changes – these need to be explained to them.

■ Always remember the effects on individuals. A 'soft' human resource approach will often bring future rewards in terms of staff loyalty when they have been supported and communicated with during the change process.

■ Check on how individuals are coping and remember to support them. Some people will need more support than others – a 'sink or swim' philosophy will damage the business if it leads to low quality output or poor customer service because staff were poorly supported during the change period.

Force field analysis

Force field analysis, first developed by Kurt Lewin, provides a framework for looking at the factors (forces) that influence a change situation. These forces can either be 'forces for change' that help the organisation towards a goal or 'forces against change' that might block or hinder an organisation from reaching its goal.

The steps to follow are:

1 Outline the proposal for change – insert in the middle of Fig. 31.1.

2 List all the forces for change in one column and all the forces against change in the other.

3 Assign an estimated score for each force – 1 is weak and 5 is strong.

Fig. 31.1 shows force field analysis of a proposal for installing IT-controlled manufacturing equipment in a factory. The numerical scores indicate whether the forces are weak (for example, 1) or strong (for example, 5).

Once this analysis has been carried out, the process can help management improve the probability of success of this major change. For example, by training staff (which might increase cost by +1), the fear of technological change could be reduced (reducing fear by –2).

Fig. 31.1 *Force field analysis of an IT-controlled machinery proposal*

Project champions

A **project champion** is often appointed by senior management to help drive a programme of change through a business.

A project champion will come from within the organisation and be appointed from middle to senior management – they need to have enough influence within the organisation to make sure that 'things get done'. They are like 'cheerleaders' for the project, but they will not necessarily be involved in the day-to-day planning and implementation of the new scheme. They will smooth the path of the project team investigating and planning the change and they will remove as many obstacles as possible. For example, they will speak up for the changes being suggested at board or other meetings of senior managers, they will try to ensure that sufficient resources are put in place and they will try to make sure that everyone understands the project's goals and objectives.

Compass Group

Jane Moger is HR Director within the restaurant business Compass Group. She has acted as project champion for the implementation of an e-recruitment system within the organisation. 'Being a project champion in HR gives you an opportunity to get involved in complex, long-term and high-valued added activities. Project champions get a new project off the ground and give the team momentum to see the change through,' she said.

www.personneltoday.com

Project groups or teams

'Problem solving through team building' is a structured way of making a breakthrough on a difficult change situation by using the power of a team.

When a difficult problem arises regarding a major change in a business's strategy or structure, one of the most common ways to analyse it and suggest solutions is to organise a **project group**. Project groups should work with the manager responsible for introducing the change. A team meeting of experts should provide a rigorous exchange of views that may well lead to an appropriate action plan being developed and agreed. The responsibility for carrying the plan out still lies with the original manager. Now, though, he or she will be better equipped to solve the problem that was preventing change from being effectively implemented.

■ Promoting change

Promoting change is an important function of management. Gaining acceptance of it – both by the workforce and other stakeholders – will be much more likely to lead to a positive outcome than imposing change on unwilling groups. According to John Kotter, a leading writer on organisational change, the best way to promote it in any organisation is to follow the following eight-stage process:

1 Establish a sense of urgency.
2 Create an effective project team to lead the change.
3 Develop a vision and a strategy for change.
4 Communicate this change vision.
5 Empower people to take action.
6 Generate short-term gains from change that benefit as many people as possible.
7 Consolidate these gains and produce even more change.
8 Build change into the culture of the organisation so that it becomes a natural process.

If change is not 'sold' (promoted) to the people most affected by it, then it is almost certainly going to build up damaging resistance that could increase the chances of failure.

■ **Key term**

Project groups: these are created by an organisation to address a problem that requires input from different specialists.

■ **Activity**

A business is planning to adopt a new IT system that will allow many staff to work from home several days a week. Some senior managers are against this as it will 'reduce control over workers'. The IT manager in charge of implementing this strategy decides to appoint a project champion to smooth the change over.

What are likely to be the key qualities of this project champion, do you think?

AQA Examiner's tip

Effective management of change should, where possible, focus on the positive benefits of change to the stakeholders most affected by it.

Resistance to change

This is one of the biggest problems any organisation will face when it attempts to introduce changes. The managers and workforce of a business may resent and resist change for any of the following reasons:

- fear of the unknown: Change means uncertainty and this is uncomfortable for some people. Not knowing what may happen to one's job or the future of the business leads to increased anxiety – this results in resistance
- fear of failure: The changes may require new skills and abilities that, despite training, may be beyond a worker's capabilities. People know how the current system works – but will they be able to cope with the new one?
- losing something of value: Workers could lose status or job security as a result of change and they want to know precisely how the change will affect them
- false beliefs about the need for change: To put themselves at ease and to avoid the risks of change, some people fool themselves into believing that the existing system will 'work out someday' without the need for radical change
- lack of trust: Perhaps because of past experiences, there may be a lack of trust between workers and managers who are introducing the change. Workers may not believe the reasons given to them for change or the reassurances from managers about the impact of it
- inertia: Many people suffer from inertia, or reluctance to change, and try to maintain the status quo. Change often requires considerable effort so the fear of having to work harder to introduce it may cause resistance.

The importance of the resistance factors will vary from business to business. In those firms where previous change has gone well, where workers are kept informed and even consulted about change and where managers offer support and training to the staff involved, resistance to change is likely to be low. Contrast this with the likely resistance to change in businesses where there is a lack of trust and little communication.

AQA Examiner's tip

When discussing the possible resistance to changes proposed by management, try to think of the leadership style being used to implement the change. This could be a major contributory factor in determining the degree of resistance.

Activity

Land Rover has been sold to the Indian company Tata. There is a new management plan to open a Land Rover factory in India making the current models, but to keep the Solihull UK plant open. If this plan goes ahead, how might any resistance to this change among existing UK workers be reduced?

Case study

Constant change: a feature of modern industry

Britax has undergone many changes in recent years. The business grew out of a diverse group of companies. The Britax names and brand were adopted at the end of the 1990s when the business decided to concentrate its efforts and sold off some of its activities. It now focuses on child safety seats and designing and building aircraft interiors. The sales of the child safety seats have been boosted by recent changes in the law. Aircraft interiors is a niche market with four international competitors. Overall turnover of Britax's aerospace division has grown from £20m to £150m in six years despite intense competition and an aircraft building industry that fears a fall in aircraft orders.

Britax has just introduced a new, complex and expensive computer system to manage its production resource planning. Stock levels have fallen dramatically and productivity has improved. But this involved changes in many people's work practices and skills. As with all changes of this nature, the crucial key to success lies not with the product but with those who have to use it. 'People react in different ways to change,' said Graham Leake, the business systems manager. 'How people approach change is a critical factor. A big factor in managing this is to build a strong project team. The right people need to be involved from the start. The next step is training and communicating the need for change. We spent a great deal of time and effort in this area and it was well worth it.'

www.independent.co.uk

Questions

1 Why is almost constant change likely to occur within businesses such as Britax?

2 Outline two ways in which Britax reduced resistance to change.

3 Analyse how either force field analysis or a project champion could have helped during this change.

4 Evaluate the most important stages in the process of implementing and managing large-scale changes within a business.

5 Research topic: Analyse how any one major change that is currently occurring within a business is being managed. It could be a merger or takeover, rationalisation or a big change in product strategy or production methods. Research in as much detail as you can how stakeholders are being communicated with and how resistance to change is being minimised.

☑ *In this chapter you will have learned to:*

- understand why the need for change is ever present in business organisations

- analyse how change can be most effectively introduced within organisations so that everyone 'buys into it'

- assess the importance of promoting change and communicating the benefits of it

- assess the factors that lead to resistance to change and how these can be best overcome.

Summary questions

1 Explain the difference between incremental and revolutionary business change, using recent examples. (6 marks)

2 Outline two likely causes of change for a business making cameras. (6 marks)

3 Why is communication an important part of the change process? (6 marks)

4 Explain the role of a project champion to a team of people who are worried about technological change affecting their work practices. (6 marks)

5 Explain how a project group could help a manager with the task of introducing important changes to the business. (6 marks)

6 a Explain any two causes of resistance to change that might occur in your school or college after the headteacher or principal has announced a major reorganisation of the departmental/faculty structure. (6 marks)

  b For each of these causes of resistance, explain how staff might be reassured. (6 marks)

Essays

7 'The effective management of change in today's world will be the main factor determining the success or failure of businesses.' To what extent do you agree with this view? (40 marks)

8 Discuss how business leaders can effectively introduce major changes within their organisation. (40 marks)

Examination skills

The AQA A2 Business Studies examinations

There are two examination papers that are used to assess the AQA A2 Business Studies course.

Unit 3 BUSS3 – Strategies for Success

- This is worth 25 per cent of the final A Level grade.
- The examination is 1 hour 45 minutes long.
- The questions are based on a business case study containing both numerical data and written evidence.
- The questions will be drawn from the Unit 3 section of the specification.
- The final question will always ask for a detailed analysis of the arguments for and against a particular business strategy and the answer should conclude with a detailed and supported recommendation.

Unit 4 BUSS4 – The Business Environment and Managing Change

- This is worth 25 per cent of the final A Level grade.
- The examination is 1 hour 45 minutes long.
- The paper will be divided into two sections.
    - Section A will examine the issues related to the pre-issued research theme and one question from a choice of two must be answered. The pre-issued research theme will be based on a key issue from Unit 4 of the specification.
    - Section B will consist of a choice of three essays from which one must be answered. All questions will be synoptic, therefore drawing upon knowledge from all four units.

Examination entries

Both Unit 3 and 4 will be offered in January and June each year. Depending on the policy that operates in your school or college, you may be entered for these in a number of different ways. These are shown in Table 32.1.

Do not forget that, in both January and June the AQA Board allows A2 students to retake either or both of the AS units – but this will depend again on the entry policy of your school or college. The main aim of the rest of this chapter is to help you prepare for the A2 units so thoroughly that you do no have retake either of them.

What examiners are looking for

The assessment objectives

As we saw in the AS book, 'assessment objectives' is a technical term used for 'examination skills'. These are the particular abilities you will be expected to demonstrate in your examination answers. These are the skills the examiners will award marks for. The four assessment objectives are the same as at AS Level. Here is a reminder:

Table 32.1 *Methods for examination*

	January A2 year	June A2 year
Exam strategy 1:		
Unit 3	1st attempt	Retake (if necessary)
Unit 4		1st attempt
Exam strategy 2:		
Unit 3	–	1st attempt
Unit 4	–	1st attempt
Exam strategy 3:		
Unit 3	1st attempt	Retake (if necessary)
Unit 4	1st attempt	Retake (if necessary)

Table 32.2 *Assessment objectives*

AO1 – Assessment Objective 1	Knowledge	Demonstrate knowledge and understanding of the specified subject content
AO2 – Assessment Objective 2	Application	Apply knowledge and understanding to problems and issues arising from familiar and unfamiliar situations
AO3 – Assessment Objective 3	Analysis	Analyse problems, issues and situations
AO4 – Assessment Objective 4	Evaluation	Evaluate, distinguish between and assess appropriateness of fact and opinion and judge information from a variety of sources

These AOs are exactly the same at A2 as at AS Level, but they are worth different proportions of the total marks. Table 32.3 gives a breakdown of how many marks are awarded to each skill in the two A2 unit examinations, which in total are both marked out of 80.

Table 32.3 *Breakdown of marks at A2*

Paper	Knowledge	Application	Analysis	Evaluation	Total
Unit 3 (BUSS3)	16	24	20	20	80
Unit 4 (BUSS4)	16	16	20	28	80
Total	32	40	40	48	160
% of A2 total marks	20%	25%	25%	30%	

It is important to note that the skill of evaluation is a much more important skill at A2 than at AS Level and that subject content knowledge is, in terms of relative marks, the least important. However, remember that you will gain *no* marks for any question that does not demonstrate *some* relevant subject knowledge – this skill must be shown before *any* marks for the other skills can be awarded.

The command words at A2

It is very important that you understand that A2 examination papers will not ask questions that *only* ask for knowledge or even *only* knowledge plus application. A2 is meant to be more challenging than AS. This is reflected in the fact that only command words that require the skills of analysis and evaluation, in addition to knowledge and application, will be used in questions.

Table 32.4 *Examples of command words at A2*

Command word/term	Skills being examined	Examples
Analyse ...	Knowledge Application Analysis	Analyse whether Project A or B gives a higher average rate of return. Analyse the profitability of Location A. Analyse whether the Finance Director is correct to say that both projects will earn a positive NPV.
Discuss ... Evaluate ... Recommend ... To what extent ...	Knowledge Application Analysis Evaluation	To what extent do you consider the 'hard' HR strategy to be a success? Discuss the importance of a marketing plan to the success of this new project. Discuss whether lean production is a suitable operations strategy for this business. Recommend which of these two options should be adopted by the business, taking both quantitative and qualitative factors into account.

We will now look more closely at the importance of these command words, and the assessment objectives that they test, by studying them in the context of specimen examination papers.

■ Unit 3

Unit 3 example scenario. Ref: (AQA, 2008)

Read the case study and answer all the questions that follow.

"Vinyl is back," announced the *Business Daily*. The upsurge in demand for turntables to play vinyl records is due to consumer preferences for the 'original sound' offered by this medium of playing music. Technological improvements in turntable design which allows transfers of vinyl recordings to either computers or MP3 players have also boosted sales. This is excellent news for Hifonics, the UK-based manufacturer of electronic goods. Two years ago it predicted this trend. To overcome problems with its outdated models, it invested in an additional UK factory to produce an advanced range of music centres with turntables using a production process that gave great flexibility and cost effectiveness. The turntables, the transfer technology and the production process were developed by Hifonics plc's medium sized Research & Development (R&D) department.

The product range

There are four models in the Hifonics music centre range which are all assembled at the additional factory. The 'Titan', the latest model, is aimed at professional DJs (disc jockeys) and allows transfers of recordings to computers as well as 'mixing' facilities for nightclub-type effects. This is the company's first entry into this fast growing segment of the market. Sales of the other three models are impressive but Titan's sales have been disappointing. "We did not know what to expect with this product but sales are much lower than competitors' models," commented the Sales Manager. "Our promotion spending might be too low. Perhaps professional DJs need more clearly focused promotion campaigns than traditional retail customers." Costs and sales data for these four products is shown in Appendix A. The Chief Executive, on seeing the data, remarked that, "If we stopped the Titan now, profits would surely rise. Is there any reason to keep production going?"

Hifonics plc's Chief Executive wrote in the latest Company Report, "Heavy reliance on solid construction and quality materials, our traditional virtues, no longer gives guaranteed sales growth. Although costly, we must focus on more research and development (R&D) spending to develop new technology products and processes. This strategy will always succeed. Our sales forecasts suggest we could sell up to 35,000 of the music centres in the 12 months starting from June 2010. (Appendix B)

The location decision

Hifonics plc has always assembled its products in the UK. The directors are now considering opening a factory abroad. Increasing imports of cheap electrical goods from China, where workers earn a fraction of UK wages, is resulting in big cutbacks in Western European factories. Apart from sites in China, locations in Poland are also being considered (Appendix C & D show forecast data for both locations). The Operations Director submitted a report to the Board detailing the location options. He made the following points.

- The opportunities for joint ventures and sub-contracts will be great in China due to the huge electronics industry there. This would give scope for economies of scale.

- Labour law principles in Poland are the same as in the UK.

- The initial investment for a five-year lease of a factory in Poland would be £4m.

- Cash outgoings are expected to be 50% of cash inflows in any one year.

The report concluded, "We need to consider many qualitative factors too. The supply of unskilled labour in China is virtually limitless but senior managers may find Poland a more appealing location."

Other decisions

Opening a factory abroad would be likely to lead to the closure of one of the two UK factories. The axe would probably fall on the company's old factory, 25 miles from the newer one. The directors disagreed on how this decision should be managed and communicated to the workers.

Several directors supported the Finance Director's views, "It would be best to tell the staff at the last possible moment, within the limits of the law. They would have less time to worry and could not take any effective industrial action." Some directors supported the Human Resources Director's suggestion, "We should discuss this issue with the workforce and union representatives in both factories and allow early retirement and voluntary redundancies. We could appear authoritarian if we do not allow detailed consultation."

The other major issue for the Board was the problem of rising head office expenses, resulting in lower than expected net profit in 2009 despite higher sales.

Appendix A: Costs and sales data (year ending 31st December 2009)

	Titan	MC1	MC2	MC3
Labour costs per unit	£120	£60	£70	£90
Material costs per unit	£180	£30	£40	£80
Fixed factory costs and share of head office costs	£250,000	£350,000	£650,000	£350,000
Selling price per unit to retailers	£500	£150	£260	£300
Sales (units)	750	5,250	8,000	6,400

Appendix B: Quarterly sales of Hifonics plc music centres

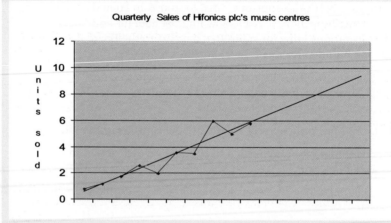

Appendix C Forecasted cash inflows from the factory in Poland

	Year 1	Year 2	Year 3	Year 4	Year 5
Forecasted cash inflows £m	2.0	4.0	6.0	3.0	1.0

Appendix D Forecasted data on a possible Chinese location

Average rate of return (ARR) for the first five years of operation	40%
Payback	3 years
Capital cost, including property lease for five years	£8 million

1. To what extent will the future success of Hifonics depend on increased Research and Development spending? *(18 marks)*

AQA Examiner's tip

Mark scheme

Knowledge (Content): 4 marks
These marks will be awarded for identifying relevant factors that show understanding of R&D, e.g. definition plus points about the potential benefits/ limitations of R&D.

Application: 4 marks
These marks will be awarded for effectively applying knowledge to Hifonics, e.g. the nature of the industry it operates in with rapid technological change; the recent innovations introduced by the company as a result of R&D.

Analysis: 5 marks
These marks will be awarded for developing a line of argument that supports either the benefits of R&D or its possible limitations, e.g. the creation of a potential USP leading to the ability to charge higher prices and earn higher profit margins; the possibility that even high levels of R&D spending might not lead to successful innovations.

Evaluation: 5 marks
Warning! These marks will be awarded for both the quality of judgement shown in weighing up the overall value of R&D to Hifonics and the quality of communication used and logical structure of the answer. For example, an answer may well be structured and draw a conclusion that R&D spending is vital to Hifonics success, but that it depends on the effectiveness of others companies' R&D programmes and it cannot, by itself, guarantee success for the business if, for instance, the new relocation project is badly managed.

2. Analyse whether or not the Chief Executive is right when he said: 'If we stopped the Titan now, profits would surely rise'. You should support your answer with relevant calculations.
(10 marks)

AQA Examiner's tip

Mark scheme

Knowledge (Content): 2 marks
These will be awarded for showing some relevant knowledge, e.g. how to calculate profit and/or contribution made by this product line.

Application: 6 marks
These will be fully awarded when the answer demonstrates correct calculations, e.g. that by not allocating fixed costs, which have to be paid anyway, this product actually makes an annual positive contribution of £150,000. Some application marks will be awarded when a candidate makes some or good progress with relevant calculations.

Analysis: 2 marks
These will be awarded for clear interpretation of results, e.g. a positive contribution means that if the Titan production is stopped, the overall profits of the business would fall.

3. To what extent do you consider the Finance Director's approach to Human Resource Management issues, such as how to inform staff of a factory closure, is appropriate for Hifonics in future? *(18 marks)*

4. Using all the information available to you complete the following tasks:

   – analyse the case for Hifonics locating a new factory in Poland

   – analyse the case for Hifoncs locating a new factory in China

   – make a justified recommendation on which option the company should choose. *(34 marks)*

AQA Examiner's tip

Mark scheme

Knowledge (Content): 6 marks
To be awarded full marks for knowledge, answers must contain development of relevant points about both locations, e.g. points in support of Poland and points in support of China. Answers that focus on just one location will only be able to gain 2 marks. Answers that refer to points for both locations but with no, or weak, development, will gain 3, 4 or 5 marks.

Application: 10 marks
To be awarded full marks, the answer must be consistently rooted in the case material. This means that points such as: 'The existence of many similar firms in China is an advantage' needs to be more fully applied as in '... and this will allow a relatively small electronics firm such as Hifonics to take advantage of joint ventures.'

Analysis: 8 marks
To be awarded full marks, answers must develop good arguments in support of both locations and these arguments should be clear and logical. For example: 'The existence of many unskilled workers in China will help to keep wage rates very low which could increase Hifonics' cost competitiveness against rival firms.' As we see below, this point can also be evaluated!

Evaluation: 10 marks
Warning again! Examiners will be asked to assess not only judgement in a candidate's answer but also the quality of communication skills used. The key point here is that the answer must contain a supported recommendation – question 4 on BUSS3 will always demand a recommendation so do not miss out on valuable marks by not giving one. Here are two examples of how evaluation could be shown:

■ 'Low wage costs of unskilled workers are only part of the argument – if Hifonics cannot recruit the skilled workers it needs in this high-tech industry, then the move the China becomes less attractive.'

■ 'Overall, I would recommend relocating in Poland as nearness to Western markets is a key factor, but I would also check on the accuracy of the financial forecasts before committing the company to such a huge investment project.'

Unit 4

Unit 4 is a new style of examination that gives you a good idea of what some of the questions are going to be months before you actually sit the paper! Section A of the examination is based on a pre-issued research topic that your teachers will be informed of in advance. They will be encouraged to guide you towards source materials that will give you access to considerable amounts of research material on the topic. The theme used on the sample paper in this book is 'Changes in business size', which relates directly to a specific area of the specification. Do not be tricked into thinking that this is the only part of the specification you should revise for the examination, however. This would be a big mistake for two reasons:

- The research topic questions will be based on recent media articles and the questions set on these will give plenty of scope for a wide variety of issues to be discussed. For example, if one of the questions concerns the impact on stakeholders of a takeover, then an awareness of social, ethical, environmental, financial and competition issues would be needed for a full answer to be attempted. So, the research topic should be looked upon as a starting point for you to analyse and revise the whole of the BUSS4 specification.

- Section B requires one essay to be written – from a choice of three – and none of the titles will be related to the pre-issued research theme. Answers should be as synoptic or wide ranging as possible so to focus revision on just one part of the specification would be unwise.

Unit 4 Examination paper

1 hour 45 minutes

Change in business size – External growth through integration (pre-issued research theme)

Candidates should consider issues such as:

- The meaning of external growth

- The different forms of external growth through integration – mergers/takeovers

- The different types of integration: horizontal, vertical (backwards and forwards) and conglomerate

- The possible reasons for adopting the strategy of external growth

- The possible costs, benefits and risks associated with these different types of integration

- How businesses may structure themselves after integration in order to obtain maximum benefit from it

- The opportunities and threats created by integration and the factors influencing how firms might respond to these

- Social, legal and ethical issues resulting from integration

- The significance of integration for businesses, shareholders and other stakeholders

- The factors most likely to influence the eventual success of the strategy of integration.

Section A

Answer ONE question from this section.

1.   Read Articles A and B and then answer the question that follows.

Article A

One reason why all shareholders should be wary of takeovers, unless they are on the receiving end of a large cash offer, is that from academic research it is obvious that many such examples of integration do not improve shareholder value for the purchasing company. They seem to be more beneficial to the ego building of management than they are to generating profits. So be sceptical of the 'synergy benefits', the 'cost savings' that will take place and the 'boundless opportunities' offered by new markets.

www.uksa.org.uk

Article B

Nine years after the announcement of the takeover of Amoco, BP is still trying to integrate the US business into the company structure. The lack of standard operating procedures for safety throughout BP's refineries, for example, created the conditions for the 2005 Texas City disaster. It is astonishing in retrospect that BP embarked on such a vast industrial merger without a carefully thought-through plan of integration. The legacy of these problems is being felt now as there was a $4bn fall in BP's operating cash flow, attributed to repair and maintenance issues. Cultural differences are very important – Americans never liked the idea of a British oil company being boss in their playground.

www.timesonline.co.uk

With reference to Articles A and B above and your own research, discuss the view that most mergers and takeovers fail to satisfy stakeholder objectives.   *(40 marks)*

2.   Read Article C and then answer the question that follows.

Article C

The statement from British Airways that it is 'exploring opportunities' with American Airlines (AA) and Continental is confirmation of how worried these airlines are by rising oil prices. Airlines are going bankrupt regularly and the big carriers are looking to cut costs through mergers and takeovers. A merger of BA, AA and Continental would create a massive airline with huge scope for cost cutting. It would also dominate the transatlantic skies, which is one reason why it may not happen. Sir Richard Branson would be determined to get the government to refer any such proposal to the competition authorities. Industry analysts have suggested that airlines could consider other forms of integration. While taking over an oil company to secure reasonably priced fuel supplies is most unlikely, other mergers and takeovers could offer advantages. For instance, integrating with businesses that offer other travel related services – such as car hire, holiday packages and even hotel chains – could be an effective strategy for airlines faced with rising costs and falling profits.

With reference to Article C above and your own research, to what extent is the strategy of growth through integration likely to be a profitable one for airlines such as British Airways? *(40 marks)*

AQA Examiner's tip

Mark scheme

This is the same for both questions.

Knowledge (content): 8 marks
For these top marks, a good understanding of relevant factors, drawn from the articles and your own research, would be necessary.

Application: 8 marks
Top marks for this skill will be awarded when the answer shows good application to the context of the articles and to the issues raised by them.

Analysis: 10 marks
Arguments must be well explained and follow a clear logic with good reference to appropriate Business Studies concepts and techniques to gain full marks for analysis.

Evaluation: 14 marks
Notice the weight given to this skill! Judgement and evaluation should not be left to your last paragraph. Try to show balance of argument throughout your answer, suggest and support the view that some issues are more important than others and, finally, give a clear and supported conclusion. Ideally, this should refer back to the question so that your final summing up is well focused on the initial topic raised by the question. For example, in question 1, it might be appropriate to conclude: 'So, it seems that in the short run there may well be stakeholder conflicts arising from integration but if it is well managed and leads to higher profitability, there may be a chance that most stakeholder objectives will be met in the long term.' Written communication is, as in BUSS3, assessed in this assessment objective too.

Section B

Answer ONE question from this section.

You are encouraged to use relevant business examples, theories, studies and data to support your arguments.

3.   'The key to successful business today is how management manage the change process.'
     To what extent do you agree with this view?   *(40 marks)*

4.   'Very large multinational businesses do not have to worry about the effects of changes in the external environment.'
     Discuss this view.   *(40 marks)*

5.   ABB is one of the world's largest engineering companies, operating in over 100 countries. 'I would define globalisation as the freedom for my group of companies to invest where it wants when it wants, to produce what it wants, to buy and sell what it wants and to support the fewest restrictions possible coming from labour law and social conventions.'
     Percy Barnevik, President of the ABB Industrial Group.

     Evaluate the likely impact on a company's stakeholders from increased globalisation.   *(40 marks)*

AQA Examiner's tip

Mark scheme

This has the same distribution of marks as for Section A.

■ Define any key terms contained in the essay title first.

■ Apply your answer clearly to the type of business or industry or market referred to in the question.

■ Analyse arguments used by including relevant Business Studies concepts and techniques learned throughout your Business Studies course.

■ Do not leave all evaluation until the final paragraph. Try to show balance of argument and prioritise arguments as you develop your answer. Written communication is again assessed in this section of the mark scheme.

■ A2 Examination Skills – final advice

■ Read each question carefully.

■ All questions will require evaluation – apart from one question in BUSS3 which is likely to use the 'analyse' command word and which will be focused on calculations.

■ Define and explain any key business terms contained in questions as your first step – knowledge must be demonstrated before any marks for any skills can be earned.

■ Allocate time carefully between each question – this is a real issue for BUSS3 in particular. Leave around 40 minutes for question 4, the report-style question.

■ Write in full sentences – and use appropriate Business Studies language where possible. Do not forget the marks for communication skills.

■ Use separate paragraphs for each separate point – evaluate in every paragraph, if possible.

■ In the BUSS3 numerical question(s), show all calculations and lay these out as neatly as possible.

Index